Sue Palmer is a writer, broadcaster and consultant on the education of young children. She is a specialist in literacy and is also a popular speaker, addressing thousands of teachers, parents and health professionals each year across the UK and around the world. She writes frequently in the national press, and has worked as a consultant to the National Literacy Trust, the Basic Skills Agency, many educational publishers, the Department for Education and the BBC.

www.suepalmer.co.uk

By Sue Palmer

Toxic Childhood
Detoxing Childhood
21st Century Boys
21st Century Girls

21st CENTURY GIRLS

How female minds develop,
how to raise bright, balanced girls
and why today's world needs them more than ever

SUE PALMER

An Orion paperback

First published in Great Britain in 2013
by Orion Books Ltd.
This paperback edition published in 2014
by Orion Books Ltd,
Orion House, 5 Upper St Martin's Lane,
London WC2H 9EA

An Hachette UK company

1 3 5 7 9 10 8 6 4 2

A CIP catalogue record for this book
is available from the British Library.

ISBN 978 1 4091 4865 4

Printed and bound in Great Britain by CPI Group (UK) Ltd, Croydon, CR0 4YY

The Orion Publishing Group's policy is to use papers that
are natural, renewable and recyclable products and made
from wood grown in sustainable forests. The logging and
manufacturing processes are expected to conform to the
environmental regulations of the country of origin.

www.orionbooks.co.uk

To Beth and Maeve

Contents

INTRODUCTION

Yesterday, I saw a 21st century Alpha Girl. She was sitting with her parents in an Edinburgh restaurant, enjoying a cheap but chic supper. It was difficult to guess her age – I thought about 11, but she could have been younger or older. A little girl dressed like a teenager, or a teenager acting like a little girl?

Stick thin, of course. Fashionably clad. Pert and pretty with just the right amount of make-up to show off her wide eyes, fresh young face and kissable mouth. She was childishly innocent in some ways – gangly, giggly, delighted to be with the grown-ups. But she was also entirely conscious of the impression she was making on the waiters and fellow diners. Sweet, winsome, flirtatious, adorable...

She looked a bright little thing, too. Mum and dad were clearly enjoying her witty conversation. In a few years' time (five, seven, or nine?), she'd be a great choice for a *Daily Telegraph* front-page photo, celebrating her brilliant A-Level results. And that Alpha Girl sheen suggested many other accomplishments. I could imagine her playing in the school orchestra, starring in the netball team, writing a delightful blog and racking up more Facebook friends than anyone else in her class.

My supper companion – a female chum who, like me, had lived through the heady days of women's liberation – turned round in her seat for a quick look. 'Yep, she's Little Miss Perfect,' she agreed. 'And you're right, she's very young to be dolled up like that. How could her parents let her? They look okay people.'

'I don't suppose it was their idea,' I said. 'It probably just happened, and they felt powerless to stop it. I hear it all the time. To start with it's a sort of joke: "They grow up so quickly these days..." And then before anyone knows it, she's on a roll and there's nothing mum and dad can do. If a bright kid like that is used to getting her own way, she'll be able to run rings round her parents.'

My friend seemed unconvinced (but then she's not a modern parent). 'Oh well,' she said, 'at least she looks bright. With any luck, she'll run rings round the boys, too. If she can get to university without anything going wrong, the world's her oyster.'

'That's probably what her parents are hoping,' I muttered. 'Good luck to them – and to her if she knows what she wants. But I doubt she does and there's always a price to pay when kids grow up too quickly.'

'Come on, lighten up,' said my friend, giving me a long, hard, old-fashioned look. 'I dare say older women in the 1960s used to worry themselves sick about us, with our miniskirts, panda eyes and prescriptions for the Pill. You're letting that girl book get to you.'

The female of the species

She was right. Writing this 'girl book' has got to me. It's my fourth book about the effects of modern lifestyles on child development, and I've vowed it'll be my last. It's taken twice as long as it was meant to, it gave me my first ever attack of writer's block and I've nearly thrown in the towel on several occasions. When friends asked why it was causing so much trouble compared with 21st Century Boys, I'd mutter darkly 'Boys are straightforward little creatures – girls are just so *complicated*.' Parents with children of both sexes smiled sympathetically, especially the fathers.

It doesn't help that I'm female, with all the usual complications. I'm also profoundly conscious that the overwhelming majority of my readers are probably female, too. No matter how hard politicians have tried to promote the idea of 'parenting' over the last decade or so, women still take most responsibility for rearing children. When I give talks about modern childhood for parents and professionals from education, health and the social services, the audiences are around 90 per cent female. So it seems fair to assume that most of my readers know exactly what it feels like to be a girl, a young woman and a mother. Like me, you know all about female complexity from the inside.

And since you're so familiar with it, you've probably never given it that much thought. Neither had I till I started writing this book. But I soon realised that, to give advice on raising girls to meet the challenges of the 21st century, I would have to. Thinking about my own convoluted female thought processes hasn't been a particularly comfortable experience.

There is, for instance, the terrible female tendency towards 'victimhood'. I don't just mean the extreme ways some women appear to embrace suffering, such as self-harm, anorexia or participation in abusive relationships. I mean our capacity to put ourselves out in ways that aren't remotely in our own interest. Female fashion victims go to far greater extremes than their male counterparts, cheerfully suffering any number of uncomfortable trends (crinolines, bustles, corsets, naked flesh in winter, monster high heels) and submitting to painful cosmetic procedures, including, increasingly these days, unpleasant surgical procedures. And why exactly is it that, despite 50 years of supposed sexual equality and the rise of the dual income household, women still shoulder the lion's share of childcare and other domestic duties?

The other way of looking at this female trait is to conclude that women *care* more than men. We care more about our personal appearance, the state of our home environment and the smooth running of our children's and our partners' lives. We want to 'get it right'. We also often care more than men about the welfare of people outside our immediate family – hence the disproportionate number of women in the caring professions. Perhaps, above all, we care about other people's opinions.

I'm not saying there's anything wrong with caring. It's vital to our own survival, as well as to that of our nearest and dearest and, indeed, our species. In fact, while writing this book, I've come to believe that the capacity to care for others is probably the greatest of human virtues, and that nowadays it's seriously undervalued.

It's also important to care about what other people think of us. If we didn't, society would soon break down. But the capacity to care shouldn't make women embrace victimhood. It shouldn't make us overly self-conscious. And it certainly shouldn't be perverted into an extreme preoccupation with the image we present to the world.

That's what depressed me about the girl in the restaurant. She was a beautiful, self-conscious, self-made Miss Perfect. She was thrilled by the pleasure she was giving her audience (waiters, fellow diners, adoring parents). She'd created a glorious, feminine persona – good, kind, clever, successful, sexy, the perfect Alpha Girl – which must be exptremely high-maintenance. And she probably isn't yet in her teens. Can you imagine carrying that weight of 'perfection' through adolescence and into adulthood? I certainly wouldn't fancy it.

The erosion of childhood

My interest in what I call 'child development in the modern world' began 15 years ago as the result of my work in literacy (see Chapter 4). It's been the most fascinating voyage of discovery for me, both professionally as an educator and personally as a mother. Not many mums get the opportunity to open up dialogues with scores of experts in fields as diverse as developmental psychology, neuroscience, nutrition, play, sleep, childcare, parenting, marketing, social science and economics. Nor do they have the chance to discuss what they've learned with thousands of people who spend their working lives with children, or with thousands of parents struggling through the minefield of 21st century child-rearing.

In the four years since embarking on this book, I've also had the chance to knit together all this received wisdom with up-to-date research about the female of the species and what makes us different from the male. This has been fascinating from a personal point of view, because it's explained a lot about why women (including me) behave as we do. It also sheds light on why the women's movement, which began when I was in my early teens, has now run into very stormy waters.

There are, of course, many reasons why the move towards sexual equality hasn't turned out as we 'liberated' young women hoped back in the 1960s; human culture is an extremely complicated phenomenon, and anyone attempting to explain it is asking for trouble. Still, over the last 15 years I've got used to sticking my neck out, so I'm going to have a go. I believe that what Dr Richard House recently described as 'the erosion of childhood' has been an extremely significant factor in the process.

Modern neuroscience has now confirmed that, as Wordsworth put it (with artless 18th century male self-regard) '*the child is father of the man*'. She's also mother of the woman. The way we raise our children determines not only the sort of adult they become but also the sort of society they forge for themselves. Girls and boys are the products of both nature and nurture, but the nurture they receive is inevitably influenced by the culture in which they grow up. And for a variety of reasons, over the last 30 years, our own culture has become increasingly careless about its young.

Childhood, as a stage in human development, has been steadily eroded. Children today are initiated into the high-tech, adult world of competitive consumerism at an increasingly early age, long before they're ready developmentally to cope with it. We expend immense time and effort attending to their material requirements (often in breathtakingly misguided ways), while neglecting their emotional needs. And I believe that if we don't get a grip on this problem soon, the increase in developmental disorders, behavioural difficulties and mental health problems recorded by experts over recent decades will soon run out of control.

It's often claimed that the contemporary idea of 'childhood' was invented by the Victorians. Personally, I prefer the theory of American essayist Neil Postman, who claims that it originated with the spread of literacy and is therefore linked to the invention of the printing press. Critics of Dr House's campaign to halt the erosion of childhood point out that, in earlier times – as in less sophisticated cultures today – children were treated as little adults. There was no concept of 'childhood innocence' and kids were perfectly aware of the way grown-ups behaved on a daily basis, including their sexual behaviour.

However, cultural concepts develop for a reason. Our modern idea of childhood emerged in response to the increasing sophistication of Western society, and the recognition among adults that children need time to mature – physically, emotionally, socially and intellectually – in order to cope with the complications of modern life (see Chapter 1).

Girls, for instance, need a period of 'childhood innocence' to develop the self-confidence, resilience and intellectual skills they need to make the most of sexual equality in a fast-moving, screen-saturated, highly commercialised world.

Mind the gender gap

In my first book on this subject, I coined the term 'toxic childhood' to describe the complicated cocktail of lifestyle factors that now affect the well-being and long-term prospects of a growing number of children. While I was writing it, it became clear that the effects on boys and girls were substantially different, and I wanted to find out why. Researching and writing 21st Century Boys (2009) and 21st Century Girls was a scary move, as it plunged me deep into the quagmire of gender politics and raised the vexed question of whether boys and girls do actually think differently.

There's still no consensus on how far gender differences in the way children think are the result of nature or nurture (see Chapters 2 and 3), so I've made the best use of the available research. For what it's worth, I think the neuroscientist Lise Eliot sums this up pretty well in her book Pink Brain, Blue Brain. She concludes that there are only very small differences in the brains and behaviour of boys and girls at birth, but that these develop into a troublesome gender gap as they grow older.

If this is the case, the lifestyle factors I've described as toxic are likely to be implicated in the way this troublesome gender gap develops. That was certainly my conclusion when I researched and wrote *21st Century Boys* – I identified many aspects of modern life that could drive young males into types of behaviour that were potentially damaging on a personal level. In fact, I chose to tackle boys' development first because there was already widespread concern about their underachievement in the educational system, their increasingly screen-based sedentary lifestyle and misbehaviour during the teenage years.

When I made my first forays into the gender politics debate, the damaging effects of that troublesome gap on girls were far less obvious. However, in the last few years, the spotlight has swung round to focus on the female of the species, and particularly on the effects of growing up in our increasingly sexualised culture. In the UK today, girls are not only more likely to engage in underage sex than boys (in 2011, statistics revealed that for the first time more girls than boys lost their virginity before the age of 16), they're also becoming worryingly self-conscious about their physical appearance at an increasingly early age (around the age of five according to recent research). Concern about these developments has led to renewed interest in gender stereotyping and the sexual exploitation of girls and women, including an outbreak of feminist writing on the subject.

I was relieved to see feminist writers tackling this topic again. The women's movement paid it great attention in the early days of 'liberation', but by the closing decade of the 20th century the movement had seemed to lose interest. Instead, feminists have concentrated on academic, legislative and political activity, leaving popular culture to look after itself, and, since the last 20 years have seen the rise of pop video channels, celebrity culture and reality TV, young girls have been provided with some highly sexualised role models.

The trouble with feminism

I have to admit to serious reservations about feminism. As a woman born right in the middle of the 20th century, I've been part of the sexual equality project from the beginning, and always felt as free as any man to earn my own living and pursue my own path in life. I was glad when the women's movement began raising awareness of gender stereotyping and sexist attitudes, but in other respects it wasn't something I wanted to sign up to.

For a start, it seemed unnecessarily antagonistic. Back in the 1960s, I couldn't see how the cause of equality was served by being 'antimen', or what was to be gained from blaming our generation of males for the sins of their fathers. Feminist vituperation also had a slight flavour of victimhood, which made their complaints sound whingeing. I suspected that, rather than furthering the cause of equality, they were merely stirring up resentment. During research for *21st Century Boys*, I spoke to many boys and men on the subject and was dismayed at their bitterness – even those who were firmly committed to equality rolled their eyes about feminism.

Second, I've never understood how a *women's* movement could be so unconcerned about children. It seems that, from a feminist perspective, motherhood is merely something to be squeezed into a woman's working life, taking up as little time as possible. The needs of the child don't even come into the equation. My own experience of motherhood was that much as I loved my career, I loved my daughter even more, and was torn between their conflicting demands. Where were the feminists who valued my instinct to provide the best possible care for my child?

So, while thoroughly committed to the cause of equality, I've never been committed to the sisterhood. This meant it was quite exciting to find myself onside with the latest wave of feminist literature about stereotyping, sexualisation and the normalisation of porn. These issues are a real threat to 21st century girls and, having read through the new books on the subject, I was keen to interest the mothers in my audiences about the implications of what one author calls 'the return of sexism' for their daughters' future.

Unfortunately, most of the mums I met turned out to have as little interest in gender politics as feminists do in motherhood. Much as I tried to interest them in gender stereotyping, they were far more concerned about the day-to-day issues of child-rearing. I soon realised that phrases like 'the objectification of women' don't cut much ice with people whose main concerns are whether or not to use a dummy, how much TV is too much, and do I think homework is a good idea for five-year-olds?

It was also clear *why* these women had trouble thinking beyond such immediate concerns. They were exhausted. More than half a century after the sexual revolution, mothers are still taking on most of the responsibility for childcare and keeping family life on track ... but now most of them also have paid work outside the home. The rise of the dual income family coincided with a massive hike in house prices, so without mum's earnings the family might not have a home at all.

The sexual revolution definitely hasn't turned out the way we hoped it would, and I suspect feminism has contributed to the problem (see Chapters 2 and 3). So, it will be up to the next generation of girls to get the equality project back on track. Since the girl is mother of the woman, they'll need the best sort of childhood in order to equip them for the task.

Science and wisdom

All the conclusions I've reached about raising girls are, of course, influenced by my own experiences as a woman and a mother, and from 40 years' involvement with children. The first 20 years were spent in primary education and the second 20 learning from other people who work with children, including nursery nurses, teachers, social workers, childminders, fosterers, psychologists and, in recent years, parents.

Until the last century, shared experience was all anyone had to go on in terms of child-rearing. Older women, who'd watched many children grow up, passed on their wisdom to younger mums. And when family lifestyles didn't differ enormously from one generation to the next, this wisdom was usually enough to see parents through. But as the pace of change during the 20th century accelerated, we began to lose faith in wisdom and turned to science.

That's why, when I started fretting about child development, I sought scientific advice on what might be happening to the current generation of children. I wanted to learn from the science available how young minds develop and about the potential effects of various social and cultural changes on developing brains. It's been a fascinating journey, but, when there's been no research into a particular aspect available to consult, also a frustrating one. Perhaps the funding hasn't been available or it's an area that no one's yet thought to investigate, or perhaps there simply hasn't been enough time to conduct adequate research.

On these occasions, one just has to revert to wisdom. But having interviewed a host of experts I realised it wasn't just their academic knowledge they were passing on – it was their own personal wisdom, born of experience. By teaming the experts' wisdom with the experience of the parents and professionals I was meeting in the field, I found it was often possible to see a way through. I began to feel like some sort of latter-day travelling 'wise woman', carting around the accumulated wisdom of the many hundreds of people whom I'd had the good fortune to meet face to face.

This book, therefore, is just as dependent on that wisdom as it is on science. It bats back and forth from research-based evidence to anecdote, opinion and occasional theorising – I hope it's always clear which is which.

Part One is an overview of some of the key issues involved:

- the problems facing parents in an age of materialism
- the origins of the 'gender wars' and how they have intensified those problems
- the debate about the female brain and girls' early development
- the reasons why contemporary culture can be 'toxic', especially for girls
- the basics of child development and the special challenges of bringing up daughters.

Part Two looks at five aspects of modern child-rearing, the problems they raise for girls and some advice about each area based on what I learned from all those experts.

PART ONE

THE POWER OF THE PERSONAL

To nourish children and raise them against odds is in any time, any place, more valuable than to fix bolts in cars or design nuclear weapons.

Marilyn French

And so our mothers and grandmothers have, more often than not anonymously, handed on the creative spark, the seed of the flower they themselves never hoped to see — or like a sealed letter they could not plainly read.

Alice Walker

There can be no keener revelation of a society's soul than the way in which it treats its children.

Nelson Mandela

CHAPTER 1

MATERIAL GIRLS

First, a flashback to a more innocent age.

> It's the early 1980s and I'm an earnest young head teacher
> berating Mrs Lavery of the infant class about the pictures on her
> cloakroom wall. Alongside the boys' coat pegs are spaceships,
> steam engines and dinosaurs; alongside the girls' are flowers,
> fairies and fluffy bunnies. Having been taught at college that
> 'gender is a social construct', I'm damned if my school is going
> to confront children with gender-specific messages every time
> they hang up their coats.
>
> Mrs Lavery is unimpressed. 'But Sue, the children chose
> their own pictures,' she says. 'The boys *like* spaceships and
> dinosaurs and the girls *like* fluffy bunnies. If we want them to
> think for themselves, what am I supposed to do?'

What indeed? It felt petty to deny children their choice of pictures.
And it was obvious from a glance at the playground that the infants
were far less committed to ironing out gender differences than my
college lecturers. From the day they arrived, they played mainly in
single-sex groups, and the boys' wild, rumbustious, risky games were
very different from the girls' more careful, contained, socially aware

activities. So I demurred. Maybe there were more things in heaven and earth than were dreamt of by the gender theorists.

Thirty years on, I know there are. No one back then could have begun to imagine children's lifestyles in early 21st century Britain, nor the consequences of giving them 'free choice' in a consumer economy. Visit any large toy store and you'll find it overflowing with expensive, sophisticated toys for children – even though, according to educational psychologists, most of them could stunt children's long-term development.

You'll also notice that the products on sale are colour-coded, in order to appeal to two different types of infant consumer. Half of them shine in blue, black and silver packaging. The other half are pink.

The plague of pink

Over the last few years, the question of gender stereotyping has once again become a hot topic among the chattering classes. It went out of fashion in the mid-1990s, when the 'gender wars' seemed to fizzle to a close. The vast majority of women had by then joined men in the workplace. There was a common curriculum for girls and boys in school, and examining boards were no longer advantaging male over female students. Legislation was supposed to ensure equal opportunities and freedom from sexual harassment at work. To most people, it no longer seemed necessary to shield little girls from pictures of fluffy bunnies or to give them toy trucks so they'd feel free to be engineers when they grew up.

> Gender stereotyping has once again become a hot topic among the chattering classes.

After earlier attempts to change children's play by parents who'd learned that gender is a social construct, we'd all discovered that little girls tend to wrap toy trucks in blankets and cuddle and coo at them. And little boys make guns out of Lego. It had become widely accepted that evolutionary influences incline female children towards nurturing play and males towards 'play fighting'. And since letting little girls express their caring side hadn't stopped women achieving equality, why not just let the kids get on with it?

But kids don't just get on and play any more. In a competitive consumer culture, they expect to have something to play with – something bought from the shops. In the latter part of the 20th century, major corporations identified children as a lucrative market with access to lots of parental 'guilt money'. Armed with the evolutionary gender theories, their marketing departments homed in on infant consumers.

The job of the marketing industry is to find out what customers want, and sell it to them. If little girls want flowers, fairy dust and fluff, marketers are delighted to develop endless products to satisfy their cravings. And if one particular colour appeals, they'll happily spray everything that colour. So when girls said they liked their products pink, that's precisely the colour the market made them. Globally.

Children's biological development helps this process along. Most start taking an interest in their gender between the ages of two and three, around the time they start at pre-school.* This is also when another deep human instinct kicks in – the instinct for inclusion in the peer group. It's a very sensible instinct because, back in our Stone Age past, if we weren't accepted by the tribe we were dead. Suddenly little girls feel a compelling urge to belong to the tribe of other small females in the playground. Given the widespread colour-coding of products, an important symbol of inclusion in recent years has been pinkness.

The combination of peer pressure and market forces is a powerful one, and so the pinking process gathered strength over the years. Girls responded to the market, and the market responded to the girls. Eventually, almost everything aimed at young female consumers – toys, clothing, soft furnishings, accessories, books, bikes, laptops – became comprehensively pinkified.

> Almost everything aimed at young female consumers became comprehensively pinkified.

* Actually, they're technically aware of it from babyhood, but not able to make much sense of the gender differences until they can talk.

About three years ago, some mothers began to worry whether this 'pink plague' could affect girls' self-image and aspirations. There was a spate of articles in the press by women (including a couple by me) about the pinkification of little girls' lives and its gender-stereotypical implications. A couple of mums set up a pressure group, www.pink-stinks.org.uk, to challenge the 'pink signposting' that pushes girls down particular aisles in toyshops, *'usually towards beauty tables, princess dresses and toys "pinked up" and "dumbed down" for girls.'*

Girls on top

For many commentators (male, in particular), the mothers' concern was baffling. Why in the world were they fussing about a bit of pink? There was no evidence of girls being dumbed down. In fact, they were now markedly outperforming boys in 21st century Britain. It's the boys whom educationists are worried about.

As one of those educationists, I can confirm this. Thirty years of paying attention to girls' achievement has paid off. They now get off to a much better start than boys in school, and maintain their lead throughout the school system. They suffer from far fewer special educational needs. They've more chance than boys of getting into university, and once there they're more likely to graduate: around 50 per cent of women are expected to have a degree by the time they're 30, but only 40 per cent of men. Indeed, many previously male-dominated professions are starting to turn female. There are more women qualified as secondary teachers, doctors and veterinary surgeons than men, and women are even making serious inroads into that traditional bastion of male domination, the law. In 2011, the average earnings of young women in their twenties were, for the first time, higher than those of men.

You can see why those male commentators felt indignant. On the surface, it seems that 21st century life suits girls better than boys. In an uptight, upfront, urban society, their sociability, emotional intelligence and language skills put them at a definite advantage. By the time they reach their teens, statistics suggest that girls are only half as likely to suffer from emotional, behavioural or mental health problems as boys. Once they start work, the female tendency to be careful and conscientious is welcome in a culture where accountability procedures and meticulous record keeping count for a lot.

But that's where the advantage ends. As time goes on, most women don't fulfil their early promise. Men still dominate the upper echelons of almost every business and profession, as well as the political corridors of power. The famous 'glass ceiling' is still in place. Men's average earnings are still, on the whole, around 23 per cent higher than women's, partly because many of the careers popular with women – such as the 'caring professions' – are not well paid, and many women work part-time.

> Men still dominate the upper echelons of almost every business and profession.

There are also significant problems for working mothers, who often struggle to combine the demands of a highly competitive workplace with a lack of good, affordable childcare. Indeed, surveys over the first decade of the new millennium showed the majority of working mums would rather be at home – they were exhausted, stressed, disillusioned and worried about the mother-shaped gap in their children's lives.

However, women who stay at home aren't all that happy either. Many full-time mothers feel they're considered socially inferior to their working sisters. Those who've taken a career break for childcare fear it condemns them to a future on the lower rungs of the promotion ladder. And then there are the single mothers, many of them raising children in gruelling conditions, who've acquired an appalling public image ('state scroungers') that's usually far from the truth.

I believe the feminist revival of interest in gender stereotyping – summed up by the ubiquitous pink – is symptomatic of a deeper disquiet about the results of the gender wars. Despite all the equal rights legislation and girls' brilliant performance at school, sexual equality still seems beyond our reach. Women may get off to a good start, but the workplace is still a man's world – probably because men don't have babies.

From pink to precocity

The more I've learned about child development, the deeper my own disquiet about what's happening to girls – commercially driven gender stereotyping is just one way in which 21st century culture is undermining the sexual equality project. However, since many of today's parents seem unimpressed by old-fashioned feminist rhetoric, at my *Toxic Childhood* talks I explain instead why it's important not to give in to 'pester power'. The mums and dads I meet – from every socio-economic background – feel increasingly helpless in the face of commercial forces. They may have no desire to buy into a market-driven craze like pinkness, but such is the power of playground peer pressure and daughterly wheedling that most find it impossible to resist.

At around the same time that journalists were fulminating about the pink plague, another phrase was beginning to circulate in the media: 'the sexualisation of children'. This really did hit a nerve with the parents of girls, and we've since had two official government reports on the subject. I discovered that it also rallied the attention of my audiences in ways that feminist slogans didn't.

So I could use my homilies about pester power to show how market pressures were driving both gender stereotypes and premature sexualisation. After all, if a girl doesn't conform to the commercial colour code, she'll be the odd one out in the playground. No loving parent wants their child to feel deprived, and they certainly don't want to risk her losing friends because she's 'different'. The thought that she might be excluded from the group seems much worse in the long run than a bit of pink ... so most of them give in.

> The thought that she might be excluded from the group seems much worse in the long run than a bit of pink.

Since babies don't come along with a crystal ball, parents don't know that, once exposed to the market, their daughter will soon be asking for a Bratz doll – a sexy little moppet that makes Barbie look positively strait-laced – or some similar ghastly toy. She'll explain that everyone has them, and her life will be a misery if she isn't part of the in-group.

Mum and dad might feel misgivings again, but the same fear of social exclusion will override them. After all, it's only a doll – surely not the first step on the road to teenage promiscuity? But then it'll be something else – maybe she'll want a bikini for the beach, even though it's nonsense for a six-year-old child to sport a bikini top. But all the other girls seem to have them... And before you can say 'object-ification', it's lip gloss, mascara and a rather sexy top...

Again, the sexualisation of children springs from an unholy alli-ance of biological and market forces. As part of the natural course of development, young human beings are driven to copy their elders – we see them do it all the time in their play. They particularly aspire to copy slightly older members of their sex whom they admire. Natu-rally, the market has responded to these aspirations, with a strategy known as KAGOY (Kids Are Getting Older Younger).

A few decades ago, marketers spotted that stuff targeted at older teenage girls – sexy fashions, make-up and magazines – were in great demand among younger teens. So of course they provided it. Once the stuff became normalised in that age group, the demand came from even younger teens. Again the market obliged. This normalisation process travelled down the food chain until items once sold only to adult women (such as high-heeled shoes and make-up) are now avail-able in sizes and packaging aimed at girls of almost any age. To add to the problem, in an adult-oriented, screen-saturated world, little girls constantly absorb messages about the importance of being physically attractive, 'hot', sassy and sexy.

From the marketers' point of view, it's all a matter of parental choice. If mum and dad are happy to buy sexy products for their pre-teenage children, the market would be mad not to provide them. So mum and dad are left to battle it out against global corporations, armed with multimillion-dollar budgets and a battery of sophisticat-ed psychological selling strategies. Since commercially fuelled peer pressure is now such a powerful force, even if the product is totally unsuitable, some parents inevitably succumb and their daughters' trophies keep playground aspiration on the boil. As long as there's peer pressure, pester power and guilt money, the combined forces of nature and market greed will ensure the KAGOY strategy keeps rolling along.

Choice and confusion

In comparison with these anxiety-inducing developments, Mrs Lavery's flowers, fairies and fluffy bunnies seem pretty tame. But I think my dilemma in the cloakroom was the same as that confronting today's concerned parents. They're both about how far caring adults should take responsibility for children's long-term welfare, as opposed to responding to their short-term desires.

In my case, I had reason to fear that the stereotypical pictures alongside the coat pegs might, in the long run, somehow disempower our girls. But I wasn't very sure of my ground, and I didn't want to interfere with the infant class's short-term right to choose, so I opted for the line of least resistance.

Parents fretting about Bratz dolls or their daughter's desire to plaster herself in make-up at the age of ten go through a similar process: '*Maybe it could be bad for her, but she really wants it, and everyone else has it so... I'll just go with the flow.*' They understand the social factors driving their child's behaviour only too well, because the same deep need to keep up with the Joneses also drives many of their own purchases. (And anyway, surely a little bit of lip gloss can't do any harm...)

Some parents are spared the dilemma, because they themselves defer to a higher authority; adults with deep religious beliefs wouldn't dream of allowing their daughters to dress in a sexualised way. Others have strong views on the subject based on political or environmental allegiances (or perhaps because they've mugged up on child development). Their strong views give them the strength to resist the culture, even at the risk of possible social consequences for their daughter in the short term. But most parents simply don't have a strong enough reason to fight the system.

Child-rearing is all about deciding what's best for one's offspring and, where necessary, exercising parental authority. But after the tumultuous social changes of the last few decades, how are parents to decide what's best, and from where do they get their authority? Very few people are sure of their ground in terms of child-rearing these days. And as for bringing up girls, we adults have just lived through a sexual revolution that's changed the way our entire world works, and we're still trying to work out what the heck the new rules are.

When you stop to think about it, the change in the role of women in society has been little short of seismic – in fact, it may be the most significant social change in the history of our species. Most of us are still grappling personally with the consequences. We don't talk about it much, but it's affected all our relationships, our self-images (male and female) and our collective confidence.

The perfect storm

It doesn't help that the sexual revolution coincided with two other massively significant social phenomena – the relentless rise of competitive consumerism, and increasingly rapid cultural change, driven by digital technology. Both these movements underwent a huge gearshift about 30 years ago. As capitalism proved the most powerful political force on the planet, free-market consumerism went global. And as advances in computer science came ever thicker and faster, new high-tech gadgets appeared in the shops every day, changing the lifestyle of the average consumer at the giddiest of paces.

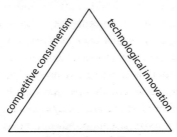

the sexual revolution

Modern men and women found themselves in the middle of a 'perfect storm': three powerful 'fronts' all hitting at the same time. It's been like living in one of those old-fashioned snow globes, where you shake up and chaos ensues. But, in this case, after 30 years, we're still waiting for the storm to settle.

Indeed, it's a tribute to the human spirit that, despite the personal and social effects of that storm, we're still here, battling bravely on and most of the time coping reasonably well. Homo sapiens is a remarkably adaptable species. But the experience has given the human spirit a battering too. It's made us much more materialistic.

As we (men and women) tried to work out our new roles in the new world order of sexual equality, our decisions were influenced at every turn by consumerism and technology. The market devised endless products (fashions, gadgets, leisure activities) to help us to establish our new identities. And the rapidly proliferating visual media showed us ways to look and act, then reflected our choices back at us.

We soon realised that, even if confused inside, it's possible to look absolutely fine on the outside. The visual media demonstrated how products can define identity; they teemed with images of successful new men and women, attractively dressed, carefully coiffed, driving smart cars, eating exotic food and living in swish designer houses. So we concentrated on earning enough money to pay for the perfect lifestyle, clinging to the belief that this would make everything come right in the end.

When you're constantly adjusting to new circumstances, there's no time to notice the unintended consequences of change, especially if you're not really sure what you're doing. So it's not surprising it's taken so long to recognise that the perfect storm has had a damaging effect on the way we raise our children. As family life turned into family lifestyle, long-established elements of a 'good childhood' disappeared. Instead, the mother-shaped gap in children's lives filled with consumer goods, including technological gadgetry ... and the inevitable screens.

Little girls are influenced by glamorous images of female-kind. They've grown up in a world where women, despite (or possibly, because of) sexual equality, are 'objectified' as never before. The images of female perfection that they see around them every day are objectifications of a dream. Screen-based culture continually tells them that image (PR and packaging) is of vital importance. Marketers convey the constant message that 'stuff' – products, goods in shops, objects – is what really matters. So they absorb all these messages, and pass them around the playground among their friends.

> When you live in a material world, it makes you a material girl.

When you live in a material world, it makes you a material girl.

★★★

The perfect storm isn't going to blow over any time soon. Human culture will continue to advance at an increasingly crazy speed, and we human beings will have to carry on adapting to it. It's anyone's guess where our current materialistic value system will take us (politically, economically, environmentally...), but the straws currently blowing about in the wind suggest that life in Western democracies will become more, rather than less, challenging. So it doesn't seem particularly sensible to encourage another generation of girls to rely on products, PR and packaging to solve the problems they encounter.

I think the best way for parents to weather the storm is to remember the power of the human spirit – the inborn commitment to life that's so far brought our species through both good times and bad – and to try to nurture their daughters' inner strengths, rather than being constantly distracted by outward appearances. This means considering what actually makes human beings 'happy and successful'.

It's a pleasure to report that, in this respect, psychologists and neuroscientists now confirm what wise men and women have claimed through the ages:

- well-being is more important to psychological health than material excess.
- much of our potential for well-being ('happiness') and getting the most out of life ('success') is shaped during childhood.

So giving your daughter a happy life is ultimately more productive than buying her a lifestyle.

We've reached a stage in cultural evolution at which women (at least in Western democracies) are supposedly as free as men to make their own choices about the pursuit of happiness and success. But since their experiences as children affect the way they make those choices, we need to know whether female psychology differs in any significant way from the male variety – are girls born to pursue happiness and success differently from boys?

> Are girls are born to pursue happiness and success differently from boys?

CHAPTER 2

STONE AGE GIRLS

It's a year or so after the cloakroom fluffy bunny incident in my tiny village school. I'm doing a project about the Stone Age with the top class of nine- to twelve-year-olds. These are the halcyon days before health and safety regulations, so I can take children out into the real world without filling in reams of risk assessment forms. We've planned several weeks of afternoons on location in the local hills, pretending to be a Neolithic tribe founding a new settlement.

So here we are on a sunny Scottish hillside, and I start by asking them to build a temporary shelter, then we'll suss out the terrain. They immediately divide into gender groups. The boys work together, with lots of shouting, arguing and jostling for position. But they soon dig out a shelter in the brushwood, and start firming it up with branches and stones. The girls watch them for a while, offering occasional spirited advice, then go off in groups of two or three, to collect sticks, leaves, moss and other useful-looking soft furnishings.

Once the shelter's more or less finished, the boys lose interest. This is when the girls move in, tidying up the homestead and making it cosy. They notice that it's not very waterproof, so some collect leafy branches to weave into the roof. The others make seats, beds and a table. Meanwhile a couple of boys find a hollow log and start trying to turn it into a canoe. The others are noisily fashioning weapons from sticks and stones.

While I'm discussing hunting techniques with the boys (and restraining them from setting off immediately into the surrounding countryside in pursuit of quarry), the girls complete their nest and sit in it, chatting happily and making daisy chains to hang around the door. I worry about the gender stereotyping and rail at them about doing something more proactive. They look at me askance: *'We're discussing the terrain, like you said. There's no water round here, you know.'*

Genes and gender

That was the day that I began to wonder whether gender is merely a social construct – perhaps something rather deeper than sexual stereotyping lay behind the way those boys and girls behaved? I hadn't expected such a dramatic division of labour on our Stone Age hillside, but it certainly mirrored the sorts of activity I'd watched in the playground.

> I began to wonder whether gender is merely a social construct.

It also mirrors the theories of 21st century evolutionary psychologists. They argue that the differences in behaviour between today's men and women link to their roles in our remote past, roles that arose from the biological drive to perpetuate the species. Since human babies are born in a highly vulnerable state and are not properly capable of fending for themselves for at least a decade, our ancestors divided up child-rearing duties along biologically determined lines.

Stone Age males – like other males across the animal kingdom – were competitive creatures, keen to beat off the opposition and mate with the most fecund females in order to pass on their genes. After their extremely brief contribution to the reproductive process, their paternal role was to protect and provide for their women and children. This involved staking and defending territory, making and using weapons and tools, finding their way around the hunting grounds, taking risks, and working as a team to develop successful strategies. Because of men's natural competitiveness and desire for dominance, the pecking order within hunting or war parties had to be clearly established.

The Stone Age females' commitment to reproduction was, of course, much greater and occupied most of their adult lives. They had to bear, suckle and socialise their offspring, maintain the commitment of their male protectors, and rub along with other mothers back at camp while the men were away. So females had to be good at nurturing and socialising, both of which involve more upfront, intimate relationships than the strategy-based social dynamics of a hunting or war party.

Evolutionary psychologists like Steven Pinker claim that, with countless millennia of evolutionary adaptation to these roles, today's men and women are genetically programmed for different types of behaviour. Data from educational and psychological research, criminal justice records, social surveys, psychometric testing, and so on, seem to support their case.

On the whole, modern males are still much more inclined to aggressive, competitive and risky behaviour than women. They're often more interested in things, and how they work, than in people, and have better visuospatial skills (such as imagining how three-dimensional objects look when they're rotated in space). At work, the pecking order matters a lot – they're motivated to achieve by recognition of their status within the organisation, especially job titles and pay differentials.

Women are usually less reckless than men, more interested in people than mechanisms, often more likely to be fulfilled in 'caring' roles,

> While women in today's workforce share men's concern for status, they don't seem so driven by the competitive instinct.

and inclined to chattier, more intimate friendships. While women in today's workforce share men's concern for status, they don't seem so driven by the competitive instinct – they tend to give equal importance to material rewards and the quality of their relationships.

Male and female brains

So far, so neatly explanatory. But does this mean there are differences in the way male and female brains have developed through the millennia that influence how men and women actually *think*? Some scientists believe there are, and one of the most influential in recent years is Simon Baron-Cohen, professor of developmental psychopathology at the University of Cambridge. In his book, *The Essential Difference: Men, Women and the Extreme Male Brain*, he describes two broad strands of thought that have underpinned human behaviour through the ages.

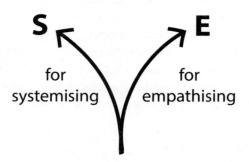

He calls them 'systemising' (S-type) and 'empathising' (E-type) thought. Systemising thought arises from the need to understand and control our environment. It's led us to form rule-based systems about how to make and build things, as well as systems of abstract ideas such as mathematics or the law. Empathising is about social intelligence – the capacity to tune in to other people's feelings, work out what's going on in their minds, connect, communicate, establish relationships and get along together.

The two ways of thinking aren't mutually exclusive – indeed, all human beings (male and female) need to be able to do both, as they're both necessary for survival. So we're all born equipped to systemise *and* empathise. But Baron-Cohen argues that males (with their long-term interest in tools, weapons, strategy and structures) have been primed by evolution to be more interested in objects and systems, while females (with their biological commitment to nurture and personal relationships) have majored in empathising and people.

He's conducted wide-scale surveys of men and women, and found that men score *slightly* higher than women on S-type tasks, while women score *slightly* higher than men in E-type skills. To check whether these differences were just the result of social influences, he studied children in their first week of life, before they could possibly have been introduced to traditional gender roles.

His team at Cambridge placed images on either side of newborn babies' cots, and counted the times they turned their eyes to look at them. The choice was between a friendly human face –

> Baby girls preferred to gaze at Jennifer, while the baby boys looked more at the alien.

Jennifer – and a mobile, on which Jennifer's features had been rearranged to look like a machine ('the alien'). On the whole, baby girls preferred to gaze at Jennifer, while the baby boys looked more at the alien.

Humans and machines

Baron-Cohen's suggestion that the male brain might be slightly more inclined towards systemised thought helped spark a furore in scholarly circles. Some academics (mostly male) claimed it explained why, despite several decades of equal opportunity, men still tend to dominate the upper echelons of academia, especially in the sciences. Others (mostly female) railed against such 'genetic determinism', maintaining it's a mixture of stereotyping and prejudice that stops brilliant women from rising to the top.

The evidence of significant structural differences between male and female brains at birth is still skimpy, although hormonal influences before birth clearly affect development (see Chapter 3). However, if the male brain should ever turn out to be slightly better adapted to scientific thought, the effects are really only likely to be noticeable at genius level. In the overwhelming majority of the population, intellectual ability appears to be evenly spread – once women were given access to education, they proved themselves just as capable of S-type thought as men.

But the reactions to Baron-Cohen's work are fascinating for another reason. Despite fierce squabbles about who has the S-type edge, neither male nor female scientists have appeared remotely impressed by women's apparent superiority on the empathising front. There seems to be an automatic assumption that S-type thought is somehow 'better' or 'more important' than the E-type variety.

There's certainly no denying that our species' talent for systemising has been significant in terms of human progress. Tools and technologies, models and machines, and civic structures and scientific knowledge are all based on S-type principles. Indeed, we value our talent for systemising so highly that we've designed entire education systems to develop it. When I interviewed Professor Baron-Cohen at Cambridge in 2008, he'd recently surveyed the subjects taught in the university and confided that 'with the possible exception of English Literature', they were entirely concerned with S-type thought.

The contribution of E-type thought to human progress is far less obvious but just as significant. If our species couldn't 'read each other's minds' and understand each other's feelings, those systems would never have got off the ground. One of Homo sapiens' greatest strengths is that we're extremely social animals, able to live and work together, sharing our S-type understanding and co-operating over complex projects. Empathy underpins the love, kindness, care and trust on which we build our personal relationships, families and communities. It's at the very root of our humanity, and without it the systems we devise can easily become dehumanised – cold, heartless and mechanical.

In fact, there's every reason for 21st century men and women to focus their attention on E- rather than S-type thought processes. In the middle of the last century, humankind's cumulative S-type brilliance led to the creation of the ultimate systemising machines: computers. These machines are now far outstripping human beings in S-type potential. If we're to use this rapidly developing technology wisely,

> Machines are now far outstripping human beings in S-type potential.

for the good of the species, we urgently need to recalibrate the S/E balance that raised us to our present dizzy heights. We have to remember what makes us human.

A man-made world

So why should highly educated men and women fret about minuscule differences in their capacity for S-type thought, while apparently ignoring the E-type? Apart from the fact that they're all talented S-typers themselves (and understandably attached to their own thought patterns), I suspect they're unconsciously influenced by another essentially 'male' personality trait, one that's directed the development of human culture since the Stone Age.

Aggressive, competitive men are, of course, all very keen to be top dog. So success in a man-made culture is all about power, measured in status and material wealth. That's why the social systems men have created are hierarchies. When there's lots of testosterone swilling around, it helps to have everyone slotted into a neat social pyramid, so that power struggles can be localised around particular rankings. But hierarchical systems also cater to the competitive instinct because individuals can improve their status by clambering up the ranks.

For anyone who wants to move upwards in such a system, empathy isn't helpful. Indeed, it's a positive disadvantage. What you need is sound, strategic S-type thinking, and a ruthless streak. So, through the ages, a talent for E-type thought has held little appeal for men (or women) whose aim is to climb the greasy pole in pursuit of life's glittering prizes – and, once at the top, to hold on to their elevated position.

On the whole, it's been left to the people in the lower ranks of social hierarchies to keep empathy bubbling through human society.

These low-ranking 'losers' have usually been too busy keeping body and soul together to dream of rank or wealth, but their poverty and vulnerability gave them good reason to value collaboration. Presumably that's why one of the world's great E-type thinkers (who summed up his philosophy as 'loving your neighbour as yourself') promised a 'heavenly' payback rather than a worldly one.

The long-term result is that empathy has no appeal whatsoever to anyone in thrall to the pursuit of power. It's low-status stuff, associated with soft-heartedness, dependence on the goodwill of others, intangible 'heavenly rewards' and poor prospects in terms of worldly success. It's not likely to cut much ice with hard-nosed scientists in elitist institutions – especially women scientists, anxious to prove themselves after only a century or so of female access to higher education. No wonder they're unimpressed by Baron-Cohen's claim that their sex has the edge in it.

But there's another reason why E-type thought wouldn't appeal to talented systemisers, and why it doesn't appear on the curriculum at Cambridge University. Empathy is caught, rather than taught. It's a human talent, rooted in our emotions and dependent on first-hand embodied experience. While education systems can transmit ideas and knowledge down through the generations, E-type talents can only be developed through real-life human relationships.

> Empathy is caught, rather than taught.

The dance of communication

Empathy is intensely personal. It involves face-to-face contact with other human beings, and the ability to tune in to their emotions and forge relationships. Since we all have our own unique emotional baggage, it's impossible to systemise this sort of human understanding – every relationship is different. And the 'tuning in' process is interactive, rooted in the here and now of human contact. True empathetic engagement involves give and take; the lead in a real conversation goes back and forth.

As the supreme social species, human beings have brains hard-wired for empathy but, like all natural human talents, empathy also needs nurture in order to develop. So how have E-type skills been nurtured through the ages? The process has, of course, mainly been women's work. Since time immemorial, mothers have passed the capacity to empathise from one generation to another through their personal, intimate relationships with their children.

From the moment her baby is born (I'll make it a boy in order to avoid confusion with pronouns), his mother has to 'read his mind', and tune in to his feelings so she can cater for his needs. In so doing she is not only refining her own E-type talents, but also modelling these skills to her son at a time when he's functioning at the deepest of emotional levels.

Developmental psychologists talk, rather delightfully, about a 'dance of communication' between mother and child – the mother responding to the child, the child responding to the mother, each imitating the other's face, voice and gestures.

This dance of communication between one generation and the next carries on throughout childhood. Children learn their emotional and so-cial skills – the essence of their humanity – from the people who care for them, play with them, talk and listen to them, and unconsciously model the endless nuances of social behaviour. Fathers who engage emotionally with their children pass on E-type skills, as do grandparents and other adults prepared to spend time communicating with the next generation. It famously 'takes a village to raise a child'.

But as long as women were trapped by their biology in a low-sta-tus domestic existence, most of the responsibility rested with them. For countless millennia, while their menfolk were out using human-kind's ever-increasing store of S-type knowledge to create ever more sophisticated civilisations, women were stuck at home bearing and raising the next generation. In a man-made culture, they valued their E-type contribution as little as anyone else. Yet as mothers sang to their infants, played with their toddlers and comforted their growing children, they were unconsciously passing on the human talents that make civilisation possible.

Women's work

The E-type skills women refined on the home front while men were out doing the moving and shaking were essential for day-to-day existence. Preparing food, fetching water and generally keeping the home fires burning are all extremely time-consuming, so to fit them all in around bearing and caring for their children, women relied on the kindness of other women. They delivered each other's babies, came together to help new mothers through the early weeks and months, and trusted each other to help keep an eye on the children as they grew. Women's survival, and that of their offspring, depended on their talent for making and maintaining strong personal relationships.

And it wasn't just relationships with other womenfolk. Their biological destiny as mothers condemned women to dependence on men for protection. So in order to keep daily life rolling along as smoothly as possible, women needed to use their E-type talents, along with their sexuality, to keep their lords and masters onside.

It really is little wonder that E-type thought is considered of so little value in today's sexually equal, highly individualistic culture. For countless millennia, men who wanted to concentrate on those things that earned kudos in the male hierarchy – physical brawn and S-type brain – could afford to leave women to specialise in empathising. Women's strength in nurturing personal relationships has always been associated with powerlessness, vulnerability and submission.

Although their position at the bottom of social hierarchies must have been extremely irksome for spirited women, biology – in the form of maternal instincts – ensured the female sex carried on passing E-type thinking skills down through the generations. And for those children (mostly boys) who gained access to education, the E-type skills acquired at home underpinned the S-type knowledge passed on by teachers.

So, even though women's work was unsung, unpaid and (consequently) unnoticed, it affected the direction of human culture slowly but surely. This continued until recent centuries when a happy combination of S-type reason and E-type humanity led to the popularising of ideas like democracy, equality of opportunity and human rights.

Indeed, it popularised them so much that by the second half of the 20th century there was no longer any excuse to regard women as inferior to men. What's more, contraception had finally freed them from the physical demands of constant procreation. They were at last free to escape from domestic servitude and join men on the wider stage.

Of course, in a culture created and dominated by male values, they still did so on 'male' terms.

From Stone Age to stereotypes

All of which brings me back to the 'Stone Age' boys and girls on a Scottish hillside 30 years ago, who conformed so neatly to the theories of the evolutionary biologists. The boys were competitive, keen to make tools and weapons, and eager to roam the hills in the hope of material reward (in the form of a kill). The girls were collaborative, taking pains to make the shelter warm and cosy, and then happy to sit quietly, discussing practicalities.

Gung-ho, status-driven male enthusiasm on the one hand, and down-to-earth, people-centred female engagement on the other. Was it nature that led them to act in such gender-specific ways, or were they just conforming to cultural stereotypes? On the basis of current scientific evidence, I think both were involved (see Chapter 3), although gender stereotypes almost certainly had the upper edge. But with hindsight, I think the real victim of gender stereotyping that afternoon might have been me. Confronted with the children's Stone Age behaviour, my reaction had been to worry that the girls weren't being as 'proactive' as the boys.

> Gung-ho, status-driven male enthusiasm on the one hand, and down-to-earth, people-centred female engagement on the other.

In fact, both boys and girls worked to build the shelter in a very proactive way. Their efforts dovetailed neatly to achieve the desired result, just as male and female contributions have dovetailed to keep the human project rolling along through the ages. But I'd been primed by a man-made value system to see male activity as somehow 'better' or 'more important' than women's work. And I fell straight into the status trap, just like the female scientists who shrug off the significance of empathy.

There's a danger that this could sound like an argument for sending women back to domestic slavery, which it most certainly isn't. I'm thrilled to have been born at a time when enlightened human thought has freed women to take an equal role in society, and I'm certainly not knocking it. What I'm arguing is that we should accord as much prestige to what the women of the past were doing on the home front as to what men were doing in the wider world. And no matter how we organise society in the future (which hopefully will be along increasingly equal lines), we have to ensure that the essential human aspects of traditional women's work are not lost – especially the transmission of E-type skills. Otherwise, we're in danger of the human project rolling right off the rails.

The value system of the 'perfect storm' described in Chapter 1 is 'male' in the extreme. Consumer capitalism stimulates a state of gung-ho, status-driven enthusiasm in pursuit of material rewards (most of which we don't really need), but allows little thought for anyone else. Computer technology encourages us to seek depersonalised, systemised ways of thinking, so we end up bedazzled by data or swamped in bureaucracy. Neither consumerism nor computer technology is a 'bad' development – the more of us there are on the planet, the more we need sophisticated, systemised solutions to ensure the well-being of the earth and our species.

But with all these new developments there are bound to be some unintended consequences. The more impersonal our systemised solutions have become, the less we've valued the E-type thinking skills that balance our S-type strength. And we're now so in thrall to values based on 'male' behaviour (and thought processes) that the balance of S- and E-type thinking has been seriously disturbed. In 2011, research from the USA showed that levels of empathy in young people have been falling steadily over the last 30 years, with an especially steep decline in the last ten years.

We can see the results of the S/E imbalance all around us. On the world stage, there are financial scandals, collapsing economies and frequent crises due to the ruthless exploitation of the world's resources, both human and material. In our daily lives, there's been a steady deterioration in personal relationships, a decline in trust in the wider community and a constant undervaluing of the personal element in care – not just for children, but for the old, the sick and the vulnerable. In our pursuit of ever more systemised solutions to the problems that confront us, we also seem to have lost sight of common sense.*

The S/E balancing act

Back in the heady days of women's liberation, no one could have foreseen the effects of the cultural storm that was brewing on the horizon. But, as one of the women who benefited from the struggle for equality, I wish the sisterhood had realised – as we marched proudly out of the home and into the workplace – how much we owed human enlightenment to our mothers, our mothers' mothers and all the women who went before them. Had we done so, perhaps we would have pursued sexual equality in ways that valued women's traditional strengths as much as those of men. And perhaps if society as a whole had been persuaded to take the significance of E-type thought on board, we would all have spent the last 50 years valuing love, trust, kindness and care as much as we value social status, material goods and all the bells and whistles of screen-based technology.

> No one could have foreseen the effects of the cultural storm that was brewing on the horizon.

Still, a couple of generations of misplaced enthusiasm aren't the end of the world. The capacity for E-type thought is still in our DNA and there are still many good-hearted men and women keeping the light of empathy burning and passing it on to children. As a travelling speaker, I meet them all the time. Like everyone else, they struggle to

---

* If you're an S-type thinker who distrusts the idea of common sense, my use of the term is defined on page 117.

establish a sensible work–life balance in a culture where work (especially the systemised, bureaucratic elements of work) is considered much more important than personal relationships and family life. But they're prepared to make sacrifices in terms of status and material wealth to achieve a personally satisfying balance of 'heavenly' and worldly rewards.

> There's also gathering evidence that women are losing interest in competing on male terms.

There's also gathering evidence that women are losing interest in competing on male terms. It appears that talented female S-brainers are beginning to recognise the downside of too much systemised success. The Canadian psychologist Susan Pinker recently reviewed research on women who've excelled in male-dominated fields. She found that, once they've shown they can succeed in a man's world, a significant number lose interest in climbing the greasy pole. They drop out, either to raise a family or to pursue a less-well-paid career that they find more rewarding on a personal level (often involving working with people).

She also discovered that in countries where women have the widest range of career options, they're *less* likely to choose high-powered jobs, leading her to comment that '*gifted, talented women with the most choices and freedoms don't seem to be choosing the same paths, in the same numbers, as the men around them. Even with barriers stripped away, they don't behave like male clones.*' Just like my Stone Age girls, they appear content to let the boys jostle, compete and rush around in pursuit of glory, while themselves engaging in other useful, and personally rewarding, pursuits. Deep down inside, they aren't really such material girls.

And, of course, that's the case with most grown men too. There's only room at the top for a handful of ruthless, power-obsessed buccaneers. Throughout history, men blessed with a reasonable balance of S- and E-type skills have been just as keen as women on a balanced life. They've known intuitively what neuroscience now confirms – that once our basic material needs are met, the recipe for human wellbeing is:

- satisfying relationships with friends and family
- engaging in activities we find personally satisfying (to the extent that we can enjoy 'losing' ourselves in what we're doing, rather than constantly pursuing extrinsic rewards)
- a feeling of being in control of our own day-to-day existence.

Our natural attachment to this formula is why the human race has continued – despite frequent appalling falls from grace – on the enlightened upward trajectory that led to the 20th century acceptance of human rights and sexual equality. And as long as we remain human, that natural attachment will continue. Twenty-first century happiness won't be achieved by neglecting personal relationships in the selfish pursuit of consumer-driven status, or by relying on technological solutions to control every aspect of our daily lives. It will rely, as it always has done, on our species' ability to balance the capacity for systemised thought with the capacity for care.

Redressing the balance

So how do we redress the balance, and start to accord as much prestige to traditionally female as opposed to traditionally male values? It seems to me that we should look at the reason why male and female behaviour diverged so dramatically over the millennia – the raising of children. If we can identify exactly what it was that women did to keep E-type thought flowing through human culture, we can look for ways of doing it just as well in a sexually equal 21st century context.

It can probably be summed up in two words: personal care. By tuning in to their offsprings' social and emotional needs with intelligence, and responding to the changing nature of these needs at different stages in children's development, talented E-type mothers (aided by loving fathers and other adults in their families and communities) were unconsciously passing on their skills to the next generation.

There's now a mountain of scientific evidence to support the

> Childcare in modern Britain isn't focused on responsiveness and empathy.

idea that responsive empathetic care of this kind – especially in the early years of children's lives – is of enormous significance in building balanced brains, with long-term knock-on effects on the way society develops and functions. But childcare in modern Britain isn't focused on responsiveness and empathy. We've come to see it as primarily a matter of tending to children's material needs – keeping them fed, clothed, safe and comfortable. Personal interaction with loving adults is often incidental rather than central to this process.

The emphasis on the impersonal is partly due to consumerist values, in which the parental role is to earn money to spend on their offspring, and partly to the depersonalised nature of technological interaction, which distracts us from real-life face-to-face relationships. But the sexual revolution has also played a significant part. By pursuing equality on 'male' terms, the feminist movement has helped to nudge E-type thought out of the child-rearing equation and redefined our cultural concept of care.

Fortunately, parents (male and female, feminist or not) still love their children – nature sees to that. If they're aware of the significance and subtleties of child development, they can make the effort to provide the sort of personal interaction needed at different times in their children's lives. If they also take the long view – imagining the world their offspring will inhabit as adults – they'll see the point of promoting personal care for all children, especially in their earliest years. So if, like our Stone Age ancestors, today's parents put the welfare of the next generation at the heart of their private and public lives, they can lead the way in escaping from the negative gender stereotypes that underpin our current S/E imbalance.

***

Central to any reassessment of child-rearing practices is our attitude towards motherhood. As a fundamental aspect of human biology, the capacity to bear and suckle children inevitably affects the development of the female of the species – not just physically, but psychologically. So when motherhood is viewed merely as an inconvenient interruption to their working lives, it's bound to have a negative effect on the self-concept of women and girls, turning their E-type talents in on themselves in ways that can be destructive on a personal level.

> When motherhood is viewed merely as an inconvenient interruption to their working lives, it's bound to have a negative effect.

This means that the parents of girls have a special interest in recalibrating the S/E balance needed to keep human culture on an even keel – and so do feminists. Raising the profile of women's contribution to human progress has to be good for the self-image of 21st century girls. If we carry on bringing them up to judge themselves by old-fashioned man-made criteria, they'll continue to find themselves wanting – and sexual equality will become an increasingly unrealisable dream. But if the girls – and their brothers – are raised in a culture that places equal value on E- and S-type thought, there's a far greater chance of that dream turning into reality.

Over the last 15 years, I've seen at first-hand how many present-day, talented E-typers (male and female) are struggling – with increasing feelings of powerlessness – to exercise their skills against a swelling cultural tide. So it seems to me that we have to rally the power of the personal pretty damn soon. As the speed of human progress accelerates, we have to turn the tide within the next couple of generations, or it's likely to become a tsunami. And a wave that size could flatten not just the dream of sexual equality, but the very characteristics that first made us Homo sapiens.

CHAPTER 3

MOTHERS, DAUGHTERS AND CHILD DEVELOPMENT

It's several years after the Stone Age project and I've left the little village school to try my hand as an educational writer. But now I'm on the verge of doing something completely different … which starts with a mystical experience.

I awake with no idea of where or even who I am, frantically trying to make sense of the movement and voices around me.

'*She's back*,' someone says, and gently lifts one of my arms, to arrange it beside my head on the pillow. I realise I'm on a hospital trolley, returning from an emergency Caesarean. Memories of thirty-six hours of labour come flooding back.

'*Where's…?*' I start to say, then there she is. The midwife lowers my newborn baby into the crook of my arm and our eyes meet for the first time. Maybe it's just the drugs, but I'm overwhelmed by the intensity of her gaze. I gaze back, transfixed and transported.

Yes, it's her – my daughter! But the weird thing is, it's not just her. Somewhere behind those deep dark eyes are *her* daughters, her daughter's daughters and all the daughters to come, stretching into the future. And I'm her mother, staring through a mother's eyes. But I'm not just me; somewhere in the consciousness behind my eyes is my own mother and an endless chain of mothers, woman after woman, stretching back into the past…

Then the midwife's back to whip her away to the special baby unit for observation. *'She has to go. Don't worry, you'll get her back.'* So I'm left alone again, no longer part of that spectacular female continuum. Just me – an infinitesimal pinprick in time and space – but a new me, desperate to mother my daughter.

So that's what it's all about, I think, as they put me back to sleep.

The eyes have it

Of course, when I awoke the next day the realities of motherhood soon pushed mystical experiences right to the bottom of my mental agenda. Looking after a small baby turned out to be nowhere near as straightforward as teaching a class, running a school, or writing textbooks about grammar and spelling. And a profound sense of the continuity and interconnectedness of human existence was of absolutely no help in getting through the day.

But I'll treasure the memory of that first meeting with my newborn child for the rest of my life. A quarter of a century later, looking back on it still makes my heart swell, and there's a tiny emotional echo of the experience whenever my grown-up daughter and I catch each other's eye. So it's been interesting to discover through research into child development that – in terms of keeping humanity on track – the cross-generational meeting of eyes may indeed be 'what it's all about'. What's more, it could also be the reason behind critical differences in male and female thought and behaviour through the ages.

All newborn babies (boys and girls) are programmed to gaze at human faces, for two very good reasons. First, it helps to trigger the deep parental love of one generation for the next, and the care that

> All newborn babies (boys and girls) are programmed to gaze at human faces.

keeps the human race bowling along. Second, it sets up the new arrivals to learn about their fellow human beings, and to gradually develop the E-type skills they'll need to survive in a social world. Babies are also programmed to imitate the adults they see and to copy them in any way they can, which at birth isn't very much, as their bodily control is practically nil. They do, however, have instinctive command over the muscles of their mouths, which they need for feeding purposes. If you put your tongue out at a newborn baby, the odds are it will obligingly struggle to stick out its tongue at you.

But the tongue thing is merely an interesting scientific snippet. It's eye contact that matters to us grown-ups (particularly female grown-ups, with our long-established interest in nurturing personal relationships). We've learned that the eyes are the windows to the soul. We look into someone's eyes to see if we can trust them, and when we fall in love we gaze deep into the eyes of our beloved. So when our newborn babies hold our gaze, we fall in love with them. As the days and weeks go on, we continue to look lovingly into their eyes. Every time they look back at us, we're deeply rewarded by their attention, so the love grows increasingly profound. And every time we look at our offspring, we're providing a model for them to copy, a model of human emotional connection.

Here's looking at you, kid

This mutual gazing becomes mutually reinforcing, cementing the deep emotional bond that psychologists call 'attachment'. There's a huge body of scientific literature showing that the quality of an infant's attachment underpins many aspects of future psychological health. So the 'dance of communication' between the 'primary attachment figure' (usually mum) and her newborn baby is profoundly significant in passing on the potential for human well-being through the generations. The more emotional connections mother and child make through meeting each other's eyes, the better.

And girls, for some reason, seem to be better at joining in this communicatory dance than boys. Research studies have found that, at birth, both male and female babies stare equally at the important adults in their lives, but by the time they're four months old, girls have improved their ability to make eye contact by 400 per cent, while boys have made no progress at all. This means girls also make faster progress in other aspects of copycat behaviour – by six months, they're more likely than boys to raise their eyebrows and widen their eyes in greeting when a friendly human approaches. Scientific researchers describe girls as 'interested and sociable', and boys as 'more excitable', less easy to soothe and settle. Wise old wives used to say that 'girls are easier than boys'.

There's plenty of individual variation, of course – some baby boys are more inclined to join in the dance than others, and some baby girls less so, depending on their inherent talent for eye contact and the type of nurture they receive during the early months. But in general, girls appear to have an edge in the sociability stakes. And this gives them a head start in many of the other skills that are valued by parents.

Girls start making social gestures sooner, such as pointing, waving 'bye-bye', and raising their arms to be picked up and cuddled. They learn to speak earlier than boys, pick up more words more quickly, and have fewer speech and language problems. And by the time they start school, girls in England (where pre-school children's behaviour must be recorded meticulously) score higher than boys in every measure of achievement – giving an academic advantage that now persists throughout their educational careers.

It seems that an early talent for eye contact gives girls an advantage in making their way in the 21st century world – at least in the short term. The fact that they're easier to socialise makes them good students who soak up the received wisdom of the culture as well as their lessons at school.

> An early talent for eye contact gives girls an advantage.

The stronger sex?

So is there a biological explanation for baby girls' ability to gaze back into their mother's eyes? At the time of writing, the jury's still out on the exact reasons behind this tiny but significant difference in early male and female behaviour. And the more neuroscientists discover about the development of the human brain, the more complicated it turns out to be, so it will probably be a long time before they come to any definite conclusions.

However, it's likely that two aspects of prenatal development combine to give girls their slight social advantage. First, their developing brains aren't exposed to such high levels of testosterone in the womb. A male foetus experiences a 'testosterone surge' that begins six weeks after conception, when the Y chromosome kicks in to start the formation of the male sex organs, and lasts about fourteen weeks. (There's a further, smaller surge just after birth that lasts another six months or so.) Perhaps, as some scientists claim, foetal testosterone inhibits the development of the social centres in the brain (psychologist Louann Brizendine speculates rather chillingly that it involves 'killing off some cells in the communication centres and growing more cells in the sex and aggression centres').

The second difference is that, on the whole, girls' bodies and brains mature more quickly. So boys' relative immaturity at birth means that, in the words of neuroscientist Lise Eliot, they're 'more needy and less ready to enter the world than girls'. They tend to be more distractible, 'fussy' babies, and perhaps slower to control the focus of their gaze.

In fact, girls don't just mature more quickly than boys; the female sex as a whole is constitutionally more robust. It's now well established that a foetus with male XY sex chromosomes is likely to be more 'fragile' than one with the female XX version. The psychologist Sebastian Kraemer, who has collated research on 'the fragile male', claims that girls 'are endowed with what is in effect an extra Duracell battery'. They're at lower risk than boys of death or damage from obstetric catastrophes during their nine months in the womb. They're also less likely to be born prematurely, and those born before their due date are more likely to survive. During childhood, they're less likely than boys to suffer from various physical ailments or from developmental disorders, such as ADHD and autism.

This male fragility has only become apparent in recent decades, as science shed increasing light on human biology and development, and medical advances ensured that more children could survive any genetic 'fragility'. Since boys tend to be larger than girls at birth, and full-grown men are physically bigger (and, pound for pound, stronger) than women, it's traditionally been assumed that women are 'the weaker sex'. But size isn't everything – male brains are bigger too, in proportion to their overall body size, but there's not a shred of evidence to suggest that there's any difference between the sexes in S-type thinking power in the overwhelming majority of the population.

An essential difference

On the other hand, there's plenty of evidence that any difference in 'thinking style' (of both the S- and E-type) owes far less to minuscule differences in brain structure than to the way children are nurtured throughout childhood. In the early months and years, when their brains are developing most rapidly, these minuscule differences seem to make girls more responsive to their adult nurturers – the most significant of whom are, of course, their parents. And if the received wisdom of the ages affects the way mum and dad think about their daughter, the sort of nurture this prompts them to offer could seriously affect the way she learns to think about herself.

For instance, in a famous research study in 2000, a group of mums was asked to assess their 11-month-old children's ability to crawl down slopes of varying degrees of steepness. They were just about spot on at judging how steep a slope their sons could negotiate, but underestimated their daughters' ability by almost 10per cent.

Presumably, the mums were influenced by the age-old belief that girls are the weaker sex, and therefore assumed they'd be less physically competent than the boys at this exercise.* If they hadn't participated in the research study, these mothers would have continued under this delusion. They'd probably have curtailed a daughter's physical exploration of the world a little sooner than a son's, perhaps thereby encouraging the girls to become more risk-averse.

What's more, socially aware little girls would be less likely than boys to push the boundaries of their mothers' tolerance (there's another research study showing that, by the time they're a year old, girls check their mums' faces for signs of approval four times more often than boys). So not only would the old gender stereotype be passed down unconsciously to yet another female generation, each little girl would learn at a formative age that she couldn't trust her own judgement. She'd have a tiny bit less self-belief than her male counterparts, and be slightly more open to social pressures.

> Girls check their mums' faces for signs of approval four times more often than boys.

Very early social awareness is a double-edged sword. On the one hand, it means girls pick up social graces more quickly than boys, conforming more easily to what adults require of 'good babies'. On the other, if the desire to please makes them a little more risk-averse, self-doubting and compliant, their search for approval could begin to affect their lives in all sorts of ways.

The drive to learn

All children are different. Indeed, child development specialists tell us there's as much variation in terms of 'gendered' behaviour between the members of one sex as there is between the two sexes as a whole. There are 'easier' boys and 'more difficult' girls. If parents want to help their baby (girl or boy) reach her or his full potential, they must tune in to the child as an individual, responding day by day to their rapidly changing – and deeply personal – developmental needs.

---

* In fact, when left to try out the slopes for themselves, the baby girls turned out to be slightly more competent than the boys. They successfully judged their ability to crawl down slopes up to 8 degrees steeper.

But although all children are different, they share the same amazing potential to learn. Unless something's very much awry, every human baby is born with a brain primed to pursue two great cognitive quests. The first is to learn about the bright, noisy, new world in which they suddenly find themselves, to explore it with all their senses and find out how it works (the genesis of Baron-Cohen's S-type thought). The second quest is to learn about the people with whom they share the world, imitate their behaviour and gradually suss out how their minds work (the underpinnings of E-type thought).

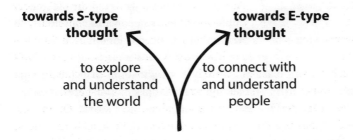

towards S-type thought **towards E-type thought**

to explore and understand the world

to connect with and understand people

The average girl is 'readier' than the average boy – in terms of overall maturity – to pursue both cognitive quests. But her slight advantage in catching adult eyes means that over the first few months she makes better progress in the second, social quest. During this period, like all babies, she's dependent on adult carers to mediate her investigations of the material world. So by the time she's sufficiently in control of her movements to start exploring for herself, she may be doing so well in the social quest that it affects her attitude towards questing in general. If her parents are worried that she might harm herself exploring the world, her increasingly sensitive social antennae will pick this up.

There's another thing all tiny children have in common. They don't 'think'. At birth, they're just bundles of physical needs, developmental drives and raw human emotion. Consciousness – the awareness that they're people in their own right, with minds of their own

– probably takes around two years to dawn, and is associated with language development. So although they start learning the moment they're born, they aren't consciously 'thinking' about what they're learning. The lessons learned in those early months and years are embedded for ever in their unconscious minds.

> Babies are programmed to attach emotionally to the adult who fulfils their physical needs.

In the Beginning is Attachment. Babies are programmed to attach emotionally to the adult who fulfils their physical needs – usually mum. But every mum was once, a generation ago, a similar bundle of needs, drives and emotion. The lessons *she* learned from *her* mum are buried in her unconscious mind. The love that binds her to her offspring is linked to long-buried memories of the love she received in her own mother's arms.

This means that a 21st century mum who wants to help her daughter to flourish in a 21st century world has to summon her adult rationality and remember that – for a child who isn't yet able to think for herself – encouraging behaviour based on outdated stereotypes may not always be in her long-term interests.

Little princess syndrome

Despite girls' slight head start on the social front and boys' slight developmental lag, both sexes pursue both cognitive quests with enthusiasm during their early years. As cognitive psychologist Elizabeth Spelke puts it: '*Infants don't divide up the labour of understanding the world, with males focusing on mechanics and females focusing on emotions. Male and female infants are both interested in objects and in people, and they learn about both.*'

The trouble is that for many millennia adult males and females have divided up their labour roughly along those lines. The world that today's infants strive to understand is awash with gender stereotypes based on that long-standing division. Despite attempts in the 1970s and 1980s to dampen down these stereotypes, which feminists could see were clearly not in the best interests of the female half of the population, they didn't go away. Indeed, as described in Chapter 1, over the last three decades aggressive marketing strategies have embedded increasingly exaggerated 'gendered' messages in every possible aspect of tiny children's lives. The most obvious example in terms of little girls is the 'princess syndrome', which is now practically endemic across society.

The archetypal princesses of old were valued largely for their looks. They were, in fact, little more than attractive objects to be traded among rich men. Since it suits a man-made culture for girls to value themselves mainly for their appearance, the appeal of princesses has been passed down through the ages in fairy tales. In the mid-20th century, Disney films began to lend a helping hand to the process, and marketers also jumped on the bandwagon with endless pink, glittery, fluffy products.

But princessdom doesn't have to be tacky. Wealthier, more discerning parents can treat their daughters to a princess-like start in life by dressing them in upmarket fashion brands. And while contemplating the contents of her wardrobe won't affect a girl's capacity to think rationally in the future, her natural sensitivity to her parents' behaviour may affect the way she feels – at a deep emotional level – about herself. If mum constantly demonstrates her love by the way she dresses her daughter, that socially-aware daughter will pick up the message that her personal lovability is closely connected with her outward appearance. Like the other expensive paraphernalia in her parents' domestic domain, she's an 'object' to be enjoyed.

The emotional lessons children learn in their first few years stay with them throughout their lives, so giving a little girl early lessons in self-objectification isn't a wise move. Though it's very difficult to resist the siren call of market forces, the less parents allow it to dictate their interactions with their daughter, the more likely she is to grow up seeing herself as a person, valued (and valuable) for her own inner qualities.

In a world awash with gender stereotypes, girls need protection from the distorting lens of the fashion industry in order to develop a strong sense of their own inner worth. So the best way for parents to dress their daughter is in practical, comfortable clothing that lets her pursue her two developmental quests as freely as possible, getting as messy as everyday exploratory activities demand.

And in an age when female problems with body image begin at an increasingly early age, girls need to feel confident in their own skin right from the beginning. So the best way to demonstrate parental love is to give girls plenty of time, attention and cuddles, and show delight in their developing personality.

Little Miss Perfect

'Oh what a lovely baby! Isn't she sweet?'

Parents out and about with their baby daughters attract demonstrations of gender stereotyping like confetti. Kind-hearted adults, anxious to involve the children in social chit-chat, shower them with the sort of compliments they assume the parents of girls will appreciate (*sweet, cute, pretty, good, clever...*). Many of these pander to the princess image, but others relate to their perceived worth in other ways.

Babies may not be able to understand language, but baby girls certainly understand adult appreciation. Their early talent for greeting visitors by making socially appropriate faces illustrates their keen interest in the sort of behaviour that goes down well with an audience.

To prevent this eagerness to please from exercising undue influence on her developing psyche, mums and dads must focus first and foremost on their daughter, tuning in to her *personal* developmental needs. If they instead focus their attention outwards, on the expectations of the world, there's a danger that their daughter will pick up these socially informed aspirations, and her performance on the stage of life will be aimed far more at the applause of others than her own personal fulfilment.

> Twenty-first century girls have a far greater range of options than their foremothers.

Twenty-first century girls have a far greater range of options than their foremothers – the future is now as open-ended for women as it is for men. So when today's girls start pursuing objectified perfection, they don't just have traditional female stereotypes to live up to, but a raft of other parental aspirations. If a baby girl is distracted from her personal developmental agenda by the quest for adult approval, she is in danger of wearing herself out by trying, like Mary Poppins, to be 'practically perfect in every way'.

I've seen plenty of these girls over the last few decades, which is why the Alpha Girl in the restaurant in which I was enjoying a meal with a friend (see Introduction) filled me with such foreboding. They expend vast amounts of physical and psychological energy on turning themselves into Little Miss Perfect – fair of face and skinny of figure, fashionably dressed and exquisitely turned out, sweet and gentle, sassy and sexy, tough and smart, and toting a bucketful of A-star exam results. The pressure of achieving and maintaining this 'perfect' persona is immense, and unlikely to do them any good in the long run.

That is why parents' personal attunement to their infant daughter's personal needs is so important. Nature equips all children with the means to pursue their cognitive missions for the sheer joy of discovery, allowing them to spend much of their young lives in the glorious state of 'flow' (complete absorption in what they are doing) that is its own reward. It's the route to long-term human well-being. So if mum and dad allow their daughter's natural exploratory drive to direct the process of discovery as far as humanly possible (basing their guidance on love in the here-and-now, not on some dream of the future or externally influenced need to control) their shared joy in her every achievement will be reward enough for both parent and child.

A baby girl already is Little Miss Perfect to the adults who love her. She shouldn't have to try.

Female fragility and female strength

Over the last 50 years, there have been endless research projects into the way adults project old-fashioned gender stereotypes onto tiny children. Gender is usually the only aspect of identity available to someone who doesn't already know a child, so it's the obvious thing to focus on, and stereotypes usually rise to the mind unbidden. The unconscious learning of adults themselves means they expect girls to be 'girly' and boys to be 'boyish'.

As little children look pretty androgynous, all a stranger has to go on in this respect is their clothing. Various cross-dressing experiments have shown that when an infant is dressed in male or female clothing, it attracts the appropriate stereotypical epithets from random adult encounters. If a child is perceived as a girl, she'll tend to be handled more gently and carefully in deference to 'her' perceived female sweetness. Boys, on the other hand, can be bounced about because they're expected to be big and strong.*

> If a child is perceived as a girl, she'll tend to be handled more gently

The slope-climbing research study described on page 46, shows that even loving mothers can be affected by the deeply ingrained gender stereotype that girls are somehow more 'fragile' than boys. Now that research into prenatal development proves that girls are not the weaker sex, there really is no excuse – we have to rally the power of rational thought to counter unconscious prejudices. As long as we allow this particular stereotypical view to affect our behaviour, little girls will learn to see themselves as somehow weak and dependent.

If adults always handle girls with kid gloves and mums restrict their movements for fear they can't assess risks for themselves, what else can a small, socially aware child conclude? When they grow up, the odds are that no matter how big, strong and sexually equal they appear on the surface, deep in their hearts will still be the suspicion that there's something essentially 'inferior' about being female. Something that might make them mistrust their own judgement. Something that makes every risk that little bit more risky for girls than for boys. Something that makes women's innermost desires less important than men's.

In her book *Delusions of Gender*, Cordelia Fine catalogues a stream of research studies into this sort of unconscious gender stereotyping,

---

* I felt uncomfortable using the pronoun 'it' in this paragraph, because it seems to treat the child as an object, rather than a person. Which is exactly what stereotyping is about – reducing human beings to objects, with certain socially agreed characteristics.

often on behalf of highly educated, apparently successful women. She calls it 'neurosexism'. It's embedded deep in our psyches and, like any kind of unconscious prejudice, it's remarkably resistant to rational argument.

I may just be indulging my personal version of neurosexism, but I think there's a way to help the next generation of girls to avoid developing this sort of deep-seated, unconscious self-doubt – and all the other harmful stereotypes that can influence their developing self-image in potentially damaging ways. It is to expose them to the great 'female' strength of E-type attunement from the moment they're born, providing them with the loving care they need to pursue their personal cognitive missions and develop minds of their own – hopefully, well-balanced ones.

It was by employing the 'power of the personal' that through the ages talented E-type mums helped civilisation develop to the point where women could use their S-type skills to achieve equality with men. So it seems to me that 'good mothering' in the early years of girls' lives will help to raise well-balanced women able to take full advantage of equality and to use it, not just for their own benefit, but for everyone's.

Tuning in to 21st century girls

At the end of the last century, Hillary Clinton convened a conference at the White House to discuss the findings of psychological and neuroscientific research into the infant brain. It concluded: 'What happens during the first months and years of life matters a lot, not because this period of development provides an indelible blueprint for adult well-being, but because it sets either a sturdy or fragile stage for what follows.'

If we want our daughters to start life on a sturdy stage – secure in themselves, keen to learn, able to make their own judgements and resist unhealthy outside pressures – the quality of care we provide in those early months and years is vital. And to avoid the type of pitfalls described in preceding sections, it's essential that we:

- tune in to girls' exploratory learning drive, rather than letting their social awareness lull us into thinking their personal exploratory mission isn't as vital as it is to boys
- avoid ancient stereotypes as far as possible, treating children as people rather than objects
- don't confuse care with control.

The last point requires a degree of old-fashioned 'female' humility. In many ways, sensitive caring for a small child involves relinquishing adult control and trusting the child's developmental drives. When a talented E-type mother tunes in to her infant's feelings, she respects the child's natural instinct to explore and learn, and does all she can to support it. Little children's self-directed learning (also known as 'play') often involves mess, dirt, adult inconvenience and sometimes the possibility of damage – so mum has to be constantly ready to intervene if necessary, and perhaps to help point the play in a more mutually congenial direction. But since she doesn't want to frustrate her little one's lust to learn, her decisions are based on common sense, personal judgement and an in-depth knowledge of the child's personal level of competence.

In the early months, mothers are, fairly obviously, the ideal carers for their own children. They're primed by nature to love them, supported by a body bursting with maternal hormones, and – with a ready-made food supply handily attached to their chests – likely to spend many hours a day in close personal contact with their infants. This emotional connection and attunement to their children's physical needs sets mothers up to tune in to their kids' developmental drives too (as long as they are aware the developmental drives are there, of course).

> Girls need this sort of constant, consistent, one-on-one personal care during the first two years at least.

For girls to have the best possible chance of a 'good childhood' and a fulfilling, happy life, they need this sort of constant, consistent, one-on-one personal care until they start to develop minds of their own, which means during the first two years *at least*.

Who cares?

There are many reasons why modern mothers may not be able to care for their own children, usually economic ones. Over the last 30 years, as women's earnings were absorbed into the economy, they became necessary to keep it on track, so the 'dual income family' is now the norm (and mums bringing up children on their own often have no alternative but to work). Nevertheless, in the choice between love and money, there may be a way to choose love, living more cheaply until children are ready for nursery school. But if that isn't possible, parents have to choose an alternative form of care – and the most common type currently available is institutionalised day care.

Over the last few years, we've been led to believe (by commercial and political forces) that childcare is a sort of commodity, to be bought and sold on the open market, its efficiency regulated and measured by government inspectors. But it's impossible to imagine the sort of one-on-one, constant, consistent loving care described above being available in an institution, no matter how well equipped and well regulated. Running a day nursery is an expensive business, and staff costs have to be kept down. As a result, carers may be poorly qualified, are almost certainly poorly paid, and turnover is often high. Nowadays, they're also kept busy with a lot of bureaucratic form filling. One way or another, the chances of anyone in an institution being available to tune in to an individual child's needs on anything other than an occasional basis are low.

It seems to me that, for most girls, early institutionalised childcare increases the danger of developing a compliant, risk-averse mindset – and indeed, there is evidence that in a 'small but significant group' of children it leads to withdrawn, compliant or 'sad' behaviour. Even those who don't exhibit symptoms in the short term may perform on a more 'fragile' stage in later life. Researchers have found worryingly high levels of the stress hormone cortisol in babies who are left in day care for long hours at a stretch, which is not good for developing brains. In recent years, many respected authorities on child psychology – including Steve Biddulph, Penelope

> Researchers have found worryingly high levels of the stress hormone cortisol in babies who are left in day care for long hours.

Leach, Margot Sunderland and Oliver James – have warned of the dangers of this sort of childcare.

The obvious alternative is some form of mother substitute, and all the evidence suggests that, as long as this substitute is highly committed and attuned to the child, another carer can be just as good as an infant's mother. There are plenty of talented E-type thinkers in the world who could take on this role. But the increasing regulation of childcare means that finding one who suits you and your baby can be very difficult. In recent years there's been a significant reduction in the number of childminders providing one-on-one care in their own homes, thanks to government health and safety rules, record keeping and other S-type red tape, which have removed much of the job satisfaction that compensated for low-paid, low-status work.

Mum's the word

These problems aren't going to disappear of their own accord. If we want to raise bright, balanced daughters, unaffected by damaging stereotypes and able to help create a genuinely equal society in the future, we have to start challenging the widespread assumption that early childcare is something that can be neatly systemised away. That means challenging the most damaging stereotype of all – the stereotype of motherhood as low-status, unimportant women's work.

I can't imagine much of a public challenge in the present cultural climate. The men who still run most of the show wouldn't care or dare to make it. And female movers and shakers aren't usually all that impressed by motherhood themselves. Some have no personal experience of it, having decided they're better suited to their chosen career rather than caring for small children. Others, who've found a way of fitting motherhood into their own career, tend to be committed to the current feminist line of 'having it all' – or perhaps prefer not to think about the subject because it stirs up too much maternal guilt (see Chapter 4). Most modern women are just too damn busy.

So, in the early stages at least, it would have to be a personal challenge, waged personally by both male and female parents. And the parents of daughters have the greatest reason to make such a stand. Unless we do, woman will continue to hand on misery to woman, until it deepens like a coastal shelf.

In his book *How Not To F*** Them Up*, the psychologist Oliver James describes three types of modern mothers: Organisers, Huggers and Fleximums – the first type is inclined to S-type thought, the second to E-type and the third group hovers somewhere in the middle. He suggests how each of them can try to ensure the best type of childcare for their babies and toddlers. When interviewed on Radio 4's *Woman's Hour* to argue what seemed to me a very reasonable case, he was torn to shreds by two women who simply could not see the issue from the child development angle. Early childcare is right up there with breast-feeding, smacking, politics and religion in terms of arousing deeply held, entrenched opinions.

James – who's very much a 'new man' – suggests that the best mother substitutes are, in order of suitability:

- dad, who also has a deep emotional attachment to the child
- another family member (which probably means granny), whose blood relationship means they're also deeply committed to the child's welfare
- another highly empathetic person (such as a nanny or child-minder).

I couldn't agree with him more. But as long as motherhood is seen as a low-status occupation, it takes a remarkable father (no matter how well balanced) to take on the role. And today's grannies are often busy with their own careers, nannies are expensive, and empathetic child-minders are becoming as scarce as hen's teeth. If we don't start valuing E-type strengths soon, this vital aspect of traditional women's work will drop from low status to no status. And if we let that happen, it's not just girl babies who'll have less chance of developing balanced brains, it's also boy babies – those needy 'fragile males' who require far more loving nurture to avoid their natural tendency towards selfish individualism.

***

In a fast-moving, materialistic world, there's a constant tension between messy, time-consuming human processes and the appeal of neat, well-marketed, man-made products. Caring for babies and toddlers is a process – and a long, hard, demanding one at that. In a world where few people recognise its importance, it often seems a thankless task, even to the most committed mum.

So it's infinitely tempting for parents to be distracted from the process of care by sophisticated products offering a quick fix for early parenting problems, commercial packages promising a head start for a daughter's lifelong success, or a cheap and simple way to make her happy. After all, the babies in nursery brochures and TV ads look really happy, don't they? But there are no quick fixes for raising babies and no products that can act as substitutes for love and human attunement to children's needs.

It's also tempting for parents to see a daughter as a sort of 'product' herself – a personally tailored human package, able to elicit admiration from other adults because of her appealing appearance or carefully controlled behaviour. But if her parents objectify her in this way, she'll grow up objectifying herself.

Children's experiences in the early months and years lay down a personal 'default model' for self-image, social competence and habits of thought and behaviour that influence the rest of their lives. Girls' genetic inheritance gives them a slight natural advantage in terms of the social awareness that can lead to E-type talent, so we must build on that strength and not let it degenerate into a source of weakness. That process starts with mothers (and, hopefully, fathers) valuing the strength in themselves.

CHAPTER 4

TOXIC CHILDHOOD

It's a rainy afternoon towards the end of the last century. I'm standing in a kitchen in Chiswick, interviewing Dr Sally Ward. Since my daughter was born, I've become a 'literacy consultant', writing primary textbooks and – in the last couple of years – giving talks around the country about the teaching of literacy. I also write articles for the educational press, and today I'm a newshound on the trail of a story.

Everywhere I go these days, teachers seem to be worrying about children's ability to listen. They claim there's a steady deterioration in attention skills that's affecting pupils' learning and behaviour. In some cases it also seems to be affecting their language; teachers in disadvantaged areas say that 'language is going down year on year'.

So I've hunted down an expert in language and listening. Sally Ward is a speech and language therapist who's been researching young children's listening skills for 15 years. To be precise, she's been testing the capacity of nine-month-old infants to 'single out a foreground sound against background noise'.

She explains that this is what little babies have to do to tune in to their mother's voice, discriminate the sounds of their native language and eventually learn to speak. When she started the research project in 1984, she was concerned to find that 20 per cent of the babies she tested weren't developing this skill on schedule. Fifteen years later she's even more concerned, because the proportion has doubled to 40 per cent.

It's a startling statistic and particularly interesting to a literacy specialist. To read and write a phonetic language like English, children must be able to discriminate language sounds. If they can't, they'll have trouble when they try to learn phonics.

'Why do you think it's happened?' I ask, suspecting I may have stumbled upon a scoop.

'I don't think there's just one cause,' Sally replies. 'I think it's lots of things coming together because of the incredible speed of change in the world. Just think, for instance, of the amount of noise these days. Traffic noise increases every year. When a baby's out in the pushchair with a parent, there's so much racket going on. Adults don't notice because we've learned to screen out background noise, but little babies don't know which sounds to screen out – and if they can't hear mum, they won't develop the skill. And for some reason, the pushchairs nowadays all face the wrong way. If children can't see their mother's face, how can they tune into what she's saying?'

How indeed? My brow furrows. Suddenly, I'm no longer a newshound looking for a scoop or a literacy specialist concerned about declining standards in reading and writing. I'm a mother experiencing a mild surge of maternal guilt because she pushed her daughter around in a buggy that faced the wrong way...

'Of course, the background racket is just as bad indoors. At the beginning of the 1980s, all-day TV arrived in Britain. And in most homes, it blares away all the time. I really do fear that, by the early years of the new millennium, half the children in this country will have trouble tuning in to their mother's voice above the noise of the television.'

I begin to feel even more uneasy. When Beth was small I left the TV on during the day. I didn't know anyone in our neighbourhood and felt very isolated. Daytime TV was a substitute for adult company...

'And then, of course, there's video. Until 20 years ago, there was only one way to comfort a fretful infant – or entertain a happy one. You had to pick it up...' Sally picks up an imaginary baby and begins gently rocking it, that automatic physical accompaniment to the ancient 'dance of communication' '... and you had to look into its eyes, and talk or sing nursery rhymes to keep its attention. As soon as video arrived, there was another way. You could pick the baby up, give it a quick cuddle, then switch on the electronic babysitter.'

Now I'm staring at her in horror. When Beth was a few months old, I bought her a video of nursery rhymes. She watched it for hours, but never learned a single rhyme. And by the time she was four, it was clear she was seriously dyslexic.

Nature, nurture and culture

Beth is in her twenties now, and has her dyslexia firmly under control, but at the time of the interview her problems with reading and writing loomed large in our lives. Throughout her school life, my daughter had to cope with the challenge of living with a learning difficulty, and the many problems that being 'different' from other children creates. I'd decided she needed me at home, which is why I persisted with a freelance writing career, rather than looking for more lucrative work in teaching.

Indeed, dyslexia was the reason I was standing in Sally Ward's kitchen with a notebook. At the age of ten, Beth concluded she was fed up with being different, and asked to become a weekly boarder at a school for dyslexic pupils, where everyone had the same problems as herself. It was a three-hour drive from home, so I took her there every Sunday evening, found speaking or writing work during the week to pay the fees, then picked her up on Friday afternoon to drive her home.

And now Sally Ward seemed to be suggesting that my early mothering had actually contributed to my daughter's dyslexia. I'd bought the wrong pushchair, filled my home with TV babble and put her in front of an electronic baby sitter instead of singing to her myself. Maternal guilt is a powerful emotion, and was about to swing my career in yet another direction.

> Maternal guilt is a powerful emotion.

As I drove off, I tried to reason the guilt away. After all, neuroscientists were now claiming that dyslexia is the result of a genetic predisposition. I was pretty sure that Beth's problems originated in a mixture of heredity, the traumatic circumstances of her birth and a medical history of intermittent hearing loss, due to glue ear.

It didn't work. She may have been predisposed to a learning difficulty, but I knew deep down that the outward-facing pushchair, the all-day TV and – above all – that wretched video of nursery rhymes had exacerbated it. I'd put too much faith in technological products and not enough in my own input as a mum.

Like most of my generation, I'd grown up assuming that technological progress is essentially benign. It never occurred to me to question whether pushchairs should face in a particular direction or whether TV might be bad for babies. As for the video, I bought it because of research showing that 'nursery rhyme knowledge' was closely correlated with success at school. It contained hundreds of rhymes, tunefully delivered by professional singers in colourful costumes. Surely this had to be better than a weary mother, dredging up a few scraps of rhymes from ancient memory.

If Beth had been born ten years earlier, there would have been no option but to sing the nursery rhymes myself, the way mothers have sung to their infants down through the ages. I would have sung them hundreds and hundreds of times, tuning her ears to the sounds of language. It didn't matter that I had a limited repertoire, or that I'm not a professional singer. What mattered was the combination of loving personal attention and *endless* repetition.

To 21st century adults, reared in a quick-fire, multimedia world, repetition doesn't seem important. We crave variety and sensation. So we assume our babies must enjoy the same sorts of 'stimulation' – TV and video to watch, a pushchair facing outwards so they can see where they're going and what's going on. And if that's what we give them, they'll gradually crave more and more variety too. But what if it's not what they *need*?

My baby, with a predisposition to poor sound discrimination, needed to hear the same songs over and over again, from the same beloved voice. Perhaps that would have strengthened the neural networks for phonological awareness so that learning to read came a little more easily. I'd assumed phonological awareness developed 'naturally', and, in the days when nurture depended on endless personal interaction, it did. But as culture and nurture changes, we can't take 'natural' development for granted any more.

> As culture and nurture changes, we can't take 'natural' development for granted any more.

The special needs explosion

Maybe 15 years of scrabbling around to find out more and writing books about child development in the modern world has just been my way of expiating maternal guilt. But I think I let myself off quite early, on the principle that it wasn't really my fault – I didn't know that I was doing anything wrong, and if I had known I would have done things differently. However, my experience in Chiswick sparked my interest in the effects of environment on development.

I'd gone to interview Sally Ward because of reports from teachers that children were somehow less easy to teach than they had been in the past. My notebooks were full of scribbled quotes:

- '*Can't seem to listen.*'
- '*Poorer concentration/difficulty focusing attention.*'
- '*Far more low-level behaviour problems.*'

- *'Don't seem to be getting along with each other as well as they used to.'*

And, of course, from less advantaged areas of the country, *'Language is going down year on year.'*

At first I'd assumed this was the ranting of grumpy old women. People have been claiming that the younger generation is going to the dogs since Cain killed Abel. But when you hear the same phrases time after time, in every part of the country, from teachers of all ages and in every type of school, you start wondering if there might be something to it. Thanks to my travels in the role of literacy consultant I met thousands of teachers every year, and a great many had the same vague but serious concerns.

Once Sally got me thinking about 'natural development', I began to wonder if there was a link between teachers' reports of behavioural changes among children in general and the explosion of special educational needs due to 'developmental conditions'. Dyslexia had become a big issue in schools during the early 1980s; ADHD (attention deficit hyperactivity disorder) came to public attention about a decade later; dyspraxia (difficulties with co-ordination) and ASD (autistic spectrum disorders, including Asperger's Syndrome) followed rapidly in their wake.

Scientists are now agreed there's a genetic predisposition for all these conditions. But the unfortunate children affected by them exhibit the same characteristics that teachers were noticing on a smaller scale across the board – problems with focusing attention, controlling their behaviour and/or tuning in to other people. All of these are higher order 'executive functions' which are expected to develop naturally over the course of childhood. Maybe aspects of our rapidly changing culture were impacting on children's development in general, and if a child had a particular predisposition to a developmental disorder it would be exacerbated?

For several centuries, lifestyles in the Western world have been changing with increasing rapidity, and our species' remarkable capacity to respond to change carries us along, taking advantage of each new cultural leap. But a newborn baby's brain in the 21st century is much

the same as it was in Stone Age times – biological evolution is a long, slow process – and
in early life in particular, children still need the
same basic experiences they've always needed.
If they get them, mild genetic predispositions
to some sort of learning problem might be
overcome; if they don't, they might be intensified.

> A newborn baby's brain in the 21st century is much the same as it was in Stone Age times.

It occurred to me that the incredible acceleration of change in recent years might have brought us to a developmental tipping point.
There might now be so many small but significant changes in the
lifestyles of little children that we are in danger of hazarding healthy
human development. It wasn't a comfortable thought. From a professional point of view, there were huge implications for the teaching of
literacy. But when I stood back and looked at it from a wider perspective, there were implications for the whole damn species.

Ballooning children

Within a few weeks, I had launched myself into a new part-time career
as a researcher. To start with, I concentrated on the development of
communication skills, since it was related to my personal interest in
literacy. I followed up Sally Ward's point about the pushchairs and
discovered that they faced 'the wrong way' because parents in the
1970s wanted lightweight, folding pushchairs that they could put in
their cars. Manufacturers discovered that to create a model that sat-
isfied customer demand, while also taking cost and safety into account, the dynamics of design required the baby to face away from
the pusher. No one stopped to think about the infant's developmental
communicatory needs.

Then, in the early 2000s, my field of study widened because the
'obesity explosion' hit the news. Suddenly, the media was swarming
with doctors and nutritionists explaining that, over the last few decades
children's diets had changed markedly, with increasingly visible
results.

I realised that I'd actually seen this happening. During my teaching years in the 1970s and early 1980s, I'd worked in schools in some very disadvantaged areas, so I knew what malnourished children looked like. They tended to be spindly, undersized and pasty-faced. But when I began visiting schools in the late 1990s, they'd changed. Disadvantaged children on poor diets were still pasty-faced, but now they appeared huge and lardy – some were mountainous.

'Why are they so big?' I asked a teacher in one school.

'Oh, they live on chips,' she said ruefully.

'But they lived on chips in Leith in the 1970s...'

It wasn't until a few years later, when I interviewed nutritionists and researchers into human physiology for Toxic Childhood, that I learned it wasn't just the chips but what they were now cooked in: trans fats. Along, of course, with vast quantities of fizzy drinks, sweets and other junk food, which our consumer culture sold to both children and parents remorselessly. And, of course, there had also been significant changes in their levels of activity, as traditional outdoor active play was replaced by indoor, sedentary entertainment.

What's more, these experts, along with others whom I interviewed, told me that these changes in lifestyle didn't just have a visible effect on children's bodies, they also had an invisible effect on brain function. Like any social problem, the effects were more noticeable in the poorest children. Health and educational achievement have always been affected by poverty – and in a competitive consumer society, the poverty gap yawns wider every year.

Toxic childhood syndrome

By the time Toxic Childhood was published in 2006, there was growing concern that something was amiss with childhood in the UK, and not just among the poor. Official reports soon began to appear, like the one from UNICEF in 2007, which found on a range of indicators of well-being, that our children were the unhappiest in the developed world.

Two huge research projects into children's lives towards the end of the last decade – the Good Childhood Inquiry and the Cambridge Primary Review – raised serious concerns about lack of play, the effects of commercialisation and increasing government control of education. And there are numerous illustrations of the knock-on effects of the pressures on children, in surveys showing UK teenagers at or near the top of international league tables listing every type of teenage misbehaviour, distress and disaffection.

When writing *Toxic Childhood* I found myself in the middle of all this angst. As well as nutrition, play and communication, I investigated changes in sleeping patterns, family breakdown, education and childcare, and the various ill effects of growing up in a global electronic village, financed by market forces. I concluded that children's well-being and healthy development are seriously threatened by a toxic cocktail of factors associated with modern lifestyles, and we really need to get our act together and sort it out.

> Children's well-being and healthy development are seriously threatened by a toxic cocktail of factors associated with modern lifestyles.

Suddenly, I wasn't just talking to teachers and writing in the educational press, I was in touch with all sorts of people – politicians, health workers, policemen, childcare professionals, town planners – and turning up in the national media pontificating about contemporary childhood. It was heady stuff.

I was also giving talks to parents. And just as the teachers had alerted me to the changes happening to children, the parents I met – most of whom were mothers – made me determined to look for a solution. It's all very well conducting an academic analysis of the way modern life damages children's chances. But in every group of parents I spoke to, I watched people embark on the same guilt trip that I'd suffered in Sally Ward's kitchen. Some actually burst into tears.

I desperately wanted them to stop worrying and take positive action. But it was obvious that – while they were naturally concerned about their children – most couldn't see any way out of the mess. They felt trapped in the culture, like hamsters on a wheel. The big picture seemed too big to deal with.

It certainly is a very big picture. At my talks, I would make a triangle with my hands to try and illustrate what it seemed to me had happened – three huge cultural movements colliding into a 'perfect storm' for childhood...

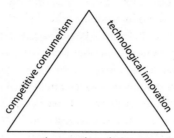

the sexual revolution

Spinning along with Moore's Law

Since the 1980s, we've all learned to take the incredible speed of human progress for granted. I first heard about Moore's Law from an ICT geek whom I met during my research. It was named after one of the founders of computer chip giant Intel, and states that the power and potential of computing technology doubles roughly every two years. Since the building of the first modern computer in 1948 (based on Alan Turing's work at Bletchley Park during the Second World War), this regular doubling act has led to an incredible acceleration in every aspect of human life.

But as our culture spins further and further into virtual realms, real-life human interactions are becoming increasingly threatened. And the consequences for children, whose brains are still maturing, are likely to be far greater than they are for mature adults who grew up at a time when a great deal of personal interaction – with the real-life world around our homes and the real-life people in our families and communities – could be taken for granted.

I'd learned from my own bitter experience that long-term consequences can result when mothers and babies focus on screens rather than on each other. My research convinced me that there can be similarly disturbing developmental consequences when children spend time playing video games rather than out in the real world, and socialise on social networking sites instead of face to face with family and friends.

For a couple of decades, the exponential rate of technological progress kept us all so busy (and enthralled) that we didn't even wonder about the possible side effects on children. It's only in the last few years that experts in various fields have started to spot the dangers, and draw attention to them.

Daniel Anderson, a highly respected producer of children's TV programmes in the USA, recently began to worry that 'We are engaged in a vast and uncontrolled experiment with our infants and toddlers, plunging them into home environments that are saturated with electronic media.' Around the same time, the eminent neuroscientist Susan Greenfield pointed out that screen-based entertainment offers 'a gratifying, easy-sensation "yuk and wow" environment ... We cannot park our children in front of the TV and expect them to develop a long attention span.'

The capacity to control the focus of conscious attention is one of the most significant factors in human thought, of both S- and E-types. It's impossible to imagine how long it took for our species to evolve this remarkable ability, but the brain of every newborn human being is programmed to develop it over the course of childhood – as long as that development is triggered by appropriate experiences.

In terms of human progress, the very word 'focus' gives us a hint about what those experiences are. I once wrote a children's book on word origins and discovered that although 'focus' had been adopted by Renaissance artists and lens grinders to talk about aspects of their work, it started life back in ancient Rome as the word for 'hearth'. Presumably the fire in the hearth was what first drew a Roman's eyes when entering a room. Families have now moved on from sitting around a fire together. In centrally-heated 21st century homes, it's usually something else that draws our eyes.

All consuming

By the early 1980s, while Moore's Law was sending technological change into overdrive, the adults of the developed world were also adjusting to the effects of increasingly aggressive marketing. Consumer capitalism had become such a successful economic system that in the nations that embraced it, most of the people lived in a state of material comfort unsurpassed in human history. But to keep the economy booming, we all had to be persuaded to keep on consuming. The marketing industry had to raise its game, and convince us that we needed more and more 'stuff'. As a result, the British cultural climate became steadily more competitive, and the national consciousness was increasingly focused on shopping.

The marketing industry soon sussed that one highly effective way of exploiting the deep emotional needs of adults is to use their children. Children are just as accessible as adults via screen-based technology, and they're also very amenable to peer pressure if a product catches on. So marketers began training the younger generation to pester their parents for products aimed at children.

It was so successful that they also began to train them to pass on marketing messages for everything their mums and dads might need (or desire), from foodstuffs and toilet paper to cars and holidays. They were delighted to find that peer pressure + pester power often met up at home with 'guilt money', supplied by parents who were so busy working to finance their families' consumption that they didn't have any time to spend with their kids.

> Peer pressure + pester power often met up at home with 'guilt money'.

Targeting children increases both short- and long-term consumption. As they pick up the consumerist messages that make them such excellent pesterers, they're also absorbing the consumerist ethic into their developing brains. The next generation is being groomed to be 'superconsumers'.

Again, it took a couple of decades for experts to start publicly questioning these marketing techniques. It wasn't until 2006 that American child psychologist Susan Linn pointed out that: 'Comparing the advertising of two or three decades ago to the commercialism that permeates our children's world today is like comparing a BB gun to a smart bomb... The explosion of marketing aimed at kids today is precisely targeted, refined by scientific method, and honed by child psychologists...'

And it took until 2011 for a UK government report to admit that: 'Parents have told us that they feel they cannot make their voices heard, and that they often lack the confidence to speak out on sexualisation and commercialisation issues for fear of being labelled a prude or out of touch.' Nevertheless, the report concluded that it's still up to parents to police the commercial world – its author, Reg Bailey, merely urged marketers to take a more ethical approach – and a 2012 follow-up report confirmed that no further government regulation would be introduced.

As a 'critical friend' to these reports, I registered my profound disbelief that the rough beasts of global capitalism would ever find it in their hearts to resist the massive profits spawned by the peer-pressure/pester-power/guilt-money combo. How could they possibly turn their backs on the long-term prizes to be gained? As the Jesuits knew, if you can hold a child in thrall until they're seven years old, they're yours for life.

> If you can hold a child in thrall until they're seven years old, they're yours for life.

Mum's the word (reprise)

The collision of these two great cultural 'fronts' – competitive consumerism and accelerating technological change – has been changing the nature of childhood for the past 30 years, in ways that can be fundamentally damaging to children's long-term psychological development and well-being. In the brave new world we all inhabit, a young child's social and emotional development is no longer influenced just by his or her own nature and the personal nurture provided by mum and dad. From the minute a child is exposed to screen-based technology, the forces of consumer capitalism also have a hand in the process.

The third element of the 'perfect storm' for childhood that also gained speed in the 1980s was the sexual revolution, sending mothers out of the home and into the workforce. Given the general cultural climate, it's no wonder the feminist dream of freedom was immediately hijacked by economic forces. Those of us who experienced the glorious dawn of women's liberation expected that, from then on, parenthood would be shared equally between men and women. As it became apparent that this was pure wishful thinking, feminist activists concentrated their attention on improving mothers' rights in the workplace.

Meanwhile, the marketing industry concentrated its attention on gaining access to children's minds. As the next generation of girls focused on the flickering screens, they absorbed messages riven with gender stereotypes that were far from consistent with feminist values. As well as the 'pink princess' image of femininity and countless stereotypical Little Miss Perfects, Mean Girls and drama queens, the visual media's portrayal of 21st century females concentrates overwhelmingly on their bodies. Young, skinny, and – above all – sexy bodies, scantily clad and cosmetically enhanced to conform to a limited number of physical stereotypes. As the mother of a daughter, I watched this development with growing dismay.

The gender wars are clearly far from over, as the recent revival of interest in feminism has confirmed. But so far the issue of motherhood has been largely ignored, except as an inconvenient interruption to women's career development. A mixture of female self-doubt, political correctness and maternal guilt mean that rational discussion of the biggest problem of all in the achievement of sexual equality scarcely raises its head. Mum is indeed the word.

★★★

When I first read Simon Baron-Cohen's work, I thought that dividing human thinking into two broad types was pretty simplistic. But the more I read about child development, the more sense it made to describe the complex tangle of physical, emotional, social and cognitive developmental drives in terms of two great quests, leading to two ways of relating to the world, ways that are fundamentally at odds with each other.

S-type thought is essentially selfish – it means shutting off from emotional engagement to focus on objects, ideas, mechanisms or systems. E-type thought is social – toning down selfishness to meet someone else halfway, focusing on the emotional reality of another human mind. In S-type mode, people are merely objects (little girls who can be dressed up like dolls), ideas (such as stereotypes), mechanisms (like computers) or elements in a system (e.g., consumers). They can also be symbols, like Madonna.

Back in the 1980s, when the perfect storm first hit, there was a dramatic shift in Western iconography. For nearly two millennia, the Madonna had been a religious icon, symbolising the emotional attachment between mother and child. But now that sex was associated less with procreation than recreation, 'Madonna' became associated with a very different sort of icon – an entertainer who, by ruthlessly exploiting her sexuality, became one of the wealthiest women in the world.

I'm fairly ambivalent about religion myself, and can see the feminist argument that the traditional Madonna images are also symbolic of the 'patriarchal oppression' of the Catholic Church. What's more, they idealise and romanticise motherhood just as much as the average Pampers ad. But they do at least suggest the centrality of the mother–child relationship in human development. I think it's pretty tragic that man-made culture's single appreciative nod at women's work has now been eclipsed by a shallow, self-referencing, utterly materialistic concept of 'girl power'.

> It's pretty tragic that man-made culture's single appreciative nod at women's work has now been eclipsed by a shallow, self-referencing, utterly materialistic concept of 'girl power'.

CHAPTER 5

GROWING GIRLS

'So why do you claim that day care is bad for babies?'

It's 2007, and I'm on the TV news, being interviewed about a letter from a group of child development experts in that morning's Times. (After a decade on the research trail, I've now turned into a child development expert.)

As I rattle through the psychological evidence that babies and toddlers are better off with their mums, my young female interviewer becomes rather tetchy. 'But nowadays mothers have to work,' she snaps.

'That doesn't make any difference to the evidence.'

'But isn't it a matter of choice? Parents want a decent lifestyle for their children.'

'I think you'll find little babies don't care about lifestyle. They just want love.'

Her eyes fill with tears.

Oh God, she's a mum. The price of her hard-won success as a TV journalist has been to hand over her beloved baby to someone else ... probably at one of the expensive nurseries that I've just argued can never do the job of a mother.

She struggles to regain control and hands over to the man who does the sports results. I leave the studio feeling really mean. After all, that poor girl is doing her best in a culture that doesn't give a damn about child development. She's been brought up during a storm of market-driven messages to the effect that babies are just one more thing for a successful woman to juggle. All she knows about care is what they tell her in the fancy brochures.

Five-finger exercise

The trouble is that almost everything children need for healthy development is now at odds with the culture in which we're trying to raise them. The further we travel from our natural biological heritage, the greater the gap between the needs of human infants and the lifestyles of the adults who care for them. But this needn't mean it's beyond the wit of 21st century men and women to recognise the discrepancy and readjust our lives to raise happy, balanced children. The challenge in the midst of the storm is to hold fast to what we know underpins human well-being.

And we know a great deal. Over the course of the 20th century, psychologists acquired many insights into the way human consciousness, personality and habits of behaviour develop. In the last 20 years, neuroscience has begun to confirm many of these insights using MRI images of developing brains.

After many years of trying to distil all my findings and translate them into everyday language, I've now got what children need for healthy development down to five ingredients that can be ticked off on the fingers of one hand. This five-finger exercise doesn't cover obvious material needs – like nourishing food, suitable clothing and a safe, warm home – because my audiences are generally lucky enough to be able to take them for granted. The difficulty in a 21st century consumer culture isn't finding enough money to keep our children alive – it's finding enough time to give them a life.

- First and foremost (so I tick it off on my forefinger), they need **love**. Unconditional love from the moment of birth is at the heart of everything a human being needs to thrive. One international expert on child development put it very simply: '*Somebody's got to be crazy about that kid. That's number one. First, last and always.*' Little babies need to know that at least one special 'someone' is always there for them, and as they grow from baby to toddler to schoolchild to adolescent, the knowledge that they're loved is the foundation for confidence, emotional resilience and feelings of self-worth.

- However, love isn't just about respecting children's needs. Children also have to learn to respect the needs of other people. So the second ingredient is **discipline.** It sounds rather harsh, but I can't think of a better word. For a parent, it means initiating one's offspring into the rhythms of family life, teaching routines and rules, setting boundaries for behaviour and expecting them to be kept. Thanks to their experience of life, parents know better than children what's in everyone's long-term best interests. Over time, as children learn to keep within the boundaries, this adult-imposed discipline is likely to develop into self-discipline, at which point boundaries can be open to negotiation. In my five-finger exercise, I use my ring finger to represent discipline because it balances the forefinger, and every research project on successful parenting stresses the constant balancing act between 'warmth' and 'firmness'.

> Successful parenting stresses the constant balancing act between 'warmth' and 'firmness'.

- But children's development isn't just up to their parents. They're naturally programmed for physical, emotional, social and cognitive development from birth. The care of loving adults is essential, but too much control can interfere with development. I use my tall middle finger for the ingredient that helps children to gradually grow away from their parents, and become autonomous, self-controlled, independent personalities. It's **play**. Children are hard-wired to play. It's the inborn spirit of exploration that drives them, from their earliest days, to learn for themselves about their surroundings and to interact with the people who care for them. As they grow older they need increasing freedom to explore the world in which they live and to learn to get along with their peers on their own. So parents have to know when and how to back off – and to be brave enough to do so.

- Then there's the thumb, which is very important in human evolution. Mankind's opposable thumbs allow us to use tools to fashion our world. I use my thumb to represent the most significant tool of the lot – the one that separates us from all the other animals: **language**. It emerges miraculously from a complex web of human communication skills – such as reading faces and body language, imitating gestures, and responding to rhythm, pitch and tone of voice – and has made us the supreme social species. To learn these verbal and non-verbal skills, children need to spend plenty of time with loving adults, who unconsciously act as models for them to imitate. Then, as they grow, children need opportunities to develop their powers of communication on their own terms, through play with other children and interaction with other responsible adults.

- Last, and definitely least in the great scheme of things, my little finger stands for **education**. In a sophisticated, modern society, children won't get far without it, especially the key skill of literacy, which hugely refines our capacity to think. But the four other components of a 'good childhood' listed above underpin education. All elements of care, these four components are the natural foundations on which formal education can be built. As long as children are raised with love, and are given sensible boundaries and sufficient opportunities to play and develop language skills, their education should flourish. Even without much education, they'd probably be in pretty good shape to meet the challenges ahead.

Natural tortoise, cultural hare

The components of my five-finger exercise should be available to every family, regardless of income, because they're all free. Unfortunately, 30 years of competitive consumerism have conditioned us to see no value in free stuff – the modern ethic is that we must buy our way to happiness. And since, for those same 30 years, we've also been conditioned to respond to constant and increasingly rapid change, there no longer seems to be any time for long-drawn-out processes like child development. So we've assumed that, just like adults, today's children can change with the times.

Up to a point, of course, they must. The experience of childhood has always differed across times and cultures – it's one of the reasons we're such a successful species. Homo sapiens' long period of physical and psychological maturation means that each new generation has time to adapt to the world it will inhabit. Children growing up in 21st century Britain naturally have to adapt to new experiences and learn new skills.

However, there's one aspect of childhood that can't change – the biological process of growth that transforms a baby into a toddler, a toddler into a child, and a child into an adolescent. It's a process that has followed the same timetable for countless millennia. In terms of physical growth, we can actually see it happen, and most of us record it with pencil marks on the wall. Psychological growth follows the same sort of biological timetable, but since the development of children's brains takes place inside their skulls, it's nowhere near so obvious.

The 'obesity crisis' of the last decade has illustrated, in graphic fashion, the dangers of a 21st century lifestyle for growing human bodies. Letting children gobble down fast junk food while sitting in front of a screen, instead of feeding them a healthy diet and making sure they get plenty of exercise, hasn't done them any good at all. It just makes them fatter, unhealthier and increasingly likely to die before their parents. The psychological effects of this and other lifestyle changes are just as significant, but take place out of sight. This means they also stay out of mind until their effects become apparent in the way children behave – which may not be for some years.

For instance, it's easy to assume that in a fast-moving society, children can 'grow up' faster, start school sooner, make consumer choices at an ever-earlier age, and share in adult entertainment such as graphically violent films and computer games, and online activities like social networking. But the reality of human nature is that it takes around three years for children to develop rudimentary self-control, about six or seven years before their brains are sufficiently developed for academic learning, and another six or seven to bring them to a level of social, emotional and intellectual maturity that still only approximates to adult understanding.

So as human culture grows more complex, children are greater in need than ever of adult care and authority and the time in which to grow up. There are no quick fixes in terms of psychological development, and there's no way of buying a 'good childhood' in neat, bite-sized chunks.

The developmental tangle

It would help if psychological development were a nice, straightforward matter that could be reduced to a neat checklist. But it isn't. However, it *can* be thought of in terms of four main strands – physical, emotional, social and cognitive – but they interweave and overlap in a messy, uncontrollable way. The brain is a phenomenally complex organ, and especially in children's early years – when they are closer to their Stone Age past than their 21st century future – adults have to respect a biological blueprint that was laid down many millennia before checklists were invented.

- **Physical** Physical development isn't just about the obvious measurable aspects of height and weight. It is also about children's control of bodily co-ordination and balance, which develops through their natural motivation to move – rolling, twisting, grasping, crawling when they're babies, then running, jumping, climbing, and so on, as they grow older. Stop children from moving (perhaps because your culture has convinced you it isn't safe or suitable), and you're setting up problems for the future. And you'll be setting up just as many problems if you insist on children

> Stop children from moving and you're setting up problems for the future.

doing something before they're mature enough physically, such as trying to write when they can scarcely hold a pencil.

- **Emotional** It's no coincidence that the word *motivation* is related to *motion*. Nor that the word *motion* gives us *emotion*. As with grown-ups, babies and children are motivated to move towards anything that arouses good emotions, and away from anything arousing bad emotions. So their motivation is deeply embedded in their feelings. Since every child's experience is different, their feelings and motivations will be different, too.

- **Social** As we're such a social species, human feelings are also profoundly affected by personal relationships. This means that social development is tangled up in there as well. We saw in Chapter 3 how the entire trajectory of girls' development can be affected (and redirected in potentially damaging ways) by their natural social awareness ... influencing their emotions ... and then perhaps impacting on physical confidence and self-image...

- **Cognitive** And since physical, emotional and social factors are all involved in the motivation to learn, they all contribute to cognitive development. This aspect of development provides the invisible foundation on which school-based learning depends. In a fast-moving world, it's tempting to try to accelerate the cognitive strand, but homing in on any one aspect of a complex process can have unintended consequences elsewhere. If we want children to grow up with balanced brains, we need to care about all aspects of their development.

Despite the obvious physical differences between girls and boys, from a few months after birth to the onset of puberty, children are untroubled by sex hormones – they are, in fact, pretty androgynous little creatures. Girls tend to be slightly ahead of boys in almost every respect on the developmental front, but that doesn't mean we should attempt to rush girls through childhood. The best way to ensure that children of both sexes grow up bright, balanced and ready to make their way in a sexually equal world is to respect their right to develop as individual human beings in their own time.

Time to grow up

If you think of it purely in terms of height, it's obvious that trying to accelerate an aspect of natural development isn't a good idea. You can't stretch young children physically to speed up their growth. Similarly, all four strands of psychological development are also subject to a biological timetable.

> **0–3 years** Before the age of about three, cognitive development occurs naturally when children interact with their environment and the people who care for them. They have minimal conscious control over what they learn, just an inbuilt lust to explore (described in Chapter 3) that needs physical, emotional and social input. Adults can teach them simple skills (such as using a potty), but since children of this age still lack the capacity for reason and control over their emotions, it's like training a dog – a matter of endless repetition and rewards. Girls' social precocity means they're often more receptive to adult teaching than boys, but there's also a danger that they'll try too hard to emulate the grown-ups and miss out on the play they need for all-round development.

> Girls' social precocity means they're often more receptive to adult teaching than boys.

> **3–7 years** Over the next three or four years, children develop increasing control over body and mind. They still learn best through play because their understanding is still embedded in physical, emotional and social experiences rather than in the conscious control of their thought processes. Increasingly, however, their self-chosen play is influenced by the adult world, and they become interested in playful adult-directed activities, such as organised games, art activities, music, drama and word play. As they gradually develop their own inner system of thought control (usually at around the age of six or seven), they can progress from this activity-based learning to learning in more abstract ways. This is when formal education can start moving them onwards and upwards, towards more thoughtful, conscious, rational behaviour.

7–early teens Even at this stage, children's brains are far from mature. Education may help them to become steadily better at rational thought, but they may still have trouble with mental tasks such as planning, decision-making, holding several ideas in short-term memory, and seeing things from other people's points of view. Some mental tasks that seem negligible to adults continue to be quite taxing for children until they're well into their teens. And, even though they're starting to look more grown-up, they still need plenty of adult care to help keep them on track emotionally and socially. As a friend's ten-year-old daughter said during a family row, '*I may look big, but I'm only little inside.*'

Early teens–twenties Once they hit puberty, gender differences become more apparent as sex hormones kick in, influencing teenagers' behaviour in traditionally male and female directions. But despite the onset of sexual maturity, other aspects of development are still far from complete. For instance, the neural networks in human brains undergo a streamlining process called myelination (aiding cognitive development) until their owners are in their early twenties. We're not truly 'grown up' in a neurological sense until at least the age of 21.

Roots to grow and wings to fly

Given this long period of maturation, the role of parents in child-rearing is clearly critical. Until their daughter is old enough to fend for herself, they have to support her physical, emotional, social and cognitive development in the most appropriate ways, at each stage of her childhood and adolescence.

Of the five components required for healthy development listed on pages 77–8, parents have particular responsibility for the first two: **love** and **discipline**. Maintaining a sensitive balance between both elements isn't easy, but the technique recommended by child psychologists is to combine warmth with firmness:

- warmth means giving daughters responsive loving care, so they always feel that they're loved and that their feelings and opinions are valued
- firmness means setting (and sticking to) clear, age-appropriate rules and boundaries for behaviour, so they know exactly what's expected of them.

A sensitive balance between these two elements is known as 'authoritative parenting' and provides the emotional security that underpins healthy development.

The research of the last 50 years suggests that authoritative parents tend to produce self-confident, socially competent children who do well at school and, as the years go by, grow steadily more independent, self-reliant and able to make sensible decisions about their own behaviour. For instance, they're less likely to engage in any sort of antisocial behaviour during their teenage years.

The success of the 'warm-but-firm' approach is probably because:

- by being warm with their daughter, parents don't just provide her with emotional security, they act as role models for the sort of person they want her to be – kind, considerate, trustworthy and rational
- by being firm about their expectations, they gradually help her to learn how to regulate her own behaviour. As she grows in confidence and competence, parents steadily allow her more autonomy, so she gets better at thinking for herself.

According to an old saying, the job of parents is to give their children 'roots to grow and wings to fly'. Since it takes a whole childhood for daughters to grow 'wings' and learn how to use them, authoritative parenting involves a significant investment in terms of time, particularly in the early stages of childhood. The process of creating 'roots' that will be emotionally sustaining requires mum and dad to be:

> The job of parents is to give their children 'roots to grow and wings to fly.

- responsively tuned in to her emotional and developmental needs
- consistent about expectations, helping her to establish 'default' habits of behaviour that will stand her in good stead as time goes on.

And as time goes on, they should be able to allow her increasing freedom, because:

- their love is translated by daughters into self-love and self-esteem
- the discipline they provide is gradually transformed by their daughters into self-discipline and self-control.

And so she learns to be warm but firm with *herself*.

The missing ingredient

The suggestions for raising girls given in Part Two of this book are based on the principles of authoritative parenting. However, convincing as the research is, I must admit to some reservations about the term 'parenting' and the way it influences our perceptions of an age-old process.

In the past, people talked about 'raising children' or 'bringing them up'. These expressions implicitly acknowledge that children, like plants, grow upwards towards the sun – their parents' job is to support that developmental process with sensitivity. 'Parenting', on the other hand, puts the spotlight firmly on the parents – it sounds like something parents *do* to their daughters.

In fact, over the last few decades, as the term 'parenting' has become common currency, there's been an increase in the phenomenon now known as 'over-parenting'. Some parents – particularly mothers – hover anxiously over their children, trying to ensure their future success by controlling every aspect of their lives. Sometimes called 'helicopter parents', they tend to be competitive and controlling. They probably believe they're being authoritative, but the level of input is completely over the top. In Chapter 3, I point out the dangers of treating a daughter as a 'product' to be moulded into an approved shape, rather than supported into becoming her own person. Parents who turn care into control don't give their children space to develop emotional resilience, self-reliance and initiative – let alone a personality of their own.

I fear that, in emphasising the parental role, the vital ingredient that children bring to their own development – their natural drive to **play** – is being diminished. While little girls delight in playing with the beloved adults in their lives when they're young, as time goes on they need to play independently and with other children. The parental role is to prepare daughters to deal with any problems that might crop up, provide opportunities for loosely supervised, then unsupervised play, and then to gradually back off.

Child psychologists have always appreciated the significance of play in every strand of the developmental tangle, which is why there's mounting concern about the startling decline in 'real play'. For countless millennia, creative, exploratory, real-life activity (frequently outdoors) was taken for granted as a natural part of childhood – at least for boys. In recent years, this freedom for children to learn under their own steam has been seriously eroded. The reasons are complex, but I suspect the rise of the 'parenting culture' is implicated.

For parents of girls, the decline of outdoor play may seem of little consequence – they're more comfortable knowing that their daughter is safe indoors. But the more I learn about the power of play, the more important it seems that girls have the opportunity to connect with nature and to enjoy what play expert Tim Gill calls 'everyday adventures'. Indeed, I think it likely that the increasing freedom to play outside the home that girls enjoyed during the course of the 20th century (including the rise of the tomboy) helped to create the generation of women behind 'female liberation'. The advantages of real play for 21st century girls – and ways of providing it – are covered in Chapters 7 to 9.

It takes a village...

The decline of outdoor play and the rise of 'parenting' are connected with another late 20th century social phenomenon: the breakdown of communities. In the words of a justly famous African proverb: '*It takes a village to raise a child.*' In most cultures parents could usually rely on the support of their extended family and wider community to keep an eye on their children. When neighbours know and trust each other, it's much easier to let children flex their wings by getting out and about. The support of fellow 'villagers' also meant parents didn't have to shoulder exclusive responsibility for child-rearing – shared values and interests underpinned a degree of shared responsibility. Indeed, one large American study concluded that authoritative parenting is possibly only achievable within an 'authoritative community'.

> When neighbours know and trust each other, it's much easier to let children flex their wings.

Sadly, there are now few close extended families and tight-knit communities in the UK. And as we've lost touch with our neighbours, there's been a gradual breakdown of trust in society. Instead, we've retreated behind closed doors and much of our experience of the outside world is via screen-based technology. So the 'village' in which 21st century girls are raised is a global electronic village of mass communications, which feeds parental anxieties with wall-to-wall news coverage on those rare occasions when children come to harm outside the home.

The forces of marketing and the media behind the ubiquitous screens also make it much more difficult for parents to maintain a well-balanced, authoritative stance. Consumer culture constantly encourages both parents and children to confuse love with indulgence. And, in terms of damaging children's long-term mental health, 'indulgent parenting' can be even more harmful than authoritarian control.

The danger for girls starts early. Small females are easily convinced that 'love = stuff', and, due to their social acuteness, they tend to be highly effective pesterers. Young girls soon become adept at manipulating their parents' emotions for a quick fix of material rewards, which becomes their substitute for emotional security. If mum and dad can't say 'no' to shopping, they'll probably find it difficult to say 'no' to other sorts of behaviour as the years go by.

In this case, parents may choose an alternative to discipline – overprotection. At its worst, this leads them to treat their daughter like a pampered pet rather than a fully functioning human being. Instead of encouraging her to think for herself, they do the thinking for her. And since they don't trust her to act sensibly without adult supervision, they keep her under constant surveillance.

Parents naturally want to do everything they can to keep daughters safe. But the long-term aim must be to equip girls to keep *themselves* safe. Authoritative parenting develops the self-belief and self-control that girls need to be able to 'fly'. Indulgent parenting leaves them materially grounded.

Build your own village

Just as in the 1990s I met thousands of teachers, over the last six years I've met thousands of parents – mostly mothers. Nowadays my notebooks are full of scribbles from conversations at the end of my talks, and some concerns are voiced time after time. For instance:

- *'I'm frightened of being judged a bad parent.'*
- *'I don't want her to be the odd one out in the playground.'*
- *'I want her to play out, but no other kids are out there to play with.'*
- *'I'm afraid she'll resent me for being too strict.'*
- *'I'm fed up with being the mean mum.'*
- *'I'm damned if I do and damned if I don't.'*
- *'I'm never sure where to draw the line – the goalposts keep moving.'*
- *'She says she's "the only one" who doesn't have/has to do something.'*

It's clear that many mums feel like 'the only one' struggling to be an authoritative parent in a climate of overindulgence and overprotectiveness. Negative emotions such as fear and guilt are exacerbated by

> Many mums feel like 'the only one' struggling to be an authoritative parent in a climate of overindulgence and over-protectiveness.

isolation, so I'm always chuffed when a few fellow sufferers go off into a huddle to carry on chatting. The best way to bolster one's own authority as a parent is to share concerns, advice and ideas with others in the same boat. I suggest they keep in touch, try to spread their net wider to embrace a few more interested parents, and build an authoritative community of their own – a home-made 21st century 'village' to support them in raising their children.

Many parents I meet already belong to a community of like-minded mums and dads. Some are united by religious beliefs – for them the shared acceptance of a 'higher authority' underpins mutual support. Some share a political ideology – adults involved in green issues, for instance, often realise that concern for the natural world extends to children's natural developmental needs.

Increasingly, however, I come across small groups of non-aligned parents – in all kinds of localities – who've got together simply because they don't like what's happening to their kids and they want to do something locally to put it right. Sometimes it's neighbours banding together to ensure their children can play out safely, close to home. Sometimes it's mums who meet up through the local nursery or school and decide they'll 'Just Say No' to make-up or sexy clothing until their daughters are a certain age. Sometimes parents who've met through antenatal classes or babysitting groups develop a small supportive community that lasts until their children grow up. Every group is different – ranging from two or three friends to large groups of parents, teachers and other interested parties who organise local events as a reason to get together and spread the word.

There are also 'virtual villages', like Mumsnet and Netmums, where parents can raise issues that worry them and share possible solutions. These virtual networks can – and increasingly do – influence political opinion in the real world, by drawing attention to problems shared by their members; Mumsnet's 'Let Girls Be Girls' campaign helped to prompt the government to set up the Bailey Review. But more to the point, they also support real-life groups of mums and dads who get together to confront local problems.

The internet is an excellent medium for tracking down locally-based, like-minded individuals, and a Facebook group is a great way of setting up a virtual village. But meeting up regularly is essential because child-rearing involves the E-type engagement of face-to-face human contact.

There have always been problems, dangers and pitfalls in raising children. The ones we currently face are completely new and may sometimes seem insurmountable. But once we get the measure of a problem, human beings are remarkably good at finding ways to solve it ... especially when they use their E-type skills to work together.

***

One of the phrases I find myself trotting out regularly when chatting with parents is that all parents need help. Maintaining an authoritative balance is tricky, not least because it involves combining S- and E-type thought – rules and strategies require S-type thinking, loving care requires E-type thought.

In terms of S-type rules and strategies, there's no shortage of books and websites advising on authoritative parenting (see Notes and References), and the second part of this book includes suggestions for authoritative approaches to five major areas of raising girls.

However, one persistent problem for modern parents is coping with constant change. As new technologies arrive on the market, and new developments appear in childcare and education, and as marketers target ever-younger age groups with established products, how do parents decide whether they are acceptable

> However, one persist-ent problem for modern parents is coping with constant change.

for their daughter? As a general guide, I recommend the 'precautionary principle'. If, based on what we know about children's development, something may be considered damaging for a growing girl, it's best to avoid it – she only gets one shot at childhood. In the final

> If something *may* be considered damaging for a growing girl, it's best to avoid it she only gets one shot at childhood.

analysis, parents just have to make up their minds on their daughter's behalf. But it helps enormously to have a village of like-minded parents to consult.

As for providing E-type, loving care, that's a question of parents tuning in to their daughter. It involves being close physically, listening to her opinions and taking them into account, providing help or comfort when she needs it, and giving explanations for the rules and boundaries that are set. The main problem is that daughters often have different ideas from their parents, and, like the marketers, tend to know how to press parents' emotional buttons. If in doubt about how to proceed, I find it helps to breathe deeply and utter the mantra 'warm but firm, warm but firm'.

But again, it also helps enormously if parents belong to a 'village' of families who share common views and values. That way, they won't have to be the mean mum or dad and their daughter won't have to be the 'only one' who has authoritative parents.

PART TWO

RAISING GIRLS

The first seven years are for play, the second are for discipline and education, the third are for keeping with the adults.

The Prophet Mohammed

The world is too much with us; late and soon,
Getting and spending, we lay waste our powers.

William Wordsworth

It would be a shame if brilliant technology were to end up threatening the kind of intellect that produced it.

Daniel Tenner (IT writer)

CHAPTER 6

SHE IS WHAT YOU FEED HER

Food and love, attachment and self-image

'When are you doing the chapter on food?' wrote an email chum who'd just given birth to a daughter. 'Ever since I was a teenager, I've been yo-yo dieting like crazy and I don't want to hand my body image problems down to Annabel. Not to mention my horrible memories of family meals...'

Since I have similar horrible memories and have spent a lifetime watching my weight, her plea didn't exactly lighten my mood about tackling this chapter. Care versus control; process versus product; reality versus perfection. All the major challenges in raising 21st century girls are summed up in our culture's complex – indeed, downright perverted – attitudes towards food and female appearance.

On the one hand, the food industry bombards girls from birth with invitations to gorge on delicious fattening snacks; on the other, the fashion industry surrounds them with airbrushed images of female 'perfection'. If these industries were parents, the food industry would be super-indulgent and fashion hyper-controlling – a well-known recipe for producing a disturbed child. Mixed messages are always damaging forchildren; to feel secure they need straightforward, authoritative guidance.

As the marketing people disingenuously point out, it's up to parents to provide this guidance. But modern parents are deeply confused too, and riven with anxiety. One day the media warns them about the dangers of childhood obesity and the next – as a celebrity is snapped looking like a bag of bones or a catwalk model dies of self-starvation – about anorexia nervosa. What's more, since today's parents were themselves raised in an aggressive market economy, there's a good chance they've picked up a fair few market-induced complexes of their own.

Indeed, according to statistics, the chances that mothers have are particularly high. At least 80 per cent of grown women are now dissatisfied with their body shape. So unless modern mothers untangle their own attitudes towards food, they're likely to hand on their cultural confusion to the next generation of girls.

Emotion and reason

The ad men are right, course. The only way to counter the effects of consumerist mixed messages is to bring up girls in a family culture based on healthy attitudes towards eating. That means 'authoritative parenting'. So the first requirement of mum and dad is, as always, love. Food is so central to human existence that it easily becomes a metaphor for love – comfort eating is famously a matter of attempting to fill a yawning emotional gap. Since love comes naturally to most parents, we should be able to take it for granted.

> So the first requirement of mum and dad is, as always, love.

However, the second requirement is 'warm-but-firm' discipline, based on what we know is good for growing bodies and minds. This, too, should be a doddle – we adults are mature, rational human beings and over the last decade we've had endless advice about healthy eating for children. Nutritionists and psychologists are in accord that children need:

- a balanced diet, based as far as possible on natural ingredients
- to eat to satisfy physical hunger, and stop when they're full.

But when mum and dad are distracted from mature, rational decision-making by their own physical and emotional issues, which are constantly being reinforced by increasingly sophisticated market messages, it's extremely difficult to be – or even to feel – remotely authoritative.

The only solution is for parents to put their own food-related issues to one side and to concentrate on doing the best they can to prevent their daughters from falling into the same trap. If warm-but-firm parental care can help a girl develop healthy eating habits in her earliest years, it reduces the chances of her being lured from the straight and narrow as time goes on. And if throughout her childhood she's equipped to resist the siren voices urging us all towards bad habits, she's more likely to be in rational control of her own food intake for the rest of her life.

There's no one-size-fits-all system for ensuring girls eat well and healthily. Twenty-first-century parents just need to do the best that they can, depending on their family circumstances. From what I've learned during my years on the research trail, I believe that I personally would have felt more authoritative if I'd:

- been more aware of why I myself had a tendency to fall from grace
- had a few simple ground rules to follow, to keep myself on the straight and narrow.

So in the rest of this chapter I cover the main points gleaned from expert opinion that seem to me useful in these respects. And since, for 80 per cent of mothers body image is a key issue, I'll start with that.

Body image and images of bodies

For most of human history, people's expectations about female body shape were determined by the real-life women they met on a day-to-day basis. Only the wives and daughters of men at the top of the social hierarchy had the time and the disposable income to indulge in fashion to increase their families' prestige. Most people were too busy keeping themselves and their families alive, so for the majority of the population perceptions of female beauty were influenced by human attributes other than looks.

But in the 20th century, the rise of the consumer culture extended access to fashion to a wider public, while screen-based entertainment narrowed the popular concept of beauty. At around the time that women won the vote, they also acquired the right to compare themselves (and to be compared) with carefully selected, highly polished models of female 'perfection' on the cinema screen. And as visual media proliferated, the influence of human reality was steadily eclipsed by the power of two-dimensional images.

By the time that women en masse had achieved economic independence, their world was awash with images. One study estimated that a teenage girl in the 1990s saw more examples of conventionally beautiful women in a week than her mother did in her entire adolescence – goodness knows how many it is today. Many women found themselves spending much of their newfound wealth trying to live up to these unrealistic role models. As the demands of fashion made the role models skinnier, the market helped out with slimming regimes and pills, exercise equipment, gyms, beauty salons, cosmetic surgery and other artificial aids. Like the fashion victims of the past, who'd crammed themselves into crinolines and corsets, women continued to define their self-worth through control of their bodies.

It's now over 30 years since psychotherapist Susie Orbach published *Fat is a Feminist Issue*, pointing out that compulsive overeating and anorexia are two sides of the same coin, born from the pressure of trying to meet increasingly artificial standards of feminine beauty. An insecure woman struggling with feelings of self-worth may either throw in the towel and overindulge herself with food (then deal as best she can with the self-loathing that results), or step up control of her food intake to increasingly life-threatening levels.

Obesity and self-starvation are both extreme reactions and are usually related to genetic factors – like other human characteristics, the appetite for food is governed by both nature and nurture. But when girls grow up surrounded by unrealistic images and expectations, nurture becomes steadily more influential. And since Orbach's warning, consumerism has raised its game, so aspirational images of the female body become more unrealistic every year.

Worryingly, the age at which girls develop eating disorders – traditionally between 13 and 17, during the turbulent years of adolescence – has dropped in recent years, and anorexia is now becoming more common in nine- to twelve-year-olds. In the BBC series *Child of Our Time*, most of the six-year-old girls in the study turned out to be disturbingly concerned about their appearance. The growth of the 'tween' culture (see Chapter 8) and pressure to achieve in the education system (Chapter 9) are creating self-consciousness and insecurity in girls at an increasingly young age. In a recent interview Orbach said: *'Now there is this expectation to copy celebrities, the images are digitally enhanced, prefabricated, ubiquitous. I think the critical feature is there is no way not to be infected.'*

A developmental reality check

But there is a very simple route out of a two-dimensional world view. It's called 'real life'. Children are born primed to live and develop in human bodies, not in an aspirational dream world, so if parents keep their family culture as real as possible, they can protect girls from early 'infection' – physically, emotionally, socially and cognitively.

Physical development To keep a girl in touch with the physical reality of her body, she needs parental touch – cuddles, caresses, hugs, strokes, hand-holding. These usually come naturally in the earliest years, when parents care for all their baby's physical needs (and if they don't, check out the International Association of Infant Massage). But they tend to die away as she grows older – in a society that values images over reality, there's a growing cultural resistance to the 'touchy-feely'.

Thanks to the porn and computer games industries, for many adults close physical contact is now associated overwhelmingly with sex (and in some cases violence), so we're all increasingly uncomfortable about casual human touch. Nevertheless, until a girl reaches puberty, when hormonal forces come into play, physical closeness to the adults who care for her provides reassurance of her physical lovability. Opportunities for physical activity – especially outside in the natural world – are also important to help her feel confident in her own body (see Chapter 7).

Emotional development Many aspects of emotional development rely on physical closeness to parents during childhood. A close family unit provides a daughter with real-life role models – and the most significant female role model for any daughter is her mother. Looks and body shape are irrelevant in this relationship – what matters is love. According to the author of *The Beauty Myth*, Naomi Wolf, '*A mother who radiates self-love and self-acceptance actually vaccinates her daughter against low self-esteem.*'

> The most significant female role model for any daughter is her mother.

Fortunately for the dietary fallen angels among us, self-love and self-acceptance as a mother don't depend on physical appearance but on the mutual love and respect between mother and daughter – emotional attachment makes both parties feel good about themselves. Spending time together, sharing day-to-day experiences, not only cements a girl's self-esteem but provides opportunities for mums to hand on their interests, attitudes and lifeskills.

Similarly, a close emotional relationship with her father has a positive effect on a daughter's self-image and self-confidence. If she spends plenty of time with him, sharing his interests and activities, she'll feel accepted as a female by the most important man in her life. This means there's less likelihood of unrealistic gender-stereotypical aspirations taking hold later.

Social development The family is the obvious starting point for a little girl to learn that she's valued for her whole self, not merely for her appearance. But for well-balanced development, as she grows older she needs to widen her social horizons. This involves plenty of opportunities for play within her peer group, which is dealt with in Chapters 7 and 8. In terms of adult role models, the best way to counter the influence of the visual media is frequent real-life contact with other adults – which brings us back to the 'it takes a village to raise a child' argument.

> A close emotional relationship with her father has a positive effect on a daughter's self-image and self-confidence.

When parents build human support networks, it's not just the parents who benefit from them. These support networks also provide their daughter with regular opportunities to meet a variety of other grown-up role models. Like girls in the past, she'll learn how much personal warmth and kindness count towards female beauty when she experiences them. She'll also build relationships that might prove useful in the future. Once puberty kicks in, girls who have older women to turn to for advice find it easier to negotiate their way through the minefield of teen culture (see Chapter 10), and it's often easier for an adolescent girl to talk openly with someone who isn't in her immediate family circle.

Cognitive development Interaction with living, breathing human beings is the only way to convey the message that beauty is far from skin-deep. The cognitive development underpinning a little girl's lifelong capacity to reason is rooted – like all aspects of human growth – in her personal experience. Before the age of three, everything she learns is hugely influenced by physical experiences, so she needs to feel at home in her body and be actively engaged with the world about her. Hands-on learning continues to be paramount until around the age of six or so, when her powers of reason develop. But if reason isn't underpinned by healthy physical, emotional and social development, it will be less than effective. She may, for instance, start believing that inane media sound bites such as, 'Nothing tastes as good as skinny feels', are actually rational.

The dance of nutrition

Indeed, all our 21st century agonising about food intake is deeply irrational in the great scheme of things. If we slough off cultural influences for a moment, it's downright shameful to think how self-indulgent our current psychological issues are compared to the problems that parents faced in feeding children in the past – and that still exist in many Third World countries today. The challenges of providing for children's nutritional needs in times of plenty are infinitely outweighed by those in times of famine. The wealthier we get, the more selfish and self-conscious we become, and the more we value status and material success over genuine human needs.

Fortunately, motherhood still provides modern women with a route back to E-type sensibilities – as long as they can detach themselves sufficiently from 21st century concerns to take it. When her baby is born, a mother is naturally equipped with the perfect, balanced food source and a hormonally-induced desire to nurture her child. It's no coincidence that breastfed baby girls are less likely than others to have body image problems in later life – their mothers feel good about feeding them, so their first encounters with food are natural and positive.

Breastfeeding is a subject that raises fierce passions. The scientific evidence that breastfed babies are likely to enjoy greater physical and emotional health than non-breastfed babies is often lost under a plethora of cultural and emotional issues. In *Shattered: Modern Motherhood and the Illusion of Equality*, Rebecca Asher describes the pressure to breastfeed exerted by NHS employees in terms that summon up images of Stalin's mum. These employees have aspirational targets to meet and little time to meet them in, so it's not surprising that, in recent years, there's been a slight drop-off in breastfeeding rates among middle-class mums who don't appreciate being bullied.

Since breast is best, we have to forgive the NHS for its oversystemised enthusiasm. But we also have to recognise that, if breastfeeding doesn't work out, fretting about it is likely to do more harm than good. All my burrowing into academic literature on the subject leads me to suspect that the nutritional aspect of putting a baby to the breast is less significant than the role it plays in attachment. Whatever the food source, when a mother is nursing her daughter, they're both in a time and space designed by nature for deep emotional connection. If mum feels anxious or insecure, she'll communicate these emotions to her daughter, which isn't a good way to initiate a child into a lifetime's relationship with food. So if you *can't* breastfeed, don't agonise about it – settle down to enjoy bottle-feeding.*

> If mum feels anxious or insecure, she'll communicate these emotions to her daughter.

Since most female anxiety results from trying too hard to live up to standards that are imposed externally, the more mothers and daughters can keep this critical time and space to themselves the better. Hints and tips – from both the trusted members of one's real-life 'village' and the non-commercial authorities in the virtual one – are useful. But unless there's a serious health problem to address, detailed schemes and systems are likely to be counter-productive.

A mother relying on a system – for breastfeeding or for anything else – is inevitably drawn to focus on procedures, schedules, measurements, targets and goals, all of which are elements of control rather than care. So she's primed to feel anxious and guilty whenever she and her baby don't come up to scratch. On the other hand, a mother who can let herself relax into empathetic engagement, responding to her baby and allowing mutually satisfying rhythms of behaviour to grow from the reciprocal 'dance', can devote her energy to care. It takes an act of will for many modern women to keep S-type habits in check and develop E-type strengths. But motherhood is the ultimate E-type experience, so it's the perfect opportunity to let love drive the will to care.

---

* And look for silver linings. One of the nicest men I ever met told me he'd been secretly grateful that his wife was unable to breastfeed, because it meant he could share the pleasure of bottle-feeding their daughter.

Tuning in and turning off

The same goes for weaning a daughter and gradually helping her to feed herself. It can be an anxiety-inducing obstacle course with a set methodology and timetable, or a shared, natural, human progression. This isn't to suggest that E-type engagement bathes everything in a glorious, rosy glow. However a mother plays it, feeding a small child is messy, time-consuming, often unbelievably frustrating and seldom looks anything like the pictures in baby books or adverts. But it's an age-old experience of human reality that offers modern women an opportunity to escape from the pursuit of perfection and to relax into being 'good enough' – which is fine by their daughters and may be quite therapeutic for the mothers too.

It's now a fact of life that, as time goes on, many mothers can't look after their own children. Sometimes it's through economic necessity, sometimes it's through personal choice. Most women can summon up E-type enthusiasm for childcare in the first few months, when they're being assisted by their hormones in a major way, but some are too personally committed to an S-type mindset and simply can't cope with the messiness and disorder.

Oliver James suggests that these 'Organiser' mothers use their capacity for reason to ensure that their daughters aren't emotionally deprived by their absence. An Organiser mum can establish a personal relationship with the person she chooses to care for her baby so they can share ground rules about diet and mealtimes. E-type 'Hugger' mums would probably move heaven and earth to stay with their babies, while 'Fleximums' who fall between the two extremes have to summon all their emotional and rational strength to work out the best possible compromise.

For children to develop healthy eating habits they have to be weaned in such a way that they associate what they put into their mouths with the assuaging of physical hunger, and not with emotional reward and/or punishment. A baby girl who's never tasted anything but milk has no prejudices about taste beyond those acquired through human evolution,* so unless we persuade her otherwise, she'll be happy to eat carefully balanced, natural foodstuffs and drink milk or water.

This sort of simple diet is likely to set her up for a far healthier attitude towards food than carefully marketed, factory-produced baby foods and drinks, whose appealing names and labels are aimed squarely at the yearning of parents to indulge their infants in the 'treats' in which they themselves indulge. So always remember:

- love is not the same as indulgence
- loving a daughter means giving them time and attention.

Sadly, in respect of the second bullet point, there's another massive problem for adults when they're feeding infants in the modern world. Since breast- or bottle-feeding a baby, or spooning mush into a tiny mouth, isn't an intellectually stimulating occupation, it's easy for carers (whether mums or mother substitutes) to lose interest. The world moves at such speed these days that we find it incredibly difficult to focus on physical, time-consuming tasks. And care isn't just about looking after children, it's also about looking *at* them. When an attentive carer feeds a child's body, she also feeds her charge's emotional needs by engaging in the communicatory dance.

E-type engagement is highly dependent on eye contact – if a carer's gaze is fastened elsewhere, the connection with the child is broken. And nowadays, with the lure of screen-based entertainment and communication all around us, it's all too easy for an adult to be distracted from tuning in to children. If adults get into the habit of multitasking (keeping one eye on a screen while they feed a baby or toddler), focusing on the child becomes more difficult and less rewarding, just as junk snacking affects our appreciation of real food. Electronic communication can distract adults from human reality in more ways than one.

---

* Well, maybe she has a few prejudices based on whatever swilled through the umbilical cord, but at this stage she's as blank a gustatory slate as she ever will be.

Attachment to junk

Throughout this book, I argue that screen-based activities and young children don't mix. The TV, laptop, tablet or smartphone is a window into a high-tech, quick-fix consumer culture that's seriously at odds with the natural, biologically-paced process of caring for a small child. Mothers don't need distraction from the real-life 'dance of communication' with their daughters – especially if it involves depressingly idealised images of motherhood, such as yummy mummies serenely tending perfect babies in nappy adverts. And small girls don't need early exposure to negative cultural influences, including images of 'perfection' and adverts that encourage them to associate highly processed food with comfort and 'treats'.

It doesn't occur to most adults that tiny children may be affected by what they see (and hear) on TV – especially programmes that are way above their heads – but marketers know that they are. They're also well aware that children's habits of behaviour are established in the early years of life. So it pays to catch 'em young.

It's part of marketing lore that, by the time they're six months old, babies recognise corporate logos and mascots that appear frequently on screen. Perched in the supermarket trolley during the weekly shop, they're likely to point to these images delightedly, often prompting doting mothers to buy the related products. As a result, huge budgets have been devoted to developing logos and cartoon characters that appeal to tiny children. Brightly coloured, big-eyed, softly rounded cartoon characters work the best – keep an eye out for them on processed food.

By the age of two and a half, toddlers – especially the more verbally competent girls – can ask for products by name. *'For example, when they think about juice, they don't just think juice … they think company!'* says marketing guru Martin Lindstrom, author of BRANDchild. Jingles and slogans repeated regularly on screen mimic the songs and 'motherese' language that teach children to speak.

If a product is sufficiently attractive, children can easily become 'attached' to it. A UK survey of food products found that *'effectively* marketed brands generate recognition, familiarity and even affection amongst children'. So they don't even need to taste the stuff to develop a preference, but when they do taste it, the artificially heightened flavours of processed foods act on the brain in the same way as drugs, and can create a mild physical addiction.

> The artificially heightened flavours of processed foods act on the brain in the same way as drugs.

Even more to the point, the foods children learn to love in their early years can become a psychological addiction. Since infant brains are steered by emotion, tastes acquired at this stage run very deep. They need 'warm-but-firm' parents who, despite their own issues about diet, display benign authority about what's best for a growing boy or girl. Allowing outside commercial interests to trump the parental hand in children's formative years is a very bad idea.

Social eating

Since all the basic principles of physical and emotional nutrition apply as children grow older, it leads us to the question of family mealtimes – an age-old human tradition that's now been clearly linked to childhood well-being and teenage mental health by innumerable research studies. This is scarcely surprising – since food and love go together, communal eating has always been at the heart of family life. As the chef Raymond Blanc said, 'To cook for family and friends is an act of love that binds together all who share it.' Mothers, fathers and other carers (paid or unpaid) have an opportunity to carry on passing down the E-type messages every time they produce and share a communal meal.

There are many ways in which this helps to raise healthy, balanced children – shared meals are an opportunity for everyone to connect and chat (see Chapter 7), a time for adults to hand on basic life-skills such as food preparation and table manners, an oasis of real time and real space in children's increasingly virtual world (see Chapters 8 and 9), and a regular routine that can enhance feelings of security and family attachment. It's also the ideal time to continue a girl's nutritional education. So it goes without saying that during mealtimes everyone benefits from switching off all electronic distractions.

Food is a natural shared focus for E-type engagement between the generations. As I sifted through the advice of nutritionists and psychologists on family mealtimes, the suggestions that made the most sense were those that emphasised the interactive nature of authoritative parenting, and the importance of seeing it from a child's point of view as well as from an adult one. For instance, involving their daughter in shopping and food preparation can be a highly enjoyable experience, as long as parents accept that it'll take a lot longer than doing it without her 'help'. When a girl has shared the human effort and care of preparing a meal, she's naturally more inclined to value and enjoy the food itself. And even if parents can't afford the time to cook a meal from scratch, once it's on the table their daughter will obviously notice that her parents are (or aren't) prepared to make the time to share it with her.

Once the meal's been served, authoritative rules and routines focus on the key aspects of (a) a balanced diet, and (b) associating food with hunger reduction. If this sort of regime is established as soon as a toddler can eat mashed-up versions of the communal dish, mealtimes need not be a battleground as they grow older, and the following regime can be applied to the whole family, for as long as they eat together:

- everyone comes to the table hungry (perhaps by having a 'no one eats in the two hours before supper' rule)
- the meals provided are nutritionally balanced and, as far as possible, composed of fresh ingredients
- children share the same meal as the adults – with the option just to eat vegetables, bread, rice, etc. (but no pudding or alternative snacks), if the main dish doesn't appeal
- food is offered in serving dishes and children are allowed to choose what and how much of each dish they want, with second helpings if they'd like more.

Young children should be encouraged to try new dishes, but not forced to eat more than a taste. The over-twos are naturally prejudiced against new foods, so it can take as many as eight to ten 'little tastes' on different occasions to establish an interest.

A simple rule of thumb from nutritionist Ellyn Satter sums up most of the advice very neatly:

Parents decide what, when and where to eat.
Child decides how much ... and even whether.

Unfortunately, many adults' own mealtime memories are of conflict and misery, as their parents struggled to cope with the pressures of late 20th century life. But if, as all the evidence suggests, the advantages of family meals are in a girl's best interests, trying to protect her from possible discomfort and discord by avoiding them is a form of short-term indulgence that may have adverse long-term repercussions. Better to establish a few simple ground rules that allow everyone to focus on the pleasurable aspects of sharing food and company ... then hope for the best rather than fear the worst.

> The advantages of family meals are in a girl's best interests.

There are bound to be occasions when girls exert what little power they have by turning up their noses at food, or days when everyone's feeling grumpy, and meals the entire family would prefer to forget. But real life's like that.

The 80/20 approach to junk food

Raising healthy children always comes down to balance. For a healthy body, a girl needs a balanced diet. For a healthy attitude towards her body, she needs a balanced view of female beauty. If she's to carry both through into adulthood, she also needs a healthy emotional balance between self-love and self-discipline.

So her parents have a balancing act to perform too. On the one hand, they have to protect their daughter from the damaging effects of consumer culture, but on the other, overprotection always carries the risk of setting up long-term problems. Their daughter is growing up in what we still call 'the real world', despite the fact that it's awash with unreal images and unhealthy, overprocessed foods. To survive and thrive, she has to learn how to deal with them herself.

A nutritionist I interviewed for Toxic Childhood told me that with her own children she uses an '80/20 approach': 80 per cent healthy food, 20 per cent fatty, sugary or junk food. *'If they don't have the occasional sweets or McDonald's they aren't part of the peer group, and that causes other problems. As long as the overall diet's healthy, a bit of junk shouldn't do that much harm. The trouble is that many parents now get it the wrong way round – 80 per cent rubbish food and 20 per cent nourishment.'*

Like Ellyn Satter's rule of thumb for family meals, 80/20 struck me as a useful guide to apply to authoritative balance, too. So did my interviewee's way of keeping the 20 per cent in its place: *'I don't give junk as treats, it's just something we sometimes get when we're out – I don't keep it in the house. And the kids are well aware of my disdain for it!'*

Since highly flavoured, processed foods are mildly physically addictive, the more children (and adults) eat, the more they want. Turning them into rewards can create an additional psychological addiction, especially if the most important childhood rewards (parental love, time and attention) aren't always available. If parents don't allow junk food into the house, it won't become associated with home comfort and no one's likely to succumb to temptation in moments of weakness. And mild disdain is less likely to turn it into forbidden fruit than trying to pursue the zero option.

There are, of course, times when a spot of dietary self-indulgence is entirely reasonable. Human beings have always celebrated high days and holidays with special sweet or tasty foods, and waiting for such pleasures helped their offspring learn to 'defer gratification' – an essential element in long-term self-control. When birthday treats, Christmas sweetmeats and Easter eggs came but once a year, they were genuine highlights in children's lives – indeed, in the life of the whole family – to be savoured both in the anticipation and in the consumption.

The 80/20 rule is of help here too. It allows for any sweets or other unhealthy snacks that do find their way into the home, for instance as gifts or part of a celebration, to be enjoyed in sensible moderation. If temptation arrives in such abundance that it seriously threatens the week's 80/20 balance, it can be rationed authoritatively. A daughter who's encouraged to defer gratification in a reasonable way throughout her childhood is much more likely to eat sensibly in adulthood than one who's grown up in conditions of feast or famine.

> A daughter who's encouraged to defer gratification in a reasonable way is much more likely to eat sensibly in adulthood.

Time to digest

Yet again, the message is that establishing a balanced attitude towards diet and body image takes time. Parents have to find the time to show their daughters what nourishment – both physical and psychological – is all about. As always in matters close to the human heart, quick fixes don't work.

Sadly, this age-old truth is in direct conflict with the culture beyond the home. Not only does an aggressive market economy encourage us to consume too much of the wrong sort of food, it also encourages us to consume it at ever-increasing speeds. The average American now takes only 14 minutes to polish off a McDonald's meal, because, as market researcher Clotaire Rapaille explains, *'pleasure in eating pales next to our need for movement... We are a country on the go and we don't have time to linger over our food.'*

Fast food is designed to emphasise the pleasure of consuming, not eating. The marketers want us to bolt down their product and, hopefully, soon fancy another because its ingredients have impacted on (carefully identified) neurotransmitters in our brains. So the products on offer tend to be high in taste and consequently also high in calories, attractive to look at, and quick and easy to consume. It also helps if we see the business of preparing and eating food in the old-fashioned way as time-consuming and messy, and see the answer to our food problems as:

- something we can gobble on the go, 'hygienically' packaged in brightly coloured wrappers, boxes and cans, or

- ready-made meals served in restaurants, or taken home in neat, non-messy microweavable containers.

A socially-aware little girl surrounded by these advertising messages is easy prey. They fit neatly with the other messages suggesting that girls shouldn't get messy (appearance is all) and that success for a 21st century female consists mainly of tearing around madly between the workplace and the shops.

Helping a girl to develop a balanced attitude therefore requires serious investment in terms of time on behalf of the responsible adults in her life – especially her parents (or the people they choose to be substitute parents). She needs to learn from experience that preparing food is time-consuming and messy, but can also be intensely pleasurable. It's also an opportunity to spend time with people she loves, doing something that shows how much she loves them. She needs to learn that the 'puff' of immediate sensory gratification pales against the long-term emotional rewards of sharing real food with those beloved people around a table, along with conversation and conviviality.

Above all, she needs to know that she's lovable enough to deserve their time, and that they care enough to make and uphold rules about eating that are in her long-term interests. 'We love you – the marketing men just want our money.' If her parents are prepared to do this, the chances of her developing a yawning emotional gap – to be filled by indulgence or self-denial – are considerably reduced.

And if they also allow her the freedom to grow into a well-rounded individual (see Chapter 7) and help her to avoid fashion victimhood (see Chapter 8), she'll be even better equipped to survive the 21st century marketing maelstrom. An 80/20 rule of thumb could also be useful in avoiding the body image problems that spring from over-immersion in screen-based culture. If 80 per cent of a pre-teen girl's waking hours are spent in the real world, with real people (family, friends, teachers, neighbours), she should be able to survive 20 per cent exposure to the unreal world of consumerist culture without too much damage.

The appliance of science

I'd love to give my 80/20 nutritionist credit for her idea. She's anonymous only because she asked to be. *'Please don't quote me on that. That's me being a mother, not an academic. The official line is zero tolerance!'* Our interview took place at the height of media interest in childhood obesity, and she didn't dare blow her credibility with mixed messages. The junk food PR men could use it against her.

Nutritionists have been warning about the dangers of junk food for decades, but it wasn't until the government grasped the economic implications of widespread childhood obesity that they gained a strong media voice. We have to hope that, in the long run, their involvement and that of other academics will help to sort out some of the excesses of consumer culture. Scientific and medical evidence is probably the only way to raise public consciousness of the damage done by the exploitation of children for financial gain.

Unfortunately, in the short term, scientific advice – based on research evidence that's extremely difficult to reduce to sound bites – often muddies the water further. Media scares about children's health, finger-wagging government campaigns and healthy-eating policies in schools (sometimes applied with draconian zeal) tend to fuel parental anxiety. Meanwhile, marketers pander to increasing feelings of insecurity with lots of new 'healthy' products (often low in one unhealthy ingredient, but chock-full of another) and cosmetic adjustments to the marketing of junk food to give it a healthier gloss.

Those parents who fret about their public image know that the judging of children as 'products' now includes their weight and body shape, and the verdicts reflect deep class prejudices. As with Susie Orbach's body image victims, parents whose children are hopelessly addicted to junk food (often from poor backgrounds) throw in the towel, while those obsessed with appearance (often middle class) exercise ever-tighter control over food intake. Extreme examples have become the stuff of urban legend: overweight mothers in Rotherham feeding their kids burgers through the school railings; thin mothers in Surrey bragging that their offspring's favourite food is broccoli.

Even those parents valiantly trying to resist the zeitgeist often find it difficult to maintain light-touch authority, when every shopping expedition is a trip through a nutritional minefield, and packing their daughter's lunchbox becomes a political act. But it's more essential than ever to keep the faith. Today's girls need the authoritative wisdom of the people who love them. And by guiding their daughters through the junk food/body image jungle, authoritative parents are passing on personal authority to the next generation.

★★★

Once upon a time, everything about feeding babies and children suggested in this chapter was simple common sense – the problem for most families was being able to find or afford enough food to keep their offspring alive and physically healthy. But at least their accumulated wisdom – based on a wide experience of human behaviour – was held in common by the women of the village. In a global, media-driven, consumerist 'village', the only thing that we atomised, isolated inhabitants hold in common is confusion.

> So we live in a society blessed with an abundance of food and a dearth of wisdom.

So we live in a society blessed with an abundance of food and a dearth of wisdom. A great deal of our modern-day agonising comes from the problem of having too much – at least in material terms – hugely intensified by the blandishments of the marketers. To be authoritative, parents must wise up to these problems and work out a simple plan of action to create a healthy family culture, based on sound reasons that can be explained to their daughter if she balks at the regime. And, of course, they need to take the time to establish that regime in a way that enhances the quality of life for the whole family.

> It should be possible to revive the ancient tradition of 'common sense'.

The good news is that if parents do devote time and attention to raising children – collaborating with other interested parties in their immediate village – it should be possible to revive the ancient tradition of 'common sense'. Taking personal responsibility for children's well-being involves accepting the here and now of real life, experienced first-hand through the senses. And if this 'sensed' experience is held in common by enough responsible adults, they'll pass it on to the 21st century girls they raise.

Food Timeline

0–1 year

Breast is best for at least 6 months (see page 102).

Relax and enjoy feeding your baby girl. Don't get hung up on systems or schedules (see page 103), or get distracted by TV and electronic gadgets (see page 105).

When you introduce solid food, remember that you are setting up her default eating habits.

Give her plenty of variety of healthy fresh foods (check out the NHS website for up-to-date advice).

Have fun sharing new tastes and textures. If she doesn't like a taste, don't push it. Introduce it again later.

Let her use her fingers. If you use a spoon, offer her one too so she can copy you. Give her plenty of time, and expect mealtimes to be messy.

From six months, offer some drinks in a cup (milk – breast or formula, or water only).

1–3 years

Serve three regular meals a day. As far as possible, eat at the same time and give her the same food, cut or mashed up (check out NHS nutrition advice). Don't worry if she doesn't finish food.

Keep mealtimes sociable, fun and relaxed.

Let her feed herself using her fingers and, as soon as possible, a spoon. Introduce a fork when she's ready.

As she gains control over her behaviour, teach her some basic rules, e.g., no throwing food. Minimise mess by giving her utensils (even if she can't hold them properly) – give her plenty of praise for good behaviour.

Establish a routine for family meals (e.g., see page 106) and begin to introduce it.

While you're in complete control of her diet, keep it nutritious. Make any snacks healthy, and don't give them before meals. Ask friends and relatives not to give her sweets or sugary drinks as treats.

3–6 years

From now on, expect everyone to follow the family meal routine (see page 106), and aim to make mealtimes as relaxed and pleasurable as possible.

Introduce table manners gradually. Praise her for good manners, but don't expect her to have perfect manners from the start. Work towards her achieving civilised behaviour by age six.

Adults and older children are her role models for table manners. The 'no toys at the table' rule includes your own electronic toys, smartphone, etc!

Teach her how to set the table (this could be her regular job), and let her help you when you're preparing meals.

The longer you are in complete charge of her diet the better, because you can help her to set up healthy eating habits for life. When contact with the outside world means it's impossible to avoid junk food completely, introduce the 80/20 rule (see page 110).

5–11 years

Try to eat one meal together as a family every day, and make it a social occasion. Keep to your established routine (see page 107) so that expectations are clear.

Encourage your daughter to help in the kitchen and gradually teach her to cook. If you're a gardener, involve her in growing food. Develop her interest in good food, where it comes from, how it's produced, etc.

Don't keep unhealthy food in the house. Allow occasional junk food away from home so that she knows what it is, but show your disdain for it.

Explain why certain foods are bad for her and why your advice trumps marketing messages (*'We love you – the marketers just want our money.'*).

Limit screen-based entertainment (no more than two hours a day) and help her to develop sensible attitudes towards her appearance (see Fashion Timeline, page 154).

Make sure that she keeps active (see Play Timeline, page 144). Along with a healthy diet and plenty of sleep, this should ensure her weight and shape are age-appropriate. If not, see your doctor.

Talk to her about marketing techniques (see page 106) and discuss how they're used in the adverts you see on TV, the internet and all around you.

11 years +

Continue to eat together as a family throughout her teenage years, and involve her in planning and cooking meals, which will provide plenty of openings for chats about nutrition. As time goes on, encourage her to take over some or all of the cooking of occasional meals.

Use any natural teenage concern about her appearance to open up conversations about the importance of diet and exercise in keeping in shape. But don't leap in too fast – let her talk through what's worrying her, acknowledge her feelings and offer comfort before suggesting solutions.

Point her towards authoritative sources of information, such as the NHS website's advice for teenage girls.

If she wants to diet, use it as a means of encouraging healthy eating habits, such as avoiding sugary and high-fat foods, eating lots of fruit and vegetables, drinking plenty of fluids and not skipping breakfast.

Continue to discuss marketing techniques, and help her to think about nutritional claims (e.g., does a 'low-fat' product contain other, fattening ingredients?).

Make sure the meals and snacks you provide contain plenty of iron and calcium, which are often lacking in the diets of teenage girls.

Almost all teenage girls go through eating fads, but if she feels loved and valued, and you've helped her lay down healthy attitudes towards food and body image, these shouldn't last long. If you are worried, check out the advice for parents about eating disorders on the NHS website.

CHAPTER 7

HOME AND AWAY, SAFETY AND PLAY

How family time, sound sleep and 'real play' develop girls'
confidence, resilience and independence

One chilly October evening a few years ago, I was giving a talk about
'detoxing childhood' in a children's centre in the north of England.
I'd mentioned the importance of a good night's sleep for healthy development, and the mums were chatting about the difficulty of set-
tling their young children at night:

'She just won't stay in her bed.'

'Mine are always wandering down, wanting a drink or something.'

'I can put her back three or four times in a night. It really wears you
down.'

Then a woman towards the far end of the room leaned back in her
chair and drawled: 'I know how to keep them in bed tonight.' Everyone turned to look, and I wondered what the heck she was going to
suggest.

'Turn the heating off,' she said.

There was a moment's silence, then an outbreak of nods and laugh-
ter. We started talking about our own early childhood, when bed was
warm and cosy and the world beyond the duvet cold and uninviting.
A half-remembered time when children's bedrooms were just that –
rooms containing beds. Most of the mothers at the meeting were in
their twenties, so I was surprised that their memories of bedtime in
their earliest years were so similar to mine. Since their own children

were all under eight years old, it was a perfect illustration of how rapidly lifestyles were changing.

And since most of these mums were strapped for cash and struggling to combine child-rearing with a job, they agreed that turning off the bedroom radiator at bedtime was a great 'common sense' idea – not only might it give them a little more peace in the evenings, it would also save a bob or two.

The reason it hadn't occurred to them before was that their little ones' bedrooms were no longer just bedrooms. They'd turned into 'personal space', used for many other activities besides sleeping. Their kids watched TV and DVDs in their rooms, listened to music, played computer games, logged on to kids' social networks like Moshi Monsters and kept in touch with friends via texting and instant messaging.

The rise of the electronic bedsit

The transformation of a quiet, dark room intended for sleeping into a noisy, multi-purpose 'electronic bedsit' began in the mid-20th century. For the past 50 or so years, older teenagers lucky enough to have a bedroom of their own have used it as a place to play music, do homework and hang out with friends – usually of the same sex, since most parents are touchy about that sort of thing.

This was probably a necessary development. Western society has grown so wealthy and sophisticated that young men and women are still in the education system, and consequently economically dependent on their parents, until their late teens or early twenties. They need some personal space in which to assert their independence and individuality. I reckon that turning a bedroom into an electronic bedsit is an excellent rite of passage birthday present for a 16-year-old.

But as the KAGOY marketing strategy steadily blurred the distinctions between age groups, bedrooms also became a 'personal space' for younger teens and then for the 'tweens', too (see Chapter 8). This move down the age-range was fuelled by cable and satellite TV in the 1990s, and a proliferation of children's and music channels. As parents

> By 2004, 80 per cent of the under-12s had a TV in their room.

upgraded their TVs, they handed the old ones to their children, providing relief from family rows about which channel to watch and the incessant racket of kids' programming. By 2004, 80 per cent of the under-12s had a TV in their room.

They also had a growing number of other technological gadgets – computers, MP3 players, games consoles, mobile phones, etc. The combined forces of Moore's Law (see page 69) and competitive consumerism led to a massive expansion in children's material 'needs'. And, since all this electronic entertainment and means of communication meant children spent many hours in their rooms, it seemed only sensible to decorate and furnish the rooms as living space.

Once the concept of the electronic bedsit was normalised in the tween age group, it spread rapidly to even younger children. In the same 2004 survey, 40 per cent of under-fives had TVs in their bedrooms.

This change in children's lifestyles – taking place over a single generation – has had profound effects on family life. Children have grown steadily more dependent on technology to fill their leisure time, spending, on average, between five and six hours a day glued to screens of various kinds, and becoming increasingly separated from their family. Love and understanding between the generations is rooted in close personal contact and interaction, so when girls spend long stretches of their lives alone in their 'bedsits', rather than sharing family time, they're deprived of the E-type loving care that they need for healthy development.

Family time – when the generations just hang out together, sharing their domestic existence – is essential

> Family time – when the generations just hang out together, sharing their domestic existence – is essential.

for parents to keep in touch with, and influence, their daughter's development. It's when they gradually pass on the life-skills (such as housekeeping, cooking, gardening and DIY) that will stand her in good stead in the future. It's also the time when mum and dad can act as role models by sharing the job of running the home, and encourage their daughter to be a fully fledged member of the family by helping with the chores. It's how their daughter establishes important elements of her identity, through the random family chit-chat and banter that are exchanged during chores or when relaxing after they're finished, including stories from her parents' past.

Semi-detached families

No one intended this splintering of the family to happen. As Sally Ward said, when she sparked off my quest to investigate 'toxic childhood', '*It's not just one thing. It's lots of things coming together.*' The things that make modern life more comfortable, convenient and safe for adults, often turn out to have unintended consequences for children. A few months into my investigative quest, some teachers and I were trying to make a list of these 'things', and one older woman suddenly exclaimed: '*I blame central heating! In the old days, there was only one room in the house that was warm, so everyone was together, sharing family life. Nowadays every room's warm, so everyone can go off and do their own thing.*'

Her remark echoed in my head at that meeting in the children's centre, and then again when I remembered the origin of the word 'focus' (see page 70). It's not just that the screen has taken over from the hearth as the focus of the family home; all too often, each member of the family now has his or her own particular screen focus – a TV, computer, console game, tablet, phone – separate from everyone else, steadily encouraging everyone into ever more selfish S-type individualism.

And these semi-detached family relationships can begin very early. I was chatting to a midwife recently, who told me how worried she was about the young mothers she works with. '*Many of them are texting their friends and family even while we're delivering the baby. They're not even properly present at their baby's birth. When they get home they can't understand why their little one doesn't like the wonderful new nursery they've spent a fortune preparing.*'

When parents-to-be believe that 'love = stuff', they naturally want their daughter to have all the latest baby paraphernalia. They look forward to welcoming her home to her own specially designed and decorated room, full to the brim with the products that show the level of their adoration (and, via 'baby showers', that of friends and family). Then, as time goes on, they want to have the same (or better) stuff as all her friends.

The harder mum and dad have to work to feed this materialist frenzy, the less time they have for forging a family life. Not only does their daughter miss out on the family time she needs to feel loved and secure, she becomes steadily more dependent on the presents her parents substitute for their presence. This can, in turn, seriously interfere with two other vital ingredients for healthy development – sleep and play – which, as their daughter grows from baby to child, should increasingly be her own responsibility

Every little girl is born with a body and brain programmed for sleep during the hours of darkness, and play (active, exploratory and creative) during the day. If she 'settles down' to sleep at night to the fret and fizz of electronic entertainment instead, and spends many hours of her waking life interacting with screens rather than with the real world, there'll be a long-term developmental price to pay.

Why girls need a good night's sleep

Let's start with sleep. Everyone needs plenty of sleep every night, and not just children. But in a world of artificial light, caffeinated drinks and constant access to electronic entertainment and communication, our capacity to switch off and enjoy an uninterrupted good night's sleep has been seriously eroded. Scientists are increasingly worried about the 'sleep debt' that the adults of the developed world are steadily racking up, because it's associated with all sorts of physical and mental ill health issues. Since human sleeping patterns are laid down during childhood, any 21st century girl who acquires bad habits at an early age won't just be unnecessarily irritable and restless on a daily basis. She'll also be programmed for a lifetime of insomnia and all the problems that come in its wake.

One physical problem associated with poor childhood sleeping patterns is obesity. It could be that children who don't sleep well have less energy during the day for active play, or that the longer they're awake the more time there is for snacking (or, of course, both). It could be that, by spending those extra waking hours in front of electronic media, they're absorbing an extra dose of damaging marketing messages. Scientists also point out that exposure to bright light during the night influences hormone balances in ways that can affect the appetite for food. Whatever the explanation, it's clear that healthy sleeping habits must go hand in hand with healthy eating habits if a girl's to steer successfully through the junk food jungle and avoid problems.

But there may be further underlying dangers for girls in the night-time hormone imbalances caused by sitting up late in an electronic bedsit. Scientists have linked low levels of the sleep hormone melatonin (secreted during the hours of darkness) with the early onset of puberty. The age at which girls start to menstruate has been dropping steadily for about half a century and, over the last decade or so, an alarming number of girls have started to 'grow up' while still in single figures age-wise, long before they're emotionally ready to deal with it. While the reasons behind this change are still unclear and probably highly complex, sleeping patterns are almost certainly implicated.

And they're definitely implicated in problems with learning. It's now well established that new information acquired during the day is transferred into long-term memory during sleep. We consolidate practical hands-on learning during periods of shallow, 'light' sleep (which is probably why babies and toddlers, who are constantly learning new physical skills, need lots of little naps during the day), while academic-style learning is consolidated during deep sleep. Natural human sleep rhythms involve several periods of deep, 'slow-wave' sleep per night, interspersed with periods when we slip upwards into shallow sleep.

So a good night's sleep, with no disruption to natural rhythmic patterns, is essential once children start school. One psychologist found that having one hour's sleep too little per night can cause a difference in performance at school *'bigger than the gap between an average fourth grader and an average sixth grader'*. Another claims that sleep disorders can impair children's IQ as much as exposure to lead.

One very obvious responsibility for loving, authoritative parents is to establish a healthy sleep regime for their daughter from the outset and to stick to it. A key element in this regime is to avoid the pressure to furnish her with her own electronic bedsit. While she obviously needs somewhere to keep her clothes, favourite toys, bedtime reading books, and so on, a pre-teenage girl doesn't need 'personal space' – she needs to be part of a family who love her.

Hush, little baby, don't you cry

Indeed, at the very beginning of her life, a girl doesn't need a room of her own at all; she just needs her mum. Babies are naturally panic-stricken when they lose sight of (and touch with) the person who's keeping them alive, and mothers are usually similarly panic-stricken when their babies cry. Until their little ones are sleeping peacefully through the night, it makes sense to stay as close to them as possible, and in many cultures there's a long tradition of babies 'co-sleeping' with their mothers in the early months, until they've sorted out a feeding routine and settled into the rhythm of a long night-time sleep.

Co-sleeping isn't popular in Western societies, so parents have a twofold problem as they try to ease their new daughter into a night-time routine. They must find ways of soothing her to sleep in a world awash with artificial light and noise, and they must also persuade her to sleep apart from her beloved attachment figure. Not surprisingly, babies aren't keen on this, and most keep their parents awake for nights, or sometimes weeks, months, even years... . As mum and dad rapidly discover how important uninterrupted sleep is to their own well-being, their exhaustion adds to the life-disrupting mix.

Sleep is therefore an area where tips and hints from experts and other parents are extremely helpful. But, just as with establishing feeding habits, trying to follow someone else's rigidly prescribed schedule in the early stages isn't a good idea. It's the family's internal dynamics that matter, and an imported schedule distracts mum and dad from tuning into their baby personally and finding out what works best for them all.

Of course, they can't let the baby call all the shots – that way madness lies – but they do need to see it from their baby's point of view as well as their own. There are now many helpful books on ways of soothing a child to sleep, and helping them to 'self-soothe' back into dreamland if they wake up, the most popular at the time of writing being The No-Cry Sleep Solution by Elizabeth Pantley.

However, five years ago, while I was researching sleep for Toxic Childhood, I really liked a book called Sound Sleep. I interviewed its author Sarah Woodhouse, whose own research in a variety of cultures had convinced her that tiny children need to sleep beside their mothers. So, although she was well into her seventies, she'd just remortgaged her house and thrown all her savings into designing a contraption that enabled mother and baby to be as close as possible while not actually co-sleeping. It was attached to the parental bed, but could be detached as the baby grew older, when it was time to ease the gradual transition in to sleeping alone. There are several models now on the market, and I wish I'd had one.

Goodnight, sleep tight

Whatever methods parents select to help their little one to wind down to go to sleep, and to stay asleep through the night, their long-term aim is to help her become an independent sleeper. That means:

- she can fall asleep under her own steam, without their assistance
- if she wakes during the night, she just snuggles down in bed until she drops off again
- if she wakes early in the morning, she lies back, dreams and dozes until it's time to get up.

They also need to ensure that she gets the appropriate amount of night-time sleep for her age, which is:

- around 13 hours a night until she's three (as well as daytime naps for as long as she needs them)
- between 11 and 13 hours until she's six
- between 10 and 11 hours up to the age of ten.

They must assume an authoritative stance and establish a bedtime routine that eases their daughter, gently, into good sleeping habits. As always, parental authority relies on balancing 'warmth' and 'firmness'.

The type of bedtime routine to aim for, as a girl moves from babyhood to around three years old, is:

a quiet, technology-free wind-down towards bedtime (at least an hour)

bathing,* washing, cleaning teeth, etc.

a cool, darkened room with no electronic distractions

a lullaby/bedtime story (with a time limit)

a goodnight kiss.

If she hasn't already dropped off, mum or dad shouldn't hang around in her room beyond the time allotted for story, song and farewells. They should also establish from the outset that getting out of bed before wake-up time next morning is completely against the house rules (except for emergencies).

Once established, bedtime and the routine accompanying it should be consistent, especially if achieving good sleeping habits has been tricky. If a girl goes through a phase of finding it difficult to fall asleep, or waking in the night and failing to self-soothe, mum or dad should settle her back into bed as quickly and matter-of-factly as possible, using their preferred version of 'controlled crying' if necessary (the Mumsnet advice on this is sensible, brief and to the point, www.mumsnet.com).

---

* The current theory is that children don't need a bath every night because too much washing may be contributing to the 21st century explosion of eczema, just as obsessive house cleaning with disinfectant chemicals may be exacerbating the asthma boom. Makes sense to me.

During the summer, it helps to put up the sort of blackout curtains that would satisfy a Second World War ARP warden.

It helps to put up the sort of blackout curtains that would satisfy a Second World War ARP warden.

The more family time parents spend with their daughter during the day, tuning in to her needs and feelings, the easier it should be for them to establish a 'warm-but-firm' authoritative stance about sleeping habits. And the clearer they are from the outset about the importance of bedtime and a good night's sleep, the easier their daughter should find it to adjust to the routine. Hopefully, by the time she's walking and talking, she'll be an accomplished sleeper who thinks of bed as a safe, cosy place where – even if she's awake – she just lies back and dreams and dozes until she drops off again. She'll also have taken a significant early step on the way to self-control and personal independence.

As girls grow up, one way of marking birthdays could be to adjust bedtime with each passing year. If the family gets up at 7 a.m., when a girl is three she might go to bed at 6 p.m., at four she'd be promoted to 6.30 p.m., and so on, until she's nine and her age coincides with her bedtime. By this time, hopefully, her sleeping habits should be firmly established and once she's in double figures bedtime can become a little more negotiable, but should still take into account a teenager's need for at least eight or nine hours a night.

Sleeping with strangers

Within a year or so, most parents want their bedroom to themselves, and most children find it impossible to make the transition to sleeping alone without some form of physical comforter to cling to until mum or dad reappears in the morning. This has traditionally been a teddy bear, but any familiar comfortable object can take on the role of substitute attachment figure during the hours of darkness. Once this attachment is firmly established, it's very difficult to break, so parents need to ensure that their daughter's chosen comforter won't cause her any long-term problems.

Unfortunately, many parents are so harassed by their early struggles with their babies' sleeping habits that their own short-term need for a little peace and quiet means they lose track of the long-term consequences. And nowadays, there are many seductive technological short cuts to a quiet life. Even the neediest baby or toddler can be hypnotised by the bright lights and sound effects on a TV screen and, once in this state of entrancement, will often obligingly drop off to sleep. So a favourite DVD can seem like a godsend for a fussy baby who doesn't get the hang of bedtime. Or parents can buy an 'electronic nanny' to act as a 24-hour attachment substitute – the Baby TV channel provides special bedtime programmes, and stays on air all night with offerings such as *Sweet Dreams* to deal with infants wakening in the small hours.

Choosing these TV short cuts isn't all that different from helping a baby off to sleep with a spoonful of gin. The American Academy of Pediatrics recommends that children under two shouldn't watch TV at all because of research linking it to developmental conditions such as ADHD and autism, and because they know that the earlier a harmful dependency is established, the harder it is to break. Sleep researchers recommend that none of us should sleep with the TV on, at *any* age, as it impairs the overall quality of sleep.

The lure of new technology is unfortunately so great that even parents who manage to establish a screen-free sleep regime in the early years often renege once their daughter goes to nursery or primary school. When she reports that all the other children have TVs, computers, and other electronic equipment in their bedrooms, they fear she'll feel left out or underprivileged if they don't succumb. The cry of, 'But I'm the only one who doesn't have one!' is increasingly difficult to resist, as Reg Bailey's 2011 report *Letting Children be Children* clearly documented. Peer pressure is enormously powerful at every age, and commercial forces know only too well how to exploit it to push girls into their role as superconsumers (see Chapter 8).

As girls grow older, they're also keen to import various methods of electronic socialising into their rooms. Specific links between electronic communication and sleeping patterns are, at the time of writing, restricted to studies showing how children and teenagers' addiction to texting each other at all hours means they're waking frequently during the night and their sleep is generally shallower; anyone who's been rudely awoken by the beep of an incoming text will understand why. This is a harmful development in many ways, but from an educational perspective it has particular relevance for growing girls, since, as explained above, successful academic learning depends on lots of deep, slow-wave sleep.

Anyway, the message is loud and clear: allowing 'electronic strangers' into a girl's bedroom before her mid-teens is an extremely bad idea. If parents want their daughter to establish and maintain healthy sleeping habits, they have to bite the bullet and insist that her bedroom remains a technology-free zone.

Insist that her bedroom remains a technology-free zone.

Sleep Timeline

0–1 year

For at least the first six months, have your daughter sleeping as close to you as possible, and work out a routine for bedtime based on what works for the whole family.

Help her to learn the difference between day and night. Establish a bedtime that suits you all and stick to it. When she wakes for a feed, keep the room dark, be quiet and calm as you feed her, and put her straight down again afterwards.

Put her to bed drowsy but awake. Leave her to drop off by herself.

If she wakes between feeds, give her a few minutes to settle before going to comfort her. Keep the comforting brief and quiet.

Aim to have her sleeping for eight or so hours at a stretch by the age of one, but accept there'll probably be problems when she's teething.

1–3 years

Establish a bedtime routine (see page 126) and stick to it.

Don't have a TV, video, tablet, etc. in the bedroom – and don't use any of them to help her drop off to sleep.

If she wakes in the night and doesn't settle, check what's bothering her and resettle her with as little fuss as possible (I like the Mumsnet advice on this).

If she gets out of bed, put her back calmly, tell her to go to sleep and leave her. Keep on doing this until she loses interest in getting up.

If she has bad dreams or bedtime fears, take them seriously. Listen to her worries and do everything you can to allay them (e.g., provide a dim nightlight, spray the room from a bottle labelled 'Monster Repellent'!).

Make sure the bedroom is dark (use thick curtains to keep out street lights and early morning light) and cool (so that her bed feels cosy).

Have a rule about when she can get up in the morning (e.g., have a lamp attached to a timer and say she mustn't get up before the lamp goes on).

If she wakes early and can't go back to sleep, expect her to play with her teddy or to make up her own games. If you provide electronic entertainment instead she won't learn to use her imagination.

3–11 years

Maintain a firm line about bedtime (adjusting it as she gets older – see page 127), the going-to-bed routine and getting-up time.

Make bedtime a special time for cuddling up, talking about the day and showing how much you love her.

Continue to take her night-time fears seriously, and comfort her. But don't talk about her fears until daytime when she can take a more sensible perspective and you can discuss ways of solving them.

Always make time for reading a bedtime story. As she gets older, you can serialise children's novels. Read until she's drowsy, give her a bedtime kiss, then leave her to go to sleep.

Don't let her drink caffeinated drinks (including cola) after around 4 p.m.

As she gets older, she'll probably value her bedroom as a private place for reading, listening to music and somewhere to take her friends, but keep it a screen-free zone.

11 years +

Teenagers often have problems with sleep because of hormonal changes, so a regular bedtime routine and environment are still important.

Make sure she knows how important sleep is for overall health and success at school (see page 124).

If she's not sleeping well, start by checking whether anything is bothering her. If not, help her to check out the NHS advice on sleep for teenagers and to work out her own plan of action.

Keep her bedroom free of all screen-based technology until she's well into her teens (see page 129). If you do eventually allow her to turn it into an 'electronic bedsit', make sure she knows the importance of switching off all screens an hour or so before bedtime.

Playing with strangers

If parents insist on a technology-free bedroom for their daughter, the chances of her becoming addicted to various plug-in drugs are greatly reduced. Sharing a family TV or computer may be inconvenient, but it means parents have far greater control of the external influences on their daughter's psyche. They can, for instance, ensure that she learns the vital difference between play and entertainment.

In the modern world, many adults find it difficult to distinguish between the two – not least because most adults have lost touch with play themselves. We grown-ups tend to divide our time between work and 'leisure' and over the years have become increasingly passive about our leisure pursuits, often preferring to watch talented professionals play, rather than play on an amateur level ourselves. Sportsmen and women play football, golf, tennis, etc., while we watch and cheer; musicians play rock music, orchestral pieces, and so on, while we listen in the auditorium; actors play their parts while we watch and applaud; writers play with words and artists with materials, and the rest of us pay to consume what they produce. And as screen-based activity has developed, we've been able to enjoy all this second-hand play at the touch of a button.

Indeed, with the advent of computer games, we can engage directly with on-screen 'play', exploring interesting environments, experiencing dramatic events, racking up immense scores and achievements, and feeling as if we're the protagonists, when all we're really doing is responding to a ready-made programme.

We have come to see 'play' as an enjoyable leisure pursuit, which nowadays can be conducted second-hand, via a screen. But children's play isn't merely a leisure pursuit – it's a developmental drive, originating in the questing instinct through which children are programmed to learn about the world and the people with whom they share it (see Chapter 3). It's also the medium through which they learn to focus their attention and exercise increasing control over body and mind. Think of the rapt concentration of a baby or toddler as they play a self-chosen game that appears meaningless to an adult (my daughter used to spend ages, brow furrowed, taking every single book out of the lower shelves of the bookcase, or dropping random objects into a bucket of water in the kitchen). This is where a child learns to tune out distraction and concentrate on their chosen investigations – just as in her mother's arms, a baby girl learns to focus on the human face and voice (see pages 31–32).

It's very easy to distract a little girl's attention from these real-life activities by switching on the TV. The colourful shapes, movement and sound grab the attention much more quickly than slow-moving, three-dimensional reality. And attending to a TV screen doesn't take any personal effort, so the child's brain becomes locked into what psychologists call 'attentional inertia' – she isn't learning to focus attention for herself.

Media guru Daniel Anderson has found that children don't even have to be watching a TV for it to affect their capacity to focus. If a girl is playing in a room in which the TV is on, her attention is constantly distracted by its eye- and ear-catching activity. '*We have a natural inclination to look at the shiny, the bright, the mobile,*' Anderson says, while watching 14-month-old Molly interrupt her play repeatedly. '*She's being pulled away by the TV all the time, rather than making a behavioural decision to watch.*' He found that children focused 25 per cent less on their play when the TV was on, and parents interacted 20 per cent less with their children. When they did relate, it tended to be passive: '*Yes, that's nice*' or '*In a minute*'.

Screen-based entertainment is as far removed from the 'real play' children need for healthy development as junk snacks are from real food. The difference first hit home for me with a horrible, guilt-ridden thump a few years ago when I was working for CBeebies on a series called *Razzledazzle*. I had enormous fun collaborating with the producers to 'originate' and plan the programmes (it was a hoot), and then with the actors, storytellers, dancers, and so on, when the series was filmed. Then one day I watched a two-year-old girl gazing at an early episode – silent, motionless and open-mouthed. *Who's doing the 'playing' here*, I asked myself, *a bunch of lucky grown-ups employed by the media or this little mite?*

'Real play' learners or 'junk play' junkies?

To learn to control the focus of their own attention, and thus grow up able to make their own behavioural decisions, girls need real play. This is defined by play-workers as *'freely chosen, personally directed, intrinsically motivated behaviour that actively engages the child'* and it's why I now believe that parents should avoid exposing their daughters to TV in the first couple of years and allow no more than a couple of hours a day thereafter.

That's not just my opinion; it's long-standing advice from the American Academy of Pediatrics. It relates specifically to TV because television has been around long enough for scientists to establish a decent research base. The jury is still out on more recent innovations, such as computer games, electronic picture books, robotic pets, social networks and other state-of-the-art technological toys that now fill children's lives. But if you measure them against the definition of play given above, they're just as likely as the 'magic box' to turn girls into 'junk play' junkies, through the long-established psychological principle of 'conditioning'.

Does the name Pavlov ring a bell? Digital technology is brilliant at providing human beings with immediate 'rewards' for engaging with a computer programme, and programme developers spend ages working out the best way to reward small females. Like a performing dog or a laboratory rat, any little girl can be trained to behave in certain ways, lured by carefully devised on-screen rewards, such as pressing a button that makes something happen, moving up a level on a computer game or acquiring another 'friend' on a social network.

> Like a performing dog or a laboratory rat, any little girl can be trained to behave in certain ways.

Some years ago, I learned from an IT expert that kids' computer games are programmed to reward them every seven seconds. So it came as a nasty shock when, at a 2011 conference on play, Suzanne Zeedyk, a highly respected authority on infant attachment, mentioned that mothers and babies engaged in the 'dance of communication' reward with each other every seven seconds. The people who make and market interactive technology to children have obviously read the developmental literature.

In a world of such sophisticated marketing techniques, it's easy to fall into consumerist traps. Many parents believe that, since 21st century girls will be dealing with technology all their lives, they should start picking up the skills as early as possible. In fact, screen-based entertainment designed for young children is little more than 'stimulus-response' gadgetry, and any computer skills involved will be long out of date by the time the current generation of three- and four-year-olds hit their teens.

But don't expect the marketing men to tell you that.

The skills a 21st century girl *really* needs to learn over the course of her childhood are the deep-seated personal skills that underpin decision-making, adaptability and resilience. These personal qualities will enable her to survive and thrive, whatever the future brings. They are developed throughout childhood, and one of the main developmental requirements is real play. That's why, in the first couple of years, when a child's default habits of behaviour are being established, experts recommend they shouldn't be exposed to screen-based entertainment at all. Recommending a limit set at two hours a day after the first couple of years, the experts are apparently opting for another 80/20 approach (see page 109).

It seems a sensible balance to me. If a girl has 80 per cent real play during childhood, she should gradually learn to make her own choices about the best way to negotiate the junk play jungle. The very activity of engaging in 'real play' (that *'personally directed, intrinsically motivated behaviour that actively engages the child'*) for 80 per cent of the time will develop her capacity to think outside the box and learn to choose freely. Since screen-based entertainment won't become her default leisure-time activity, she'll grow up able to control her own media use, and be less likely to let the media control her (see also Chapter 8).

Unfortunately, for most 21st century girls the proportions are now reversed.

Something to play with

Most of the problems parents face in helping their daughters to develop healthy play habits spring – just like the problems of developing healthy sleeping and eating habits – from the unholy alliance of modern technology and competitive consumerism. And they've been building up for a long time.

The cultural historian Howard Chudacoff believes that the demise of real play began on 3 October 1955 – the day Mattel aired its first TV ad for a toy (a Thunder Burp gun). Until then big business hadn't thought of children as a particularly lucrative market so, except for some low-grade adverts around Christmas, toys hadn't featured in commercial breaks. But once they were depicted as desirable objects on screen, adult perceptions of play began to change. Instead of seeing it as something children *did* (freely, actively and under their own steam), adults increasingly associated it with the ownership of objects. From then on, the market expanded rapidly and by the 1980s, as Eric Clark describes in his book *The Real Toy Story*, toys were a multi-billion-dollar business. Taking their lead from the grown-ups, children began to feel they needed something to play with.

In fact, the more toys parents lavish on their offspring, the less mental effort is required during play. Take pretend play, for instance. A little girl playing 'let's pretend' without adult input has to use her imagination and explore her own ideas. There'll be innumerable opportunities for her to think, experiment and learn from creating costumes and props out of the bits and pieces she finds around the house. On the other hand, if she's presented with a ready-made princess outfit or a doctor's kit, at least half the work has been done already.

She'll doubtless be delighted with her present, just as she'd be delighted to be handed a fistful of sweets, but it won't help to develop her powers of self-control, creativity or independent thought (see also Chapter 8).

As far as real play is concerned, the job of loving parents is simply to light the blue touch paper and stand well back. In her earliest years, their daughter needs as much of their presence as possible (or that of a substitute attachment figure who knows and cares about her) to support her in becoming an independent player – see Chapters 3 and 9. But from the age of two or three, creative and pretend play takes place when she's left to her own devices or is playing with other children. She (or they) won't think of things to do with-

> As far as real play is concerned, the job of loving parents is simply to light the blue touch paper and stand well back.

out adult help unless allowed to be 'bored'. Parents don't need to be playmates in their infants' free play. Their major input takes place in family time – handing on life-skills, sharing stories and songs, chatting about what's going on in their child's world.

Of course, there are a few tried-and-tested toys that it's fun to share with a daughter, such as:

- toys that develop specific skills – jigsaws, bat and ball, skipping rope, board and card games, and so on
- toys that stimulate creativity, like building blocks, arts and crafts materials and construction toys.

But, apart from showing her how to use them and explaining any rules, take care not to take over the play. It's the development of the child's skills and creativity that matters, not those of the parent. The authoritative parental role is to support her wide-ranging, active, free play – not to control it.

A great leap backwards

Developmental psychologists are increasingly worried about the decline in children's capacity to focus their attention and thus to 'self-regulate' – i.e., to control their own behaviour. *'Self-regulation predicts effective development in virtually every domain,'* says psychologist Laura Berk, reporting on a US study that found five-year-olds in 2010 with self-regulatory skills equivalent to those of three-year-olds in 1950, while those of seven-year-olds in 2010 didn't even compare with the five-year-olds in the days when play was about what children did rather than what they owned.

Real play involves plenty of activity – not just mental but also physical. As pointed out on page 77, emotional, social, cognitive and physical development are all interrelated in an intricate fashion. So the concern of developmental psychologists about declining attention and self-regulatory skills is mirrored by that of medical doctors about the widespread deterioration in basic physical skills. In 2011, the UK's four Chief Medical Officers published a report called Start Active, Stay Active, making recommendations such as:

- babies should be allowed to crawl, play and roll around on the floor
- as soon as children can walk they should have plenty of opportunities for unstructured, active and energetic play.

The fact that this now has to be issued as 'medical' advice indicates how seriously the bulk of the adult population is out of touch with children's developmental needs. Many babies and toddlers scarcely move at all nowadays. For all sorts of reasons, mostly connected with materialistic values and a lack of inter-generational attunement, they spend much of their time strapped into baby seats, pushchairs and car seats. Babies and toddlers who are prevented from being active don't develop physical control, co-ordination and confidence, and so tend to become more sedentary as they get older.

Girls are less active than boys from the outset, and their levels of activity decline against those of their male counterparts as time goes on. The false premise on which this discrepancy between the sexes is based is described on pages 234–237, and it's been perpetuated throughout the millennia. Little girls have traditionally been given less freedom to play actively (meaning outdoors), not just because everyone assumed they were the weaker sex, but because, being female, they were expected to stay at home and help mum.

Everything I've learned about the developmental significance of play convinces me that this lack of freedom in infancy has always contributed to women's meek acceptance of their cultural lot. It wasn't until female emancipation in the early 20th century that girls of all social classes were given the same rights to childhood freedom as boys.

So it's tragic that the rise of the 'tomboy', whose lust for outdoor thrills and spills was equivalent to that of her male peers, lasted only about 50 years. Instead of getting out and about, and learning through play that they're capable of taking and managing risks for themselves, countless potential tomboys are now penned up safely in their electronic bedsits, learning that real-life risk is something to be avoided at all costs. (So, incidentally, are most of their brothers.) I hate to think what Lady Allen of Hurtwood would think of this. A campaigner for adventure playgounds and outdoor play, her robust rallying cry was, 'Better a broken bone than a broken spirit!'

Lock up your daughters?

It's difficult to say which was the chicken and which was the egg – the rise of the electronic bedsit or the explosion of parental paranoia about letting children play out unsupervised. But screen-based technology is clearly implicated in the latter as well as the former. According to neuroscientists, when disturbing information is repeatedly absorbed in a highly realistic visual form, it profoundly affects the emotional centres of the brain. So although it's completely irrational, parents viewing TV footage about the deaths of children fear that their own child is in danger.

Play campaigner Tim Gill dates the change in parental attitudes to a TV programme called *That's Life!* in the early 1990s, when the tragic death of a little girl falling from a swing led to a campaign for soft surfaces in playgrounds. The presenter, Esther Rantzen, dropped a china plate onto a soft play surface and watched it bounce. She then dropped another onto a hard floor, and it shattered. Gill believes this image profoundly affected adults' perceptions of children's fragility. It certainly affected playground design; they became increasingly 'safe', anodyne and – since soft surfaces are extremely expensive – rare. At any rate, it heralded an escalating national obsession with health and safety, and a drive to remove all possible risk of injury from children's lives.

> An escalating national obsession with health and safety, and a drive to remove all possible risk of injury from children's lives.

Saturation media coverage of other tragedies in the first decade of the 21st century – the murders of Sarah Payne, Holly Wells, Jessica Chapman and Milly Dowler – ratcheted up parental terror about 'stranger danger'. Again, it was highly irrational to conclude from these four terrible cases that any girl might be snatched off the street by a homicidal monster, but perceptions of risk escalated steadily. Child surveillance reached new heights after the mysterious disappearance of Madeleine McCann. From that time on, parents weren't just afraid of what might happen to their daughter if they let her out of their sight – they were frightened of what other people might think about them. At the time of writing, a trial in Wales relating to the disappearance of another little girl called April Jones seems likely to reignite parental anxiety.

In fact, the dangers of physical injury, abuse or violent crime are no greater than they've ever been. Children still suffer tragic accidents – nowadays they tend to occur in the home because that's where children spend their time – and children are still sometimes abused and occasionally murdered; the most likely perpetrators of these crimes have always been family members or other people known to them. A child protection officer once asked me to pass on this message to parents: 'The nasty men aren't in the park any more. They're online.' Another reason not to leave children alone in an 'electronic bedsit'.

> The nasty men aren't in the park any more. They're online.

Fortunately, the dangers of overprotecting children are at last being recognised officially. The Chief Medical Officers' report mentioned above is one of several recent high-profile documents about the need for active outdoor play. But scientific advice isn't enough. Unpicking such a widespread cultural mess depends on the reinstatement of common sense – which is why parents are so important.

Re-establishing free-range play

The potential long-term damage to a girl's overall development if she doesn't play out is infinitely greater than the possibility of serious physical injury. So the authoritative parental attitude towards outdoor play must be to:

- set sensible boundaries for their daughter to play out
- ensure she knows how to avoid and/or deal with dangers
- help to establish 'streetwise' habits of behaviour that will keep her safe.

Although the dangers highlighted in media scares are highly unlikely, there is one 21st century danger that actually is much greater than at any time in the past – traffic. There are more cars on the roads every year, and more cars parked in residential areas, making road safety procedures more difficult to follow. Ironically, keeping children indoors (and adding to the problem by driving everywhere) doesn't protect them in the long run. It just makes them more dependent and less able to look after themselves when they are eventually released from captivity.

The authoritative course of action is to ensure that as soon as she's able to walk (then scoot, then cycle), a 21st century girl learns the ropes of road safety through real-life experience. Children who go out walking in the streets regularly with caring adults learn through imitation and repetition how to survive in a traffic-filled world. They don't learn just the rules of the road, but how to judge real speed, real time, real distances and other 'intuitive' multidimensional lessons that can only be absorbed through endless experience. As the years go by, parents who watch their daughters grow in competence and confidence through frequent encounters with the outside world feel happier about allowing them increasing levels of freedom than those who keep girls closeted at home, or ferry them back and forth by car to supervised activities.

Determining what those levels of freedom are, and the right age at which to let their daughter walk or cycle to school and go 'out to play' during leisure time, has to be up to her parents. But it's much easier if, right from the beginning, they've made the effort to establish a relationship with other members of their local 'village' – neighbours, shopkeepers, and other adults in the area such as policemen, postmen and traffic wardens – so that both the parents and their daughter feel there are 'eyes on the street' to help to keep her safe. If they've also developed relationships with the parents of their daughters' schoolmates and those of other children in the immediate locality, these adults can band together to share supervisory duties and to make the neighbourhood as safe as possible for children to play out.

> We'll never be able to eradicate all risk from our daughters' lives, but we can nurture their capacity for risk assessment and risk management.

We'll never be able to eradicate all risk from our daughters' lives, but we can nurture their capacity for risk assessment and risk management, and in doing so, we will help them to develop the skills of self-regulation and common-sense understanding that willl truly provide them with 'roots to grow and wings to fly'.

Pass it on...

The love and discipline underpinning authoritative parenting is transformed into self-love and self-discipline in the next generation of women, only if, as girls, they have opportunities to try things out for themselves. For instance, a girl learns to make a cup of tea, first by watching her parents, then by being allowed to 'help', then by being helped to do it herself – building up her skill and confidence gradually. Then one day, she's ready to go solo. The same applies to every life-skill that parents teach their daughters.

As long as the drive to play isn't inhibited by hyper-control, as girls grow older they develop interests that take them beyond their home, such as sport and other outdoor activities, dance, music and drama. Parental role models* are the best way to inspire children's interest in recreational activities (the most active children tend to be those with active parents), but interests and passions can also be developed at school and through clubs and classes.

Interestingly, once an interest is conceived there's a significant

---

* It goes without saying that adult role models should be both male and female. Girls who have a close relationship with their father and other male carers during childhood tend to be more self-confident than those who grow up in a female-dominated environment.

difference between boys and girls in the way these formal activities are approached. Boys tend to focus more intently on 'product' – winning a particular race, rising up the league, and so on. Girls, on the other hand, are generally more interested in 'process' – improving aspects of their performance, honing particular skills, becoming the best they can possibly be.

For both sexes, however, there's no doubt whatsoever that of all the types of play described in this chapter, it's 'real play' that will help children to become more healthy, rounded and confident individuals, rather than a diet of screen-based entertainment and socialising.

***

In his book *The Meaning of the 21st Century*, Oxford academic James Martin ('Britain's leading futurologist') describes today's children and young people as 'the transition generation'. They are the future citizens whose thoughts and actions will, for good or ill, see the human race through the fastest-changing and potentially most challenging period of our history. Despite all the doomsayers, he thinks that our increasing technological know-how will help us to solve the problems of living on an overcrowded planet with depleted resources.

Martin's faith in technology goes hand in hand with his faith in human nature. He believes that, as computers overtake human beings in terms of systemised thinking, we can use them to solve problems that we can no longer solve ourselves. But in doing so, we have to draw on the biological strengths that computers lack – the capacity to *feel*, the ability to experience through all our senses and empathise.

In this respect, tomorrow's women may have a head start on tomorrow's men. Girls' greater potential for E-type thought should help them to process feelings and emotions more readily, and to take advantage of intuition – understanding garnered through the senses. If we allow mother nature's daughters to develop every aspect of their personalities during childhood, they should be well equipped to play their part in the new world they're about to inherit.

> In this respect, tomorrow's women may have a head start on tomorrow's men.

Play Timeline

0–3 years

Give your daughter plenty of freedom to move about and explore her environment with all her senses. Take sensible precautions to keep her safe, but don't constrain her more than absolutely necessary (see page 139).

She doesn't need many toys because she'll want to play with whatever's handy: household items indoors; sticks, stones, grass and leaves outdoors.

Make a box or basket of interesting but safe items, such as wooden spoons, large pine cones or shells, crackly packaging, discarded lids or boxes, bits of fabric, ribbon or fur. Let her experiment. Save large boxes too – an empty cardboard box is one of the best toys in the world.

Play with her – singing, clapping, tickling games; pretend play using your imagination; building, mixing and making things; moving to music; anything that you and she find fun. This provides models for her own play.

Let her play outdoors as often as possible, in the garden or the park, on visits to the seaside or the countryside.

Read stories with her and talk about them – she'll want to hear the same stories time and again.

Keep the TV turned off until she's two, and then restrict it to no more than an hour or so a day. Avoid technological toys (see page 134).

3–6 years

Continue with the sorts of play listed above, particularly outdoor play (see page 00).

Make sure she has lots of opportunities for social play (see Friendship Timeline, page 167).

Expect her to play increasingly without your involvement, but continue to have fun with her. Many fun activities at this age lay the foundations for later learning (see page 212 and Education Timeline).

Carry on sharing books together, and support your daughter in turning the stories into role play. Talk about shared TV too – good children's programmes will stimulate ideas for play.

Create a dressing-up box of old clothes, hats, shoes, fabric, beads, charity shop finds, etc.

Help her to make a 'den' (it could also be an imaginary cave, a house, a shop, a castle...), such as by putting a blanket over a table.

Provide equipment for arts and crafts activities, and suggest she makes pictures, greetings cards, scrapbooks, models and scenarios for pretend games with her toys.

Go collecting: leaves, stones, shells, cones, insects, worms, tadpoles – if it's alive, help her to look after it and watch it grow.

Prepare her for greater independence in the future by familiarising her with the local area and teaching her safety procedures (see page 140). The best way to do this is to walk (at least part of the way) to and from school, to the local shops, the library, etc.

Limit screen time of all kinds to a maximum of two hours a day.

6–11 years

Continue to limit screen time and to support your daughter in imaginative, creative, active and social play – especially outdoors.

Support her school in ensuring there are opportunities for this sort of play during break times and 'around the edges' of the school day, and that learning is as 'playful' as possible (see Education Timeline, page 212).

As she grows older, interests may turn into hobbies, such as cooking, sewing, making things, gardening or science. If you share her interests, you will have a common bond to enjoy for the rest of your lives.

As soon as you feel confident that she's ready to take on more independence, find ways of giving her the freedom to play outside the home.

Encourage her interest in more formalised play (such as sport, artistic or musical activities, dance or drama) by joining clubs – but not too many. If she's really interested, she'll want to practise and play at such activities for fun in her spare time.

11 years +

Teenagers still need to play, but they call it 'hanging out'. Give your daughter and her friends the space to hang out in your home.

She'll also want to hang out away from home – if your daughter has already been given the chance to develop self-reliance and common sense, you'll feel easier about her ability to look after herself.

Continue to encourage her established leisure-time interests. As school pressures and teenage socialising increase, it's easy for girls to neglect hobbies or other activities, but they're a good way of maintaining family ties as her focus moves increasingly away from home.

Keep up family play too: board, card and communal computer games; musical evenings or raucous karaoke sessions; a weekly 'movie night' with a DVD and popcorn; family outings, picnics and parties. These are all ways of maintaining connections between the generations.

CHAPTER 8

FASHION, FRIENDSHIP AND FUN

Girls in the social world beyond the home: the battle
between parental love and commercial exploitation

Poppy was a bright, happy three-year-old, who loved playing and pottering around the garden. Her family didn't have a TV so she was used to amusing herself. Then she started nursery school ... and began her education.

The first day she came home singing a little song she'd learned in the playground: 'Lelli Kelly, the cutest shoes, oh yeah!' Her mum and dad didn't think anything of it ... until a couple of weeks later when they took her to buy shoes.

As soon as they entered the shop, Poppy made a beeline for the Lelli Kelly stand. When dad explained they weren't the sort mum and dad wanted to buy, she threw (for the first time in her life) a raging hissy fit. She lay on the floor, kicking her heels and screaming 'Pleeease! I need them!' In the end, she had to be picked up bodily and taken home.

I met Poppy's father when giving a talk on Toxic Childhood a couple of weeks later. By that time the family had recovered from the experience and his daughter was perfectly happy with the shoes mum had chosen on a second shopping expedition. But dad was worried about the effects of peer pressure on her behaviour: 'She'd worked out that owning those shoes would make her popular,' he said, 'and it put real pressure on us to buy them.'

'Why didn't you?' I asked.

'Well, partly because they were so "girly" and didn't fit Poppy's life-style – they'd have been ruined in no time if she played out in them. They were fairly pricey too. But the thing we really didn't like was that they came with a little bag containing lip gloss. I mean, what's going on when people are selling lip gloss to three-year-olds!'

A question of identity

What indeed? Fashion, whether it's 'sexy' or not, is an adult concept. Grown women use clothing, shoes, hairstyles, cosmetics, and so on, to project not only their sexuality but their personality as a whole. And great fun it can be, as long as one has money to spend and enough self-confidence to enjoy fashion rather than becoming a slave to it. It's particularly good fun for young women in their teens and twenties, when they're establishing their adult identity and individual style.

But what's fun for adults and teenagers isn't necessarily good for children, and over the last 20 years the fashion industry has set its sights first on 'tweens' (older primary-age children who are 'too old for toys, too young for boys') and then on ever-younger girls. The earlier a girl becomes hooked on fashion, the more likely she is to be a fashion victim in the future, desperately searching for an off-the-peg identity, rather than developing a fully-rounded personality of her own.

We've already seen that children don't become conscious of themselves as thinking beings until they're around two years of age, and conscious control of their thought processes takes several more years to refine. The roots of their self-image are set, during that period, deep in their emotional core. So, as pointed out in Chapter 3, a girl who, feels loved for herself rather than for her appearance from the moment she's born, has a much better chance of growing into a well-balanced woman capable of making rational fashion choices. Parents who consciously resist the temptation to treat their daughter like a lit-tle doll enhance her chances of developing a well-rounded personality and a mind of her own.

In the same chapter, we saw that parents' unconscious preconceptions concerning gender (rooted in millennia of sexual inequality) may lead them to deter their daughters from active, exploratory play. Girls' early E-type perceptions concerning adult expectations may lead them to grow up more risk-averse than boys, and more compliant and open to social pressures – such as those exerted by the fashion industry.

One sure-fire way to discourage active play is to dress a child in inappropriate clothes. So until their daughter has developed some sense of herself as a thinking individual, it's up to her parents to buy the type of clothing that meets her developmental needs, rather than the kind that satisfies market-induced desires. Apart from 'best clothes' for special occasions, children need outfits that allow them to play freely: sensible footwear and practical, easy-to-clean clothing in which to run, jump, climb and generally mess about.

As girls develop the ability to make rational decisions, they need plenty of parental help to understand the marketers' wiles, and guidance in balancing an interest in fashion with other considerations about the way they dress, including, of course, the family budget. In today's highly sexualised culture, most girls need this sort of parental guidance until well into their teens, to help them to think critically about the messages conveyed through the fashion choices of the day.

Parents have to be aware of the potential dangers right from the start, and to be constantly on the watch for the thin end of the wedge. If they give in to 'pester power', their daughters learn to associate love with 'stuff', and to judge their own lovableness in terms of the way they look and the things they own. This, of course, is exactly what commercial forces want in order to turn out another generation of dedicated consumers, convinced they can buy their way to happiness.

In his book, BRANDchild, marketing guru Martin Lindstrom explains the importance of winning children for brands as young as possible. He approvingly quotes a twelve-year-old girl, whose parents have clearly confused love with indulgence: '*I love brands. Brands not only tell me who I am, they protect me from others in my class.*'

The princess culture

The most frequent route to hyper-consumerism for the current generation of girls starts with the commercial hijacking of fairy stories and pretend play. Traditional tales such as Cinderella and Sleeping Beauty have been popular female fare for centuries, and there can be few women who didn't go through a phase of playing 'princesses' in their youth. But the relentless proliferation of screen-based entertainment means that today's children share a particularly vivid impression of princess-like demeanour and dress code, and the toy and fashion industries have combined forces to allow them to buy into the dream. Since the 1990s, for instance, Disney films have been backed up by Disney shops, with a complete range of princess personae to choose from – a range that was developed, incidentally, by the marketing genius who made Nike the global leader in sportswear.

Mothers who were themselves raised on these films naturally enjoy indulging their daughters' childish dreams, and fathers are usually entranced by the cute appearance of their own 'little princess'. But strutting around in shop-bought finery is not the same as imaginative play, and buying into any dream is all too often the beginning of a slippery consumerist slope. It's also an extremely gender-stereotypical slope, leading girls down the age-old route to female objectification. In the words of Abi Moore, founder of the website Pinkstinks: 'The princess culture starts from the minute a child is born and it ends up, for teenage girls, with Paris Hilton'.

There's now an immense amount of prettified paraphernalia out there – indeed, it's becoming difficult to tell the difference between those products that are officially toys and the clothing, shoes and accessories aimed at small female consumers. Unless parents are careful, the dream could become an everyday reality and their daughter could slip into the princess role on a full-time basis. Since princesses are traditionally self-obsessed and high-handed, she may then start acting like a small, pink potentate. If, when she starts pre-school, she meets up with other girls who've adopted the same persona, the princess culture may begin to threaten parental authority.

In recent years I've met many mums who've told me their daughters refuse to wear anything but party dresses, or to take off their tiaras to go to bed. *'It's not worth arguing.'* *'In the end, I gave up and let her – all her friends do it, so what's the point?'* *'It's just a phase after all.'* I've also heard similar tales from teachers, including the reception teacher who confided that the previous week she'd had to go out to buy several pairs of pink knickers – if the five-year-old girls in her class had an 'accident', they refused to change into dry underwear unless it was pink. The world now teems with cute little moppets, all exercising their royal right to choose ... and all safely aboard the gender-stereotypical consumer bandwagon.

> The world now teems with cute little moppets, all exercising their royal right to choose ... and all safely aboard the gender-stereotypical consumer bandwagon.

Of course, all children go through 'phases' and whoever said that parents should 'pick their battles' gave genuinely wise advice – it's often better to turn a blind eye to a small child's irritating behaviour than nit-pick about things that don't really matter in the great scheme of things. But when a girl's self-perception becomes dependent on aspects of her appearance even before she starts school, there is a real risk of long-term repercussions, such as problems with body image (see Chapter 6), issues around sexuality (see Chapter 10), and the social and emotional vulnerability of the 'brandchild' mentioned earlier.

Dressing down for play

Fashion also encourages premature self-consciousness in children, cutting them off from the 'real play' described in Chapter 7. It's obvious that a girl wearing fashionable but impractical clothes is hobbled in terms of activity and exploration, especially if the clothes are expensive and she's anxious about getting them dirty. It's perhaps less obvious that if she's overly concerned about her appearance, it can affect her capacity to 'lose herself' in play of all kinds. And 'losing herself' is what play is all about.

> There are few more delightful sights than a small child singing or dancing unselfconsciously.

I can understand why some adults rhapsodise about childhood innocence. There are few more delightful sights than a small child singing or dancing unselfconsciously, running and jumping in puddles for the sheer joy of it, messing with paint, mud pies or sandcastles, or immersing herself in a spontaneous game of 'let's pretend'. When we adults lose ourselves in an enjoyable activity (that state of 'flow' where we're so totally engaged that we lose track of time), we reconnect with our natural playfulness, and it's very good for our mental health. The more of this state of complete absorption that children enjoy before they start worrying about what other people think of them, the better they'll understand – at a deep emotional level – what real human well-being is all about.

As a way of cutting off a child from the instinct to play, fashion is every bit as effective as the toy consumption and screen saturation described in Chapter 7. For a socially sensitive young female it's perhaps an even greater danger, since it provides a short cut into the adult world, leading to precocity – or, in modern parlance, 'cuteness' (see Chapter 10).

Precocious behaviour was generally frowned on in the past because childhood was accepted as a distinct stage of development (and big business hadn't recognised the market potential of children), but in recent decades many parents have been quite proud that their daughters are *growing up more quickly nowadays*'. Unfortunately, as shown by the research on page 137, they may appear more grown-up on the surface, but in terms of physical and emotional development they lag well behind their counterparts of 60 years ago. The knock-on effects can be seen in terms of the burgeoning mental health problems among children and teenagers.

After raking through the developmental literature, my rules of thumb about fashion and play for the under-sevens are:

- Keep commercially produced, pretend-play paraphernalia to a minimum. A dressing-up box of old clothes, fabrics, beads and perhaps the odd charity purchase encourages real imaginative play, as opposed to an early introduction to consumerism.

- Discourage 'toy consumption'. Dolls like Barbie and Bratz are obvious symbols of female objectification and, like all collectibles, are designed to promote the joys of shopping. As with junk food, banning them completely would just increase their desirability, so the 80/20 rule is probably the best way to ration any type of 'junk play'.

- Choose everyday clothes, footwear, etc., on the basis of practicality, the needs of a girl's growing body and the demands of 'real play'. This doesn't mean clothing has to be unattractive, just that fashion isn't a particularly important factor in children's clothing compared to other criteria. If she yearns for fashionable items that don't fulfil these other priorities, parents should resist being drawn into an argument. Like Poppy's parents, mum and dad should explain the reason they don't like them and then stick to their guns. By making it clear from the very beginning that they never give in to pester power, parents will avoid a lot of emotional turmoil over the years.

- Until a girl is old enough to reason, parents should use a mantra like, 'We love you; the marketers just want our money.' Just like an advertising jingle, the more she hears it, the deeper it will lodge in her psyche.

- Help her to see that in real life 'dressing up' is for special occasions, such as parties and other public outings when we want to make a particular impression. Social life demands a degree of self-objectification from us all, and of course parents will want their daughter to care about looking well turned out when circumstances demand she's on display. But always make it clear that she is loved for her inner self, whether she's dressed up for public appearances or dressed down for play.

- Let a girl help to choose what clothes to wear each morning, depending on the days' planned activities, the weather, and so on. As long as parents set the fashion boundaries, it's an opportunity for their daughter to learn about making rational choices, and paves the way for her involvement in shopping for clothing when she's older.

Fashion Timeline

At all ages, always show that you love your daughter for **herself**, not for her appearance – by the way you behave.

0–3 years

Dress her in clothes that are appropriate for who she is – a little girl, who needs to move, play, explore (not a doll, a status symbol or a mannequin).

Explain why you choose certain clothes (the weather, where you're going, etc.).

3–6 years

Let her help you to choose suitable clothes for the day's activities and learn to dress herself.

As a general rule, clothes should be appropriate for active, creative play – comfortable, practical, non-constrictive and easy to wash.

Enjoy choosing 'best' clothes that you both like for special occasions.

Draw a clear line between toys (including pretend play) and clothing.

When you shop for her clothes together, take her tastes into account but ensure you make the final decision.

By the age of six, she should be able to dress herself (appropriately) and help to look after her clothes – folding them, putting them in the wash, sorting and putting away washing, etc.

6–11 years

When shopping, continue to take her tastes into account, but help her to recognise that there are other considerations beside fashion (e.g., cost, quality, practicality, longevity) and explain that – since you're paying for the clothes – you make the final decision.

When choosing clothes, help her to develop her personal style rather than to follow trends slavishly.

Discuss the pros and cons of fads and fashions, and what they say about the wearers.

Talk about what you think is appropriate/inappropriate fashion for different age groups, and why.

Draw her attention to marketing strategies that affect girls' perceptions of brands (see page 163).

Don't give in to peer pressure. If her friends make fashion choices you don't like, explain why you don't think they're good for her, and stand firm.

Decide well in advance what age *you* think is appropriate for certain fashion choices (e.g., make-up, high heels, ear-piercing, tattoos) and stick to it. If there's something you really don't approve of, claim the right of veto as long as she's living at home.

11+

Accept that, once in her teens, she needs increasing freedom to make fashion choices (other than those for which you've already set boundaries). If you're not happy with what she wants, talk it through and negotiate a compromise.

When you think she's capable of sensible budgeting, give her a clothes allowance for non-basic clothes purchases.

Encourage her to think about the ways marketers manipulate consumers (e.g., the concept of 'cool', product placement, the use of celebrities to promote trends).

Keep chatting about the pros and cons of fashion trends and exchange ideas and advice. But remember that you're her parent, not her friend – if you have concerns about the way she's dressing or behaving, speak up.

Let's be friends

From the moment a girl takes her first steps away from the family circle, there's another reason for parents to ensure she's dressed appropriately for play – play is the natural context for honing her social skills. Parents and other caring adults can provide role models for social behaviour but, in the end, every girl has to take the values and attitudes she absorbs from the grown-ups and learn how to apply them for herself, on her own terms. We can teach children that good manners smooth the way in social relationships but, as pointed out in Chapter 2, the realities and subtleties of human interaction can't be taught. Frequent, first-hand, personal experience is vital for learning how to make friends, take turns, share, co-operate and deal with conflict.

For most children, social play starts some time in their third year, when they start attending playgroups or pre-school. Before that, they tend to play alongside, rather than with each other – so-called 'parallel play'. In her book *The Nurture Assumption*, American author Judith Rich Harris points out that the onset of social play is part of a natural human timetable. In all times and cultures prior to our own, mothers had no more than a couple of years in which to concentrate on nurturing one baby before another arrived, so toddlers were passed into the care of other children for much of the day – usually older siblings, cousins, and so on. Children have always taught each other far more than adults give them credit for, and from the moment social life outside the home begins, the influence of peers is arguably as significant as that of parents in all aspects of child development.

Since they're more acute observers of human interaction from their earliest months, girls are generally ready to socialise earlier than boys. The activities they choose have a more 'female' element too, as do their relationships with playmates. They seek out more intimate relationships from the beginning, use language that is more socially aware. '*Let's play at...*', '*Do you want to...*', '*... Okay?*', and their play is more 'domesticated', and generally less wide-ranging and physical than boys' play.

Perhaps, as Harris and other evolutionary theorists argue, this is connected to girls' biological role as nurturers, or perhaps, as most feminists would maintain, it's because they're imitating the behaviour of the adult females they've observed. As usual, I suspect it's a mixture of both. However, once under way, girls' social play isn't always as sweet and civilised as their conciliatory language suggests. Learning to reconcile one's own unfolding sense of self alongside other developing personalities is an emotionally demanding business. In the inevitable playground power struggles, girls are less likely than boys to resort to physical aggression, but just as likely (if not more so) to get 'lippy' with each other. Name-calling, tale-telling and general nastiness are par for the course in early childhood.

> Name-calling, tale-telling and general nastiness are par for the course in early childhood.

However, little children aren't strong or savvy enough to do each other much damage, either physically or psychologically – and there are usually adults or older children around to stop things getting too serious. Little ones are also easily distracted, and can rapidly forget minor bruises to their egos, just as they forget bumps and scratches, provided no one turns them into a big deal. As long as a girl feels loved and cared for at home, she'll usually feel secure enough in herself to weather the ups and downs of infant social life. When mum and dad listen sympathetically to tales of playtime dilemmas, help her to think through her options and encourage her to make her own decisions, she'll learn through experience how to solve her own social problems.

Parents can help their daughter to work out, for instance, that:

- other children are more inclined to play with her if she plays fairly
- if playmates turn nasty, she can tough it out and defend herself, or walk away and play on her own until the persecutors lose interest
- if a friend changes into an enemy, it's possible to seek out new friends
- • what the grown-ups call 'good manners' – that is, consideration of other people's feelings – are very helpful in smoothing over a temporary emotional disruption.

Stand well back!

Most playtime spats blow over very quickly – in the early years, friends can turn into enemies and back into friends again within a matter of minutes. A child who finds ways of coping with such fallings-out under her own steam, while she's still relatively unselfconscious, develops social competence and emotional resilience that stands her in good stead in the future.

> The lesson that *real* friends value her for who she is, not for what she's wearing, is one that a 21st century girl needs to learn very early.

From the parents' point of view, the emotional roller coaster of the pre-school playground needn't mean bowing to commercially induced peer pressure either. As Poppy's story illustrates, small children from loving homes tend to get over their social frets pretty quickly, and learn to thrive in the playground whether they have fashionable footwear or not. The lesson that *real* friends value her for who she is, not for what she's wearing, is one that a 21st century girl needs to learn very early.

The role of adults in supervising young children's play is to know when (and how) to stand back and let them learn from experience. As long as children are actively engaged in '*personally chosen, intrinsically motivated behaviour*' the chances are that they'll find ways to sort out their own problems. If a grown-up steps in to sort things out the moment something goes awry, the opportunity for an important social and emotional lesson is lost. It is, however, much more difficult for adults to maintain this distance if physical space is limited – the best setting for early social development (as with other aspects of development through play) is outdoors, where there's room for children to escape when relationships aren't working out, and plenty of other activities in which to immerse themselves.

The parents of daughters are often less concerned than the parents of sons to find a nursery with good outdoor facilities but, if they want their child to develop the social and emotional skills that underpin a healthy attitude towards friendship, it's worth hunting one down. There is now a growing Forest School movement in the UK, which offers children the opportunity to spend at least a few hours a week in the great outdoors.*

Parents can also take their own positive action by arranging for their daughters to play outdoors when friends visit, and fixing 'play

---

* Sadly, we've a long way to go to catch up with the Scandinavians, where three- to six-year-olds can spend all day playing in the woods at a forest kindergarten. But there are now a few wonderful outdoor nurseries scattered around the UK. As time goes on, I expect their excellent results to convince more parents of the worth of 'natural childhood'.

dates' with other parents for outings to local parks, nature reserves and wild spaces. Taking holidays with an outdoor element helps too, providing opportunities to meet and make friends with other 'free-range' children and their families.

Cool tweens!

Parents are by far the most important influence in a child's pre-school years. So, providing mum and dad are alert to the dangers and ensure their daughter takes her first steps beyond home in environments where 'real play' is possible and highly valued, they should be able to steer her safely through the princess years. But inevitably, as time goes on and she spends more time away from home, it's difficult to avoid the influence of screen-based, market-driven culture. This is when girls need support in weathering the next great market-driven storm – the cult of the 'tween'.

Marketers invented 'tweenagers' in the late 1980s, originally defining them as girls between the ages of 10 and 12 who are starting to show an interest in fashion, shopping, pop music and celebrity gossip. However, as screen-based technology proliferated and 'kids grew older younger', the demographic extended steadily downwards, and the tween market has now expanded to cover almost the entire primary school age range.

The original marketing motto for tween girls was therefore abandoned ('too old for toys, too young for boys'), and by the simple expedient of changing the spelling, both 'toyz' (like Bratz dolls, with their 'passion for fashion') and 'boyz' (like 2010 tween pin-up Justin Bieber) were made 'cool for kidz'. At the time of writing, some of the coolest pursuits for tweenagers are the online games on GirlsGoGames, with titles like Cute Girl Dress Up, Beauty Salon Makeover, Princess Room Decoration and First Classroom Kissing.

'Cool' has been a teenage term of approval for at least six decades, and is beloved by big business because its definition is constantly changing and every change can be linked to products that can be sold in shops. Sometimes cool new trends are identified among young

> 'Cool' also helps to maintain the generation gap between youngsters and their parents (who are, by definition, uncool).

people, then packaged for mass consumption; sometimes they're actively created, usually on the back of movies, pop music releases or TV programmes. Every craze opens up endless opportunities for sales of clothing, accessories, technological gadgetry and games, furnishings for 'electronic bedsits', and so on. 'Cool' also helps to maintain the generation gap between youngsters and their parents (who are, by definition, uncool).

In the days when this culture of cool was directed at teenagers, it could arguably be viewed as a consumerist rite of passage, an initiation into the adult world of consumer choice. But during the pre-teen years children aren't mature enough to make choices for themselves – they still need plenty of authoritative guidance from the loving adults in their lives. As the tween culture has boomed, the peer-pressure/pester-power/guilt-money cycle described on page 19 has steadily undermined parental authority in a growing number of families.

Most parental concern about peer pressure (at least as reported in the media) has so far centred on sexualisation. Tweenage popular culture has intensified the stereotyping of gender roles in the playground and normalised the idea that girls of this age are supposed to be 'attractive' to boyz. This is summed up in the DVD *Consuming Kids*, in which a group of US psychologists analyse the marketing and media world in which today's tweens live: '*There's a clear difference between what boys learn and what girls learn. Boys have to be tough, strong, ready to fight. Girls have to be pretty, sexy, and how they look determines their value. It objectifies both of them.*' The potential harmful effects of early sexualisation are covered in Chapter 10, but they shouldn't blind us to other significant effects of allowing girls to buy into cool culture at an increasingly early age.

Junk play and junk friendship

For a start, commercialised 'junk play' can have a serious impact on children's lifelong interests and concept of self. It distracts them from 'real play' during which they can discover their own inner strengths and talents and hone the physical, social, emotional and cognitive skills required to pursue those talents. By expending time and energy on *'personally chosen, intrinsically motivated'* play, girls learn the satisfaction of engaging in demanding activities just for the heck of it, rather than for an extrinsic and/or immediate reward. They discover that persisting with a task can result in a deep sense of personal achievement, and that they don't need anybody else's approval to feel good about themselves.

Along with the influence of family and school, it's this pursuit of personal achievement that, as they grow older, underpins girls' commitment to sport, hobbies and artistic and/or intellectual pursuits. Real play not only guides them towards the sorts of activities that help to create a well-rounded personality, it also develops their powers of perseverance, self-discipline and a realistic understanding of the effort required to achieve their aims.

If, on the other hand, they devote their leisure time to the largely sedentary, quick-fix 'fun' of junk play – such as online games, electronic chatter, pop and celebrity gossip, fashion makeovers and mimicking what they see on the TV – they're likely to reject real play activities as childish and 'uncool'. Instead they'll learn at a deeply impressionable age that the route to female satisfaction is an obsession with superficial appearance, a deep dedication to shopping and an in-depth knowledge of the world of celebrity.

There's considerable evidence that this is already affecting young girls' long-term aspirations; surveys of female role models reveal they are disproportionately skewed towards pop divas and celebrity fashion victims. As Sharon Lamb and Lyn Mikel Brown, the authors of *Packaging Girlhood* put it: *'At a time when daughters could be developing skills, talents, and interests that will serve them well their whole life, they are being enticed into a dream of specialness through pop stardom and sexual objectivity that will derail other opportunities.'*

Spending their childhood in this manufactured dream world also has profound effects on children's friendships and therefore on social development. Marketers are well aware of universal patterns of friendship, and of the claim by evolutionary biologists that it's programmed into female DNA to seek close, intimate relationships. For the tween market, therefore, best friends are now packaged as BFF (Best Friend Forever), who bond joyfully over the sort of lifestyle that can be bought in shops. Images of BFF role models are everywhere – sharing quality time on adverts, greetings cards, product packaging and websites, and on TV and in magazines and movies aimed at their age group. These images affect girls' expectations of how friends should look, what they do together and what they talk about.

There's a world of difference between real friendship – where girls learns how to trust and be trusted – and a two-dimensional depiction of saccharine female intimacy, especially when relationships are conducted, to a great extent, via the screen – see Virtual social life, page 174). This commodified version distracts girls from developing real-life intimate relationships, and encourages them to objectify the very idea of friendship. A BFF is at least as much a trophy as a friend.

And 21st century girls probably need the experience of real friendship more than girls in the past. Unlike the children of a few generations ago, they're unlikely to have many siblings at home, so their playmates are the only people of a similar age with whom they can practise the social skills they need to forge lasting relationships throughout their lives. The give and take of play is where girls discover banter and bickering, co-operation and competition, and the significance of considerate, well-mannered behaviour in getting along with others (of both sexes) on a day-to-day personal basis.

It takes real-life experience to recognise the difference – in themselves and in their playmates – between assertiveness and aggression, and to learn how to deal with both. Friends who stay the course may be lucky enough to develop the genuine intimacy that comes from facing real challenges together, and supporting each other through difficulties. This is a long way from immersion in the trivial, girly pursuits aimed at BFFs, which seem unlikely to develop anything more than a surface veneer of friendship.

Parent power and tween culture

It really is up to her parents whether a pre-teenage girl succumbs to the lure of tween culture. If they, as the authorities in the family home, follow the suggestions given in previous chapters, their daughter will have the childhood experiences that support healthy all-round development. By ensuring that the TV and computer are located within family space, parents can keep an eye on their daughter's screen use, and share and discuss the programmes she wants to watch and the games she wants to play (see also Virtual social life, page 174). They can also draw her attention to everyday examples of marketing strategies, such as:

- deceptive visual techniques, like airbrushing
- stereotypical and idealised depictions of girls, women and families
- associating products/brands with social status, sexual desirability, feelings of self-worth, security, etc.
- the use of special offers to sell products we don't actually want or need.

The more a girl is involved in family life, the more her attitude towards shopping will be grounded in reality, rather than in tween dreams. As pointed out in Chapter 7, one of the best ways to spend family time with children is to involve them in cooking, household chores, gardening, and so on – all of which involve planning, budgeting and shopping. Over the years, this provides a great introduction to critical consumerism, which can be extended to clothes, shoes, and so on.

> The more a girl is involved in family life, the more her attitude towards shopping will be grounded in reality.

Friends from other countries tell me how much they've come to envy the long-established British tradition of school uniform. Fashion is kept at bay during the course of the school day, so that choosing what to wear is restricted to leisurewear (based on the sort of activities that girls engage in), public appearances and special occasions.

Dressing to go out in public and for special occasions are still matters for family consultation – at least until a girl reaches her teens. As she gradually moves towards her teens, her parents can:

- allow her increasing freedom to develop her personal style in terms of clothing, etc., while making it clear that, since they earn the money, they obviously have a say in what she buys
- decide well in advance at what ages they're happy for her to try out more 'grown-up' fashions, such as make-up, high heels, ear-piercing, and so on, and stick to their guns (see also Chapter 10)
- keep an eye on developments in tween culture, chat with their daughter about fashion trends, music, celebrities, etc., and en-courage her to think critically about the way these influence her and her friends' behaviour.

Put like this, it should be relatively easy for parents to support and guide their daughter through the tween jungle, especially if they've got her off to a good start by avoiding the princess culture during her earliest years.* But, as most parents discover, if the majority of their daughter's friends behave in ways that are completely contrary to the family ethos, maintaining an authoritative stance is often far from easy. Tween culture pits cool peers against uncool adults, creating the sort of generation gap once associated with adolescence. As their daughter moves towards double figures in terms of age, this means that she – and perhaps even her parents themselves – may start to see their stance as authoritarian rather than authoritative.

Parent power and girl power

When members of a family start questioning parental authority, there are bound to be power struggles. All too often, they lead to arguments or even outright rebellion, resulting in a girl following the tween herd along the commercialised primrose path while her parents either stand helplessly by or make things worse by ranting and raving.

---

* If your little girl seems to be turning into an unmanageable little princess or tween, I recommend Noël Janis-Norton's book, *Calmer, Easier, Happier Parenting*.

Other girls may internalise the power struggle, desperately trying to reconcile the need to please both family and peer group.

So parents can't afford to wobble. If they trust the source of parental authority (i.e., love), it should help them to keep their tempers and to reason their way through domestic traumas. Children who feel loved (cared for, listened to, respected and valued to their very core) are unlikely to rebel against this sort of reasonable 'parent power'. Indeed, if mum and dad always try to balance firmness with warmth, their daughter will probably realise that 21st century parents are themselves engaged in a power struggle, but with forces they believe will do her harm.

The ultimate aim is for parents to equip their daughter with the 'girl power' she needs to survive and thrive throughout her life. This means the parent–child 'dance of communication' is vital throughout her childhood. Girls need their parents' time and attention (see Chapter 7), and mum and dad need to tune in to their daughter's feelings and keep abreast

> The ultimate aim is for parents to equip their daughter with the 'girl power' she needs to survive and thrive throughout her life.

of her changing emotional needs. Since they can't possibly fulfil all these needs themselves – particularly those relating to social development – they also have to know when to stand back, and let her learn to deal with the outside world for herself. They can help their daughter to ride the roller coaster of juvenile social life by:

- listening to her talking about her friends, and encouraging her to think through any problems that arise and to work out her own ways forward
- offering comfort when things go wrong, and making sure she knows that real friendship involves ups and downs, that falling out with friends is inevitable, and that learning to deal with conflict and loss is a natural part of growing up
- demonstrating that well-mannered, reasonable behaviour helps adults to exercise consideration towards others, and also to maintain their own self-respect.

And, of course, parents with friends of their own who share their values and attitudes are much better placed to stand their ground – especially if their friends include the parents of their daughter's friends. So it's worth looking out for fellow 'villagers' or like-minded people who believe that 'girl power' doesn't come from commercialised cool, but from inner qualities such as:

• self-confidence, self-respect and assertiveness
• self-awareness, self-discipline and the ability to think for oneself
• strength in both E- and S-type thought
• resilience, to bounce back from difficulties
• sufficient powers of reason to keep cool and considerate under pressure.

In fact, I think these qualities sum up 'boy power' and 'parent power' too – not to mention the meaning of the word 'cool' as a character trait, before the marketers got hold of it.

Friendship Timeline

0–2 years

Make sure your daughter mixes with other children – but don't expect real social play until her third year.

If she's involved in a tiff, take her away from the situation. Comfort her if necessary, and explain what went wrong and how to put it right.

You're her social role model, so always demonstrate good manners.

2–6 years

Ensure that she has plenty of opportunities for social play – playgroup, nursery, Rainbows, etc.

Get to know the parents of special friends – they're potential fellow 'villagers' – and organise shared play at each other's homes, on joint visits to the park, etc.

Outdoors is best for social play (there's more to do and the space in which to avoid conflict).

Let children direct their own play and sort out their own problems. If you have to intervene, help them to seek their own solutions.

If your daughter has a problem with another child or children, comfort her, listen to her worries and help her to work out ways of dealing with it.

If she's having frequent problems at pre-school or nursery, discuss it with the teacher and work out a plan of action.

Most problems at this age have simple solutions, so don't overreact.

Don't give in to 'peer pressure' regarding purchases. Explain that friends judge each other on what they're like inside, not what they own.

6–11 years

Discourage BFF syndrome (see page 162) – discuss the difference between 'packaged' friends and real friends, and encourage 'real play' with her friends.

Keep up with her friends' parents – share your concerns about tween culture and try to develop a united front. Always meet the parents of friends before she visits their home.

Involve yourself with her school (see page 87).

Keep out-of-school friendships real (rather than virtual) through play dates, joint trips to the swimming baths, the library, and so on.

If she doesn't already belong to any social organisations for her age group, encourage her to join one (e.g., Brownies/Guides).

Falling out and having tiffs are common among girls. If she's having a problem, don't panic. Try to help her to solve it for herself (see page 180).

If you think she's being bullied, listen calmly. Check out advice for parents on www.bullying.co.uk and www.kidscape.org.uk.

If she's being bullied at school, make a diary of incidents and see her teacher. If you aren't happy with the response, check out the school bullying policy and take it from there.

11 +

Accept that you won't like all her teen friends – as long as your daughter's okay, hold your tongue!

Invite her friends home, and get to know them. If you're worried they might be a bad influence on her, try to be a good influence on them.

Continue to keep in touch with her friends' parents, and support each other.

Encourage her to join sports clubs or other clubs, to develop particular interests and meet others with similar interests.

If she's being bullied, follow the same advice as above, but send her to the websites herself to check out the advice for kids.

To prepare yourself for any Mean Girl incidents (see page 180), get hold of a copy of Rosalind Wiseman's *Queen Bees & Wannabes.*

School versus 'cool'

In the battle against market forces there is *some* good news for parents, as long as they're cool enough, in the non-commercial sense, to make use of it. Once girls reach the age of five, the state provides a local centre for the village or town in which they're raised – the primary school – where there are bound to be other children whose parents are also worried about commercial pressures. What's more, primary teachers are generally interested in their pupils as individuals and are concerned about their welfare on a professional level, so they are natural allies in the quest to detoxify childhood.

As the point of education is to develop children's powers of disciplined thought and to introduce them to human culture in its widest sense, primary schools are the natural hub from which responsible adults can mount a counter-offensive against the influence of commercialised trivia. Parents and teachers just have to get together.

Many schools already organise parenting groups and meetings about aspects of modern child-rearing, such as internet safety. They also often provide after-school care and clubs where parental help is always appreciated, and class teachers organise outings that need adult volunteers to fulfil health and safety requirements. At the very least, parents have the chance to chat with each other informally at

> At the very least, parents have the chance to chat with each other informally at the school gate.

the school gate, or when classmates gather at family homes for 'play dates' or parties. So there are plenty of opportunities for concerned parents to seek out like-minded adults to share their anxieties and experiences, and to support each other in giving their daughters a childhood, rather than leaving them to the mercy of marketers and the media.

Sadly, in a competitive consumer culture, where everyone worries about what everyone else thinks of them, many parents feel too embarrassed to enrol in a parenting group, although all the parents I know who have gone along to one have found it extremely useful, including me. Just as sadly, with so many demands on parental time, it's always an effort to turn up at parent meetings or to help with school events. And anyone who pauses to think about the social ramifications of a wrong word at the school gate or at a juvenile social function is unlikely ever to utter it. So, concerned parents have to decide whether their own social and emotional difficulties trump those of their daughters.

If parents can overcome this natural reticence and forge supportive relationships with other parents and sympathetic teachers, there are many ways in which schools can help to develop their support systems, as well as spread the word so that more members of the local village become involved. For instance, committed members of the school community can make use of:

- school websites, newsletters and message boards to circulate information and stimulate discussion about children's developmental needs, and the ways that tween marketing and the media can hinder development
- school buildings for gatherings – formal and informal – where parents can make personal contacts, exchange ideas and advice about 21st century child- rearing, and provide personal peer support, as opposed to impersonal peer pressure
- school playgrounds and fields for outdoor play during evenings and school holidays, with parents collaborating to share supervision
- school facilities to organise 'family days', outings to local parks

and wild places, barbecues and other non-commercialised gatherings that bring parents and children together.

I know from my wide experience of UK schools that initiatives like these can create a real sense of community among the adults involved, forging an adult alliance that's strong and supportive enough to stand up to commercial forces.

Unfortunately, I also know that most parent-teacher liaison doesn't take these forms. It's more likely to focus on the traditional school fund-raising activities (such as Christmas fetes, summer fairs, sponsored events of various kinds), or the setting up of children's clubs run by volunteers (sport, art, gardening, cooking, music, drama, etc.). While these activities are undoubtedly valuable, and I have enormous admiration for the people who give their time and energy freely to organise them, they don't address the problem of juvenile peer pressure. Indeed, they may sometimes even inadvertently perpetuate it.

It's no coincidence that the commercial hijacking of children's minds has gone hand in hand with the institutionalisation of childcare. When parents hand over young children to professional carers for several hours each day, it's all too easy for both parent and child to fall out of step in the dance of communication, and for marketers to usurp parental authority at home. Primary schools can contribute unintentionally to this parental disempowerment, by providing more out-of-school care.

Fortunately, it's still possible for parents who have inadvertently 'tuned out' to reconnect with their children during the primary school years, and if there's sufficient adult peer support in their local village, there's a good chance they'll find a way. For a neighbourhood's school to do battle with commercialised 'cool', the task of activists is to spread the word about the potential of buying in to the tween dream, and empower more parents to regain the authority of love.

What's hot and what's not?

It seems to me that the quickest way of rallying the parents of girls to this task is to latch on to the concern about early sexualisation. Since the popular press takes a prurient interest in anything to do with sex, the topic is often in the news, keeping parental anxiety on the boil. This anxiety tends to be highly generalised and is usually centred on atavistic fears about paedophilia, which merely increases most parents' feelings of helplessness (*Who are these paedophiles? Where are they? It could be anyone...*).

The obvious way forward for responsible members of a school community is to defuse anxiety and encourage parents to take action by providing useful information about how they can tackle the sexualisation problem at source, in their own home. That means spreading the word about:

- the ways the media and marketers are currently luring little girls into sexualised, self-objectifying behaviour
- the real and profound long-term dangers of this behaviour for their daughters (see Chapter 10)
- expert recommendations for parental control of children's media use (see Parent power and girl power, page 165, above and Virtual social life, page 174).

Issuing from a trusted local source and backed up with plenty of word-of-mouth support, this sort of information can help a community to establish its own standards of responsible parental behaviour and to start to shift social norms in the neighbourhood. And, since it's impossible to combat premature sexualisation without confronting the value system that drives it, an alliance of responsible adults is likely to find itself challenging every aspect of tween culture.

Schools don't have to rely on scare stories in the media to rally concerned parents to action. They have their own information sources much closer to home – parents and grandparents who've noticed children's behaviour changing with the changing times, and primary teachers who watch each tween craze arrive and take root in the classroom. As described in Chapter 4, it was concerned class teachers who alerted me to the contributory factors of 'toxic childhood' (all of which I later found to be substantiated by research) long before the media noticed them. Thanks to Moore's Law, trends now infiltrate themselves into childhood culture with remarkable speed, and unless adults spot them at an early stage, the tween bandwagon rolls remorselessly on and the behaviour becomes accepted as 'normal'.

A school community can influence parental attitudes when a trend is in its infancy – no one wants to be the only parent who lets their daughter do something that might be bad for her – and thus create an oasis of sanity in an increasingly naughty world. That's why it's tragic that many parents and teachers have so far kept their concerns to themselves, rather than creating a school-based forum in which to raise them.

For instance, it was late 2009 when I first heard uneasy murmurs from teachers about girls as young as seven spending time on Facebook – the lower age limit is 13. Since this social networking site didn't arrive in the UK until 2006, and, until late that same year was only available to university students, the KAGOY effect had clearly worked at speed. The teachers were worried that little girls might blunder onto sexually explicit conversations or be approached by online predators. It was a perfect opportunity to rally parental concern about online safety, and to start a debate on the pros and cons of social networking.

> It was a perfect opportunity to rally parental concern about online safety.

But self-consciousness makes cowards of us all and, when people didn't speak up, the tween bandwagon gathered speed, making it more difficult to address the problem. It wasn't until 2011 that research confirmed the teachers' anecdotal evidence – by which time Facebook was the website most frequently cited as 'favourite' by girls between 5 and 10 years of age, and by 2012, 58 per cent of under-12s had their own Facebook account. Of course, by that time big business had recognised the site's usefulness for influencing tween purchases – in fact, the 2011 research was carried out by a marketing company called Childwise. So, alongside a short bout of press outrage, it was no surprise to see

> By 2012, 58 per cent of under-12s had their own Facebook account.

other news stories questioning the US law that requires a lower age limit for social networking sites.

A couple of years is a very long time in the world of childhood 'cool'. The major tween celebrities when I started researching this book (Miley Cyrus and Justin Bieber) were grown up by the time I had finished. And by the time it's in the bookshops, I suppose the GirlsGoGames site cited by my eight-year-old interviewees as their favourite for online 'play' will be old hat, or indeed, with ever-improving digital interfaces, will probably appear quite quaint.

But the developmental needs of pre-teenage girls won't change at all. They're predetermined by a biological timetable that carries them from babyhood to puberty, and doesn't vary, whatever the culture. I fear the unholy alliance between market forces and juvenile peer pressure won't change soon either ... not until enough grown-ups get together and put a stop to it. So, whatever commercially induced tween craze is in vogue, responsible parents and teachers should apply the 'precautionary principle'. If there's any chance that the tween craze will sabotage the chances of girls' physical, social, emotional and cognitive needs being met, they can't afford to just stand back and let it happen.

Virtual social life

One of the hottest 21st century trends is the transfer of social interaction from the real to the virtual world. Online socialising (chatting by text, email, message boards and posts, in a chat room, forum or on a social network) is, for most adults, a convenient and enjoyable addition to the human social repertoire. Not surprisingly, little girls are keen to join in the fun as soon as possible. But since – like fashion – virtual socialising is an activity originally designed for adults and teenagers, it's likely to have long-term ill effects if children are hooked by it too soon.

Online chat is nowhere near as demanding as the real-life experience of reading other people's facial expressions, body language, tone of voice and the pauses between their words. It is, however – as many readers may know from personal experience – very time-consuming and even addictive. Girls can't afford to get locked into an electronic, quick-fix version of communication until they've had plenty of three-dimensional, embodied experiences in the tried-and-tested social arenas of family time, play, hobbies, sport and other childhood activities.

Despite the marketing hype, there's nothing children can learn through online socialising that they can't learn better in real life. For youngsters who are still learning to get along with others, this is mere 'junk interaction', to add to the growing mountain of mind-sapping 'junk fun'. Even learning to negotiate their way around the electronic interfaces has no long-term value – as Moore's Law rolls on, anything a child learns today will be out of date within a year or so. The main argument for early immersion in the virtual social world is that children need to learn the safety rules, but these are, in fact, rules of common sense that also apply in real life.

> There's nothing children can learn through online socialising that they can't learn better in real life.

'Stranger danger' is one of the first lessons that responsible parents din into their daughters, and with plenty of opportunities to play with their peers, girls discover through experience the importance of trust, including how to judge who's trustworthy and who isn't. So there are universal rules such as:

- be polite to everyone, but wary of people until you know them well
- bear in mind that a stranger may not be what they seem (or claim) to be, and could intend you harm
- only give out personal information to people you know well and whom you know you can trust.

These rules can be covered on a day-to-day, real-life basis, so there's no particular advantage in logging girls into tween s such as Club Penguin to learn about interaction in the online world. In fact, some of the main lessons children learn on these sites are about the joys of shopping.

But the internet is a fact of daily life, and children obviously want to explore it, so every 21st century girl needs a supervised, authoritative introduction to the entire online environment. The expert advice to parents has always been:

- keep the computer located within the family space
- share activities with your children.

And it still is. See, for instance, the information for parents on the CEOP* website. (It's also worth looking at the CEOP YouTube clips 'Girls Think U Know'.)

This means that when parents decide to introduce their daughter to electronic communication, it can be integrated into her daily screen-time allowance (see page 134). They might, for instance, let her help them to update a family Facebook page or accompany her to a trusted children's site such as the CBBC website. Once she's learned her way around a site, she can be allowed to visit it herself, with mum and dad nearby in the background to keep an eye on her.

Face to virtual face

As time goes on, their daughter will probably want to access the sort of sites her friends talk about, and if parents visit them with her, they can decide whether they're happy to add them to her screen-time repertoire.

Sharing early visits to plenty of sites is an opportunity to prepare girls for using them unsupervised, and to:

- talk about any worrying features of the site – commercialisation, gender stereotyping, and so on
- repeatedly model sensible online behaviour repeatedly
- discuss issues such as cyber-bullying, internet predators, and accidentally accessing harmful material like porn.

While it's sensible to fit internet filters, when daughters do start going solo, experts stress that these aren't a substitute for adult involvement.

The above advice is much more difficult to follow if a girl is given a smartphone or a tablet, which provides her with internet access wherever she goes. Ownership of these devices among children has

* Child Exploitation and Online Protection Centre, a branch of the police.

mushroomed in the last couple of years, with a 2012 YouGov survey finding that a quarter of 8- to 12-year-olds now owns a smartphone, and that in 87 per cent of cases, parents hadn't set any filters on their children's phones. In the summer of 2012, parents buying smartphones from the four main broadband providers (BT, Sky, Virgin and TalkTalk) have been asked if they want to screen out 'adult content' so that their children can't stumble across pornography – but phones bought before that date, or from other suppliers, aren't automatically covered in this way. And, of course, plenty of other sites – games, social networks, and so on – are instantly accessible on any handheld device.

The market has obligingly responded to this development with a variety of apps allowing parents remote control of their offsprings' access to the internet. But the dangers to children alone on the global superhighway are every bit as great as those in a busy city street. They need caring adults to hold their hands, explain the rules, talk about what's going on and demonstrate, time and again, how to negotiate their way around hazards and deal with unforeseen circumstances. By spending time online with their daughter, parents can watch her grow in confidence and competence, and will know when they feel safe to let her go it alone. Authoritative parenting involves the gradual transfer of skills from one generation to the next. Remote control is no substitute for personal care.

> By spending time online with their daughter, parents can watch her grow in confidence and competence.

As she nears her teens, a 21st century girl does need increasing freedom to use the internet to chat privately with her friends, which can be arranged via email and instant messaging. But she doesn't need her own Facebook page yet. No responsible parent would dream of letting their preteenage daughter out on the town with a crowd of unknown adolescents, so why should they let her log on to social networks frequented by millions of unknown teenagers and adults? Until she's mature and experienced enough to cope with the real-life world of teen fashion and flirting, social networking sites designed for teenagers and adults should remain off-limits.

In fact, I'd question the current lower age limit of 13. The subject cropped up recently when I was interviewing a group of 14- and 15-year-old girls, and asked them what they felt was an appropriate age to join Facebook. After a few minutes discussion, they suggested 18.

'But you told me you'd all been on it for years,' I said. 'Wouldn't you have been furious if your parents had stopped you?'

'Yes,' said one. 'But I wish they had.' Her friends nodded. Although they'd been naturally anxious to join teen social networks, they found that keeping up with their peers on Facebook taxed their social powers and made them feel very vulnerable. It's difficult enough being a young teenager in the real world – negotiating their way through bewildering hormonal upheavals, discovering the opposite sex, and confronting the long uphill struggle of the public exam system. A girl with her own Facebook page has to cope with this real-life social and emotional turmoil while simultaneously conducting a personal PR campaign in front of the entire online community.

Media Timeline

0–2 years

Don't use 'electronic babysitters' (TV, DVDs, talking books) in the first two years. Your daughter needs real-life interaction with real people in the real world see pages 187–188

Don't give her technological toys that will distract her from active, creative play.

2–6 years

Maintain the emphasis on real life and real play.

Limit screen time to no more than two hours a day. Try to avoid exposing her to advertising (stick to DVDs or the BBC, or record programmes and fast forward through the ads).

If you're happy for her to play computer games, make them games that don't rely on going on the internet – it's probably the most commercialised environment in existence.

If you want her to visit children's websites (e.g., CBeebies), make sure you have good parental controls on the computer, and accompany her on early visits. Be very selective about the sites you visit, as most are highly commercialised.

Avoid virtual socialising unless it's essential for keeping in touch with the family (e.g., family Facebook contacts, Skype conversations with grandparents, etc.). Give her time to learn to socialise in the real world.

7–11 years

At the age of seven or eight, she should be able to discriminate between advertising messages and other information.

Help her to think critically about the content of adverts (see Food and Fashion Timelines), TV programmes and games.

She's also had the time to acquire social, attentional and basic literacy skills, so she's ready to learn about the online world. Prepare her carefully by always keeping her company in the early days.

Introduce the rules for online friendships in a gradual way (see box on page 179), and the reasons behind them. Talk about the differences between real-life friends and online friends.

Set limits for time spent online – the medical advice is no more than 45 minutes per session – and include online time within the limit of two hours a day for general screen time.

Visit the CEOP website for 7- to 10-year-olds (www.thinkuknow.co.uk). Explore it and talk about it together.

Don't let her go solo until you are confident she knows the rules.

Keep all devices used to access the internet within the family space where you can supervise their use, and install parental controls to limit the sites available.

Don't give her a smartphone, tablet or other internet device unless you are happy for her to access the internet unsupervised. If you do give her an online device, use parental controls to opt out of adult content and restrict access to any other sites you think inappropriate.

11 years +

Visit the CEOP thinkuknow website (see above) for 11- to 16-year-olds.

Don't allow her on social networks until she's officially old enough – usually 13+ (see page 172).

Until she's 16, insist you can access her social network page. As long as she's a minor, you are just as responsible for her in the online world as you are in the real one.

If she experiences cyber-bullying, save the messages, and report it to the provider. If she's upset, suggest she visits www.cybermentors.org.uk.

Rules for Online Friendships

• Don't give out personal details, such as your name, address or school, to people you meet online.

• If anyone ever asks to meet you, save the message and tell a trusted adult immediately.

• Don't say or do anything online you wouldn't be happy to say or do in real life.

• Save any messages that upset or worry you and show them to a trusted adult. Don't reply to any nasty messages.

• Never open an email or text from someone you don't know (delete it immediately as it may contain a virus).

• Don't post your photo online or send it to anyone who is not well known to your family.

• Don't give your mobile number to anyone you don't know in the real world.

• When logging on to forums, chat rooms, online games or social networking sites, always use a nickname.

• On social networking sites, use the privacy settings to make sure only those people you choose can see your profile.

Mean Girls

I've mentioned several times that competence in dealing with social conflict comes from personal experience. As the years go by, most girls will encounter bullying behaviour, and while adults can give advice and support (see Let's be friends, page 000, and Parent power and girl power, page 165), children gain more in self-confidence by dealing with mild forms of bullying themselves, starting in the pre-school playground. With girls, fallings-out often lead to name-calling, petty harassment such as hiding an ex-friend's belongings, giving her the 'silent treatment' and other sorts of nastiness. But if the 'victim' is able to rise above it (neither retaliating nor allowing herself to appear particularly distressed), the bullies tend to lose interest.

If, however, the persecution goes on for more than a day or so, involves more than one perpetrator and escalates into the spreading of rumours, divulging embarrassing secrets, or other attempts at public humiliation and exclusion from a social group – what psychologists call 'relational aggression' – it can be too much for even the most resilient girl to deal with. Parents need to contact the school, and it helps to provide a list of the incidents to explain their concern. All schools now have an anti-bullying policy, and there's plenty of advice and support available from charities such as Kidscape or BeatBullying.

School bullying is traditionally the harassment of vulnerable children by other children with emotional and social problems of their own. Victims are usually selected because they're 'different' in some way, often due to a disability, obesity or lack of social status, which makes them feel vulnerable and gives the bullies an obvious angle for 'objectifying' them. However, over the last couple of decades, there's been a huge increase in reported bullying, with 46 per cent of children claiming in a 2011 survey to have been bullied at some time.

I suspect this increase is related to children having missed out on family time and outdoor play with their friends. This means they're less socially and emotionally robust, and more likely to fall into the role of victim or bully. But the popular media has also undoubtedly played a part, with its ever-increasing dependence on public humiliation in comedy shows and reality TV, and frequent displays of malice aforethought in soap operas, and so on. Whatever the reason, it's certainly not for want of anti-bullying campaigns and educational initiatives – we've had them in abundance.

Indeed, we've had them long enough to know that *teaching* children how to deal with bullying doesn't make a great deal of difference. What matters is that the child is – deep down – unimpressed by the bullies. The girls who are least likely to become bullies or victims are those who feel secure in their own identity, are able to forge firm, lasting friendships, and who recognise the need for human beings to exercise consideration and respect to everyone (good manners), regardless of who they are and what they own. So the best way for parents to help their daughter to avoid the cult of bullying is to cleave to the twin pillars of authoritative parenting and 'real play', keeping the marketers at bay as far as possible, and providing role models of civilised behaviour at home.

Unfortunately, between the ages of about 10 and 14, outbreaks of relational aggression among girls have always been a normal part of teenage behaviour. As puberty strikes, all girls can be thrown off balance, so any girl can be drawn into the fray. The combined effect of dawning sexuality, the move from primary to secondary school and the impact of another marketing bombardment (this time traditional, teenage cool) is a powerful one. By the early teens, the influence of her family is also, quite naturally, lessening, while the influence of the peer group grows ever stronger.

> By the early teens, the influence of her family is also, quite naturally, lessening, while the influence of the peer group grows ever stronger.

It's also a time when girls' social life tends to revolve around friendship cliques, membership of which often depends on certain dress codes or tastes in music. The popular girls at the top of these mini-hierarchies (usually spoilt little madams) are deeply conscious of any perceived threats to their status, and hormonally heightened emotions lead to power struggles within and between cliques. Any social event that unsettles the balance can trigger a spate of nasty, spiteful behaviour, just at a time when everyone is feeling fragile.

Social networking adds another dimension to the dark side of teenage social life. It's easier for girls to be nasty from a distance than when confronting their victim face to face, and the potential to cause distress is hugely expanded online. There's no longer any sanctuary for the victim – the bullying behaviour follows her home on her laptop or smartphone – and the cruelty is very public. (As one 13-year-old girl put it, *'It's worse being bullied over the internet because everyone can see and it makes you feel really little and small.'*)

Although most of these Mean Girl eruptions fizzle out fairly quickly in schools where good manners are valued, even mild ones can be destabilising for everyone concerned. However, a girl who has learned from her earliest years that true friendship has nothing to do with appearance or status is less likely to be seriously undermined than one who started life as a little princess, graduated through the tween school of BFF and is now trying to look like a cool younger version of Paris Hilton. She's also more likely to have established genuine friendships that will see her through her teenage years.

★★★

One of the most depressing statistics in the 2007 UNICEF survey of childhood well-being was that fewer than half the children in the UK answered 'Yes' to the question 'Do you find your classmates kind and helpful?' In countries at the top of the league, the 80–90 per cent answered in the affirmative. It appears that British children trust each other less than those in other developed countries. To some extent this lack of respect must be down to the ethos of UK schools, but I believe that our schools' difficulties are rooted in the general loss of adult authority when commercial forces are allowed to hijack playground culture.

And the research backs me up. Recent studies have all concluded that the UK's dismal performance in the UNICEF survey is down to our unquestioning acceptance of the ethics of hyper-competitive consumerism. The Good Childhood Report, published in 2009, pointed out that a key reason for children's social and emotional problems was a national culture of selfish individualism, and in 2011 a follow-up report on the UNICEF survey stated loud and clear that infant lack of well-being is rooted in our ma-

> A key reason for children's social and emotional problems was a national culture of selfish individualism.

terialistic culture. It found that, while parents believed their children needed lots of fashionable gadgets and other consumer goods, their children said they'd prefer more family time and the opportunity to play out.

It's a tribute to the dark arts of the marketing industry that, in only a few decades, it has managed to corrupt the purest and most basic of all human emotions – parental love – to create this state of affairs. But now that we know why British childhood has become increasingly toxic, parents should no longer feel pressurised by market forces to turn their daughters into 'material girls'. However wildly the 'perfect storm' rages around family life, the five components for raising bright, balanced children – love, discipline, communication, play and education – remain the same.

CHAPTER 9

A MIND OF HER OWN

Education from birth to sixth form: raising girls with the confidence and mental discipline to think for themselves

A decade or so ago, I was invited to a summer party in an old university town, given by a family of academics. I had visions of floating around the garden with a glass of dry white wine, chatting to dons and their wives (or husbands) about Wittgenstein. But, as usual, once my fellow partygoers learned about my professional interest in children, they were keen to tell me, in some detail, about their own.

This particular evening, most of the conversation centred on girls. It seemed their teenage daughters were all doing really well at school, sailing through GCSEs and clearly on course for glittering academic careers. They excelled in extra-curricular activities, too – sport, art, music, dance, drama, debating – but still had the time to take an interest in fashion and frivolity. I was uneasy about the competitive edge to these conversations, because I cling stubbornly to the idea that childhood (and education) isn't a race, but these super-bright mums and dads were so proud of their girls that it seemed churlish to comment.

Then, as the wine worked its magic, the conversation took another turn. Someone mentioned being a little worried by anorexia. And, one by one, parents began to confide concerns that their own daughters might be anorexic ... then it turned out they probably *were* anorexic (they'd been to the doctor) ... then people started comparing various therapies for trying to get their girls to eat.

Although I know eating disorders have a long history in well-to-do circles and are ten times more common in females than males, it was rather alarming that – in this small sample of educated families – so many talented girls seemed to be putting themselves on starvation rations. Education is supposed to lead to a broadening of the mind, not a diminishing of the body... Could it be that the effort of living up to their high-flying reputations was causing cracks in their psyches? Had the extreme self-discipline required to be paragons of 21st century female virtue somehow been converted into physical self-punishment?

Not long afterwards, I was speaking at a very posh pre-prep school in London (one with several A-list celebrities among the parent body, as well as bankers, politicians and other worthies). Although the talk was supposed to be about spelling and grammar, my research on child development kept leaking through. Afterwards I found myself surrounded by teachers, worrying about the pressure on children to achieve at an increasingly early age.

'The parents just don't get it,' one of them said. 'As far as they're concerned, their kids are doing fine – especially the girls. They can't see that the effects of pressures now might not show till years down the line.'

The perils of people-pleasing

It's only natural for loving parents to want their daughter to do well at school, especially parents who have themselves flourished in the system. They know from personal experience that the world of work is a highly competitive place, and for a girl to take advantage of all the opportunities open to women, a good education is essential.

It's also natural to assume that good progress in today's school system depends on hitting the ground running. Children who get off to a good start tend to do better throughout their school careers than those who don't, so most parents are thrilled at any indication that their pre-school daughter is ahead of the game, such as an interest in the sort of activities marketed as educational. Indeed, it's considered a mark of good parenting to seek out such activities, and to help their infant daughters to rattle through developmental 'targets' as quickly as possible.

> Girls outperform boys in every area of the pre-school curriculum by the time they're five years old.

And in many cases, their efforts are rewarded; in England, where infant performance is recorded meticulously, girls outperform boys in every area of the pre-school curriculum by the time they're five years old. As described in Chapter 1, they maintain this advantage throughout their school careers, and have a better chance than boys of going on to university or college to prepare for a career.

Sadly, once girls reach adulthood, this early promise doesn't always translate into lifelong career fulfilment. Over the last quarter-century, it's become clear that success in the educational system doesn't necessarily mean satisfaction in the workplace – or in other areas of life. Life choices for women have turned out to be more complicated than those for men, and a personally fulfilling work–life balance seems more elusive.

Indeed, for many girls problems begin to surface in their teens. So perhaps it's worth considering the suggestion of the teachers at the posh pre-prep school that the effects of pressures in children's early years may not show until many years down the line.

Back in the early 1990s, the feminist psychologists Lyn Mikel Brown and Carol Gilligan made the link between gifted girls and eating disorders when they described how trying to live up to the contemporary ideal of female perfection (that apparently effortless combination of brains, beauty and feminine 'goodness') put them under immense psychological strain. Their concern wasn't taken very seriously at the time – feminist pride in girls' steadily increasing academic achievement tended to override it. But in recent years, the idea has resurfaced. Courtney Martin, author of *Perfect Girls, Starving Daughters: How the Quest for Perfection is Harming Young Women*, puts it very neatly.

She says that, for many 21st century girls, the feminist exhortation,

'You can be anything' has been personally reinterpreted as 'You have to be everything'.

So how can parents help their daughter to avoid the over-compliance trap, and grow up believing in herself and her power to make rational, realistic life choices – to do what she can, and enjoy doing it well, rather than trying to do everything? How can they nurture her natural drive to learn so that she's motivated to achieve at school because she actually likes learning? Although there's obviously no way of controlling the future, there are plenty of hints from authorities in psychology, education and neuroscience about the best ways to support children during the different stages of their development.

She can be anything: 0–3 years

This is a period of extraordinarily rapid brain growth, so it is critically important. As described in Chapter 3, parents' first task is to resist falling prey to gender stereotypes that could affect their daughter's self-image throughout life. But they've also got to resist the temptation to confuse care with control. Authoritative parenting means providing the conditions for healthy development, and that involves a balance between security and freedom.

A baby girl's security comes from knowing that mum – her source of food and comfort – is there when she needs her, and that dad or other 'attachment figures' are there if mum isn't. But she also needs the freedom to explore her world. Her parents have to value her self-chosen play as a thrilling – and challenging – process of exploration and self-discovery. This play is often pretty bewildering to an adult, and once a girl is mobile parents may need to reorganise the furniture and put valuables in to storage for a year or so. But if they spend time tuning into her feelings – following her lead rather than their own adult expectations – their daughter's play is rewarding for both parties. She has adult support to explore and experiment with the world around her, while mum and dad get to see the world afresh through infant eyes, and share their daughter's achievements and discoveries.

Alongside this personally chosen play, all little children delight in the social play that adults initiate – peekaboo, tickling games, songs, rhymes, and so on. Since these activities make more sense to adults, it's easy to favour them over small infants' self-chosen play. And as time goes on and children enjoy stories, construction toys, drawing, painting, counting and memory games, etc., it's clear that these activities are educational, which makes them even more attractive to ambitious parents.

The danger with girls is that recognising the satisfaction that this adult-directed play affords to their nearest and dearest, they give up their own explorations. Boys, being less sensitive to adult reactions, are more likely to hang on to freedom. Girls, on the other hand, may need to be given it, so parents must ensure that their adult choices (or, even worse, those of marketers) don't dominate play proceedings. To retain her confidence as an intrinsically motivated learner, a girl also needs to set her own challenges, devise her own experiments and learn her own lessons.

She can be anything: 3–6 years

Over the second three years of children's lives, the adults who care for them (at home or at nursery, and in the early stages of schooling) still need to trust the remarkable power of play for developing self-motivated, independent learners. As time goes on, a skilled early years teacher interlaces children's self-chosen play with more structured activities to prepare them for the nuts and bolts of reading, writing and sums – and girls are often quick to pick up these basics and keen to apply them for themselves. But the skilled teacher also knows that they don't need to be rushed into more formal learning, and that there are plenty of other physical, social, emotional and cognitive skills to develop before adult-directed activities take centre stage.

Girls need to pick up the emotional message – from personal experience and observation of their adult carers – that education is a continuation of their inborn drive to learn. In particular, they still need time to wonder, wander, explore, pretend and create in the great outdoors, where young human brains were designed to develop.

If, during her first half-dozen years on earth, a girl has opportunities to explore the world through all her senses, rising to the challenges of self-chosen play of many kinds, she has far more chance of developing into a well-rounded individual – confident, resilient, open-minded and enthusiastic about learning. And far less chance, as time goes on, of succumbing to emotionally loaded messages about what it is to be 'perfect'.

The risks of early schoolification

Over the last decade, there's been much controversy about pre-school education in the UK, and whether we put too much emphasis on adult criteria and not enough on the developmental needs that individual children bring to their first experience of institutional life. In England, the introduction in 2008 of a 'nappy curriculum' for children between birth and five (the Early Years Foundation Stage or EYFS) added to the pressure on parents and carers to take a 'schoolified' approach to children's early learning – by which I mean *teaching* skills like phonics, handwriting and calculation, rather than supporting children's own *learning* in ways that respect their developmental stages. While the EYFS is supposedly based on a developmental model, it's not easy to write personal, E-type responsiveness into a statutory framework for a wide range of institutions.

In many pre-school settings, the EYFS has had the effect of turning 'developmental milestones' (devised by paediatricians and psychologists to give a rough idea of what can be expected of children at various ages) into goals or targets for carers to tick off on lists. Combined with the bureaucracy that inevitably accompanies state intervention in human affairs, it all seems a long way from the personally chosen, intrinsically directed play through which nature designed small children to learn.

What's more, school itself starts very early in the UK – at the age of four or five, compared to six or seven in other European countries. This has always been a source of anxiety for early years experts because, for all the reasons outlined above, most internationally respected authorities on early education have always recommended that formal schooling shouldn't begin until children are at least six.

No matter how committed infant teachers are to a developmental approach, once children have started school there's pressure to conform to a traditional school ethos and curriculum. And when parents and politicians want to see evidence of 'school readiness' well before children are four or five, early years practitioners feel obliged to provide it ... and their practice is skewed in that direction.

Early pressure to read, however, doesn't seem to make a blind bit of difference in the long run – a recent study in New Zealand by Sebastian Suggate showed that, by age 11, children's achievement in literacy evens up, whether they start at five or seven. On the other hand, an early start can have long-term social and emotional repercussions. International research shows that the younger children are started on formal learning, the more likely they are to encounter personal difficulties in adulthood. They're more inclined to have problems with mental health and personal relationships (including the breakdown of marriage), they're less likely to bother to vote and there's more chance they'll break the law. According to a recent study, they even die earlier.

Unfortunately, in the UK education is shackled to political short-termism (elections every four years), so parents tend to take a short-term view too. So far, parental dissatisfaction about our early starting age has focused on the problems of boys, who generally do badly in the mandatory assessment at age five. Girls, on the other hand, take to the schoolification of their early childhood much more easily, and their higher scores keep the government's statistics on track. Their parents, pleased with their daughters' flying start, haven't taken much interest in the debate.

But it's time they took an interest. The danger of neglecting free play in the early years isn't just that it might encourage over-compliance and 'perfect girl syndrome'. It may also leave girls less capable in adulthood of assessing, taking and managing risks – a personal skill that's essential in every area of life. It's particularly important in a world where gender roles and responsibilities are being rewritten, but traditionally female E-type strengths are constantly sidelined by traditionally male S-type ones. Whatever their chosen path in life, 21st century girls need the inner confidence to take calculated risks, and the courage to stand up and fight their corner for what they believe in.

Like over-compliance, risk aversion is a habit learned during childhood, one which girl-children were traditionally encouraged to embrace because their adult role was merely to keep themselves and their offspring safe. But, if adults can manage to slough off their own fears, little girls can learn the skills of risk management just as easily as boys. During play – particularly active, outdoor play – children constantly confront small real-life challenges and test their personal judgement.

> Risk aversion is a habit learned during childhood.

Sound foundations

Everything I've learned from experts in brain development convinces me that children don't need to rush into formal learning. And long before neuroscientists found out how to watch what goes on inside the human skull wise adults recognised the same basic truths about human development. The words of the prophet Mohammed, quoted at the beginning of Part Two of this book, accord pretty well with what science now tells us about the timetable of the developing brain.

Early childhood isn't merely a preparation for school, but an important stage in learning how to be human. That's not to say that pre-school teachers don't have an important role in laying sound foundations for the 3Rs of reading, writing and reckoning. As well as encouraging free play, they can – like parents – also engage children in playful activities that are culturally useful. And since human brains formed human culture, it's not surprising that the sort of cultural activities children enjoy at different stages follow a similar trajectory to the evolution of human culture.

In pre-literate civilisations, knowledge was passed down the

> Singing, dancing, moving to music, recitation and storytelling are still highly effective ways of socialising young children.

generations through songs, dances, poems and stories. These activities came naturally because – over countless millennia – musical ability and language proved so important to our species' survival that they were integrated into our DNA. Even though they're no longer in the daily repertoire of the average adult, singing, dancing, moving to music, recitation and storytelling are still highly effective (and enjoyable) ways of socialising young children, while simultaneously developing their language skills.

In countries that take a truly developmental approach to education, they're key components of the kindergarten curriculum, alongside opportunities for drawing, painting, and other arts-and-craft activities that develop visuospatial skills and the skills of physical manipulation that children need for writing. In these countries, it's accepted by parents, politicians and the general public that these are essential foundations upon which subsequent cultural achievements are built. Like the foundations of a building, they may later be out of sight and therefore out of mind, but that doesn't make them any less important.

It makes great sense to me, as a language and literacy specialist, to devote time and energy to developing small children's sense of rhythm and their ear for sound through plenty of music, dance, songs, rhymes, poems and stories. Indeed, it seems particularly sensible for 21st century children. In an increasingly visual world, their auditory memory is much poorer than in the past, so today's girls and boys are likely to benefit from pursuing an oral curriculum for several years.

I came to this conclusion after watching three- to six-year-olds in Finland (the country that always comes top of the European charts for literacy, does almost as well in numeracy, and came fourth in UNICEF's geographical ranking for children's well-being). Musical activities, songs, storytelling and recitation were threaded through the Finnish children's day; groups of children collaborated enthusiastically in turning their favourite stories into plays (making their own costumes, scenery and props), while others went on 'field trips' or spent hours engrossed in artistic projects of various kinds. They also had constant access to outdoor wooded areas, where children of both sexes could run about whenever they felt the need to let off steam.

This play-based, child-centred curriculum, with its heavy emphasis on all-round development, oral language and memory skills, is a long way from the sort of thing I regularly see in English pre-schools and early primary classes. Although many of our early years practitioners yearn to copy the Scandinavian approach, the bureaucratic constraints of EYFS and a national obsession with literacy and numeracy targets make it very difficult. But if parents support teachers in resisting the schoolification of early childhood, it's perfectly possible. And girls should benefit every bit as much as boys.

The 3Rs – slowing down to learn

Once girls reach the age of about six, most are capable of personally directed, systemised thought and – with enough early play experiences – they're ready socially and emotionally to benefit from instruction while simultaneously thinking for themselves. The mental discipline of school-based learning traditionally begins with the 3Rs.

But literacy isn't just a question of learning how to read and write, and numeracy isn't merely a question of learning simple arithmetical procedures. Both involve the orchestration of a wide range of intellectual skills, and constant practice until they become second nature, so it usually takes several years for young children to reach the point at which the basic skills are automatic. To children reared in a world where endless entertainment and information is available instantly at the flick of a switch, all this painstaking effort can seem extremely tedious.

Why bother reading books when you can watch a film or check out facts on Google or Wikipedia? Why waste time writing something down, when you can speak it into a smartphone or tablet? What's the point of struggling over a sum when electronic calculators provide the answer in seconds? In previous generations, primary teachers could rally the troops by explaining that the 3Rs were keys that opened the vast treasure house of human knowledge. In the 21st century, many of their pupils have gadgets in their pockets offering effortless short cuts to that treasure house ... and to much else besides.

However, in terms of children's intellectual development, the long-drawn-out process of learning to read, write and reckon is still hugely important. All those years of practising literacy and numeracy skills literally change children's minds, rearranging the architecture of their brains in ways that improve their capacity for rational, logical thought.

> The long-drawn-out process of learning to read, write and reckon *is* still hugely important.

There are no short cuts here. It takes time and effort to lay down and consolidate the neural networks that characterise the educated brain. All those years of practice – gradually turning comprehension, composition and calculation into second nature – develop skills of reflection, analysis and organisation. As the essayist Neil Postman put it 30 years ago: *'Print means a slowed-down mind... The written, then the printed word brought a new kind of social organisation to civilisation. It brought logic, science, education, civilité.'* All modern education systems have been designed to take children through the same process, based on the mental discipline of the 3Rs.

The trouble is that as Moore's Law trundles on, and children have access to increasingly wonderful gadgetry at ever-younger ages, it's getting harder to keep their noses to the grindstone. *'Electronics speeds up the mind,'* said Postman, and – as the primary teachers I met in the late 1990s were beginning to recognise (see page 67) – it's much more difficult to help children focus their attention on academic study when they're growing up in a world of instant gratification and digital quick fixes. These days, even adults who've already learned to read, write and reckon find it increasingly difficult to focus their attention for long. In the words of neuroscientist Robert Rekstak, *'attention deficit is the paradigmatic disorder of our time'.*

21st century learners

This presents schools with an interesting dilemma. The advantages of screen-based, multimedia resources are obvious: a picture (or diagram) can be worth a thousand words; animations can illustrate complex processes with minimal need for language; video clips provide pupils with a ringside seat at events they could never experience in real life. But if this plethora of visual information speeds up infant minds so that they can't settle to learn the 3Rs, will they be able to make good use of it? And what's the point of instant access to all the facts and statistics in the world if students can't think about them reflectively and analytically?

Debate around the issue is only just beginning, and is bound to intensify over the coming years. As I was drafting this chapter, Louise Robinson, president of the Girls' Schools Association in 2012, and headmistress of Merchant Taylors' Girls' School, predicted that smartphones and e-readers would soon replace textbooks: *'They'll be able to access anything they want to, in advance of your lesson, so if you say, "the next lesson's going to be on the skeleton", what you can now see online in terms of the skeleton and where you can go with it makes children have far more control of their learning than they could ever do before. One click and you're in another world.'*

A few days later, Barnaby Lenon, chairman of the Independent Schools Council and ex-headmaster of Harrow School (for boys), decried the use of smartphones in school, and recommended that secondary students shouldn't spend more than two hours a day on computers, partly because of the danger of addiction to screens, partly because they're easily distracted by irrelevant (and often inappropriate) material, but mostly because *'The main issue is that children spend far too long on computers and, as a result, they are not doing the two things that we want [them] to do, which are reading and conversation'.*

> Secondary students shouldn't spend more than two hours a day on computers.

I suspect Mr Lenon's perspective is due to his experience of working with bright middle-class boys who've been hooked on screen-based technology since early infancy (paying just enough lip service to literacy to get by), and who are now struggling with concentration, written language and the coherent expression of complex ideas. It's always been more difficult to interest boys in reading than girls, but this generation has been exposed to so much electronic distraction – mainly in the form of computer games – that many are almost incapable of 'slowing down their brains' to engage in sustained linear processing of information.

Ms Robinson, on the other hand, is used to bright middle-class girls, who are much more likely to have applied themselves diligently to reading and writing in primary school. For most of her pupils, reading is probably still a regular leisure-time activity and they may well enjoy writing for personal purposes too (diaries, emails, Facebook conversations, their own stories and poems). So they'll be much better at sustaining attention than their male counterparts, as well as better at expressing themselves in spoken and written language to convey a logical train of thought. I'm not surprised that their teachers are more sanguine about their potential to wander around the online world and then snap back to follow a lesson in the real one.

I'm basing my suppositions about these head teachers' students on what I've heard on my rounds of the UK educational scene over the last dozen or so years. Teachers and parents began worrying about the amount of time boys were spending playing computer games in the late 1990s, but most girls weren't hooked on screens in the same way. That, however, is no longer the case.

Kids' game-based websites are now as popular with primary age girls as boys, and there are increasing numbers of girl-friendly online games that can be played with chums on smartphones. The popularity of social networking since the advent of Facebook in 2006 means the female of the species is now just as capable as the male of whiling away much of her life online.

When this torrent of attention-grabbing trivia threatens the acquisition of vital intellectual skills, it's time for parents and teachers to take authoritative action to limit the damage. To ensure girls continue to acquire the skills that they need for academic learning, my recommendations would be:

- 0–2 years: no screen time; lots of songs, stories, rhymes, talk and play
- 2–6 years: maximum of two hours a day screen time at home, none in school, a play-based curriculum with lots of music, songs, stories and oral learning
- 6–12 years: maximum of two hours a day screen time at home; technology used with discretion in school; emphasis on the 3Rs within an *active*, creative curriculum – and on helping pupils establish a 'reading habit'.

Once girls reach secondary school and homework runs over into screen time, rigid boundaries for home-based computer use don't work so well. Anyway, by this age they should be learning how to organise their own time, so screen use at home must be open to negotiation. School can help in this respect, ensuring pupils understand the conflicting mental demands of old-fashioned and digital literacy – including the uses of both for learning – and teaching them how to use new technology critically and with discrimination.

Computers in schools

This isn't to say that in the modern world digital literacy is less important than the 3Rs. It is just that the 3Rs come first. Children have to slow down their thought processes to learn the basic skills of reading, writing and reckoning, and then to practise these skills till they become automatic. Remembering that, '*electronics speeds up the mind*', if we start teaching digital literacy too soon, the two types of mental activity work against each other.

In the words of psychologist Aric Sigman: '*There is a conflict between multitasking and sustained attention. These things cannot and should not be developed at the same time. Sustained attention must be the building block. The big problems we are seeing now with children who do not read, or who find it difficult to pay attention to the teacher, or to communicate, are down to attention damage that we are finding in all age groups.'* He recommends that computers shouldn't be used for educational purposes until children are at least nine, by which time they're hopefully well on the way to fluency in 'old-fashioned' literacy.

I'm sure it's no coincidence that Finland – with its remarkable record of achievement in literacy and numeracy – uses no high-tech equipment at all in the play-based kindergartens I described on page 193, and very little in primary schools. Nor does it surprise me that many high-flying parents in California's Silicon Valley – mums and dads who know a thing or two about the digital world – now opt to send their primary-age children to a Waldorf school that doesn't let computers over the threshold.

Unfortunately, the politicians who run UK education embarked on a love affair with information technology way back in the 1980s, and since then schools at all levels have been expected to integrate IT into all their work across the curriculum. Vast amounts of money have been invested in electronic resources, with teachers no sooner learning the basics of one generation of hardware before it's overtaken by another. Not surprisingly, with constant retraining, and generally a shallow understanding of the resources, their level of expertise isn't wonderful. In primary schools it often results in pupils being required to use computers for tasks that could be done much more productively in real life, and recorded with pencil and paper.

> The politicians who run UK education embarked on a love affair with information technology way back in the 1980s.

The biggest investment of the last decade has been in electronic whiteboards, which have been installed in almost every classroom in the country (including nursery classes). When I visit schools, it's depressing to see how much of their day young children spend staring at screens. But teachers feel obliged to use this equipment, because school inspectors mark them down if they don't include IT in their lessons. So they upload the latest educational software onto their whiteboards, or set simple tasks in the computer suite. In the last couple of years, there's also been a craze for providing individual pupils with tablets, frequently starting in the nursery class – I've met many early years teachers who are appalled by this, but don't dare object, as their head teachers 'think it's very modern and progressive'.

From what I hear out in the schools, a great many teachers of the under-eights now agree with Aric Sigman – not out of technophobia, but because they don't see any advantage in using high-tech equipment with young children. They'd like to concentrate on consolidating the 3Rs within a stimulating, three-dimensional curriculum and leave the teaching of IT to specialist staff in upper primary and secondary classes.

Specialist teachers have the time and personal commitment to keep up to date with technological innovation, so they can teach pupils genuinely useful IT skills, such as writing programs, designing websites, making films and animations, inventing new apps and so on – the sort of skills young people enjoy learning and that their future employers might actually want. And specialist IT teachers can do this much more effectively if pupils have a solid grounding in old-fashioned basic skills.

The IT curriculum is currently being overhauled and schools are being given more freedom about the way they teach it, but, after so much financial investment in expensive hardware throughout the system, it's unlikely that nurseries and early primary classes will be allowed to drop it altogether in the near future. Commitment to the use of IT in every age group is now an established part of the UK's 'too much too soon' orthodoxy, and the commercial interests that furnished every classroom with a whiteboard will no doubt continue to influence government policy.

> The use of IT in every age group is now an established part of the UK's 'too much too soon' orthodoxy.

Nevertheless, evidence about the effects of too much computer use is growing every year, and I'm sure the government will eventually have to listen to the growing body of expert opinion, summed up by American professor Paul Thomas: 'Teaching is a human experience... Technology is a distraction when we need literacy, numeracy and critical thinking.'

Tests, targets, structures and   standards

It's not just overuse of IT in the classroom that distracts teachers from teaching and pupils from learning. Over the last couple of decades, political faith in the power of technology has led to a steady devaluation of the human element in education. As computers offered ever-greater opportunities for micromanagement of classroom procedure, teachers found themselves spending increasing amounts of time on planning, record keeping and preparing pupils for standardised assessments.

This was especially the case in England, where centralised control of state education escalated at an amazing rate between the late 1980s and the late 2000s. It began with a national curriculum (much fatter and more detailed than those in other countries) linked to a system of standardised testing and a rigorous inspection regime. These were followed by targets for achievement at national and local level, generating more tests (English children were soon the most tested in the world), and even more detailed targets for schools. It also led to increasingly prescriptive direction for teachers on how to 'deliver' the curriculum to raise achievement (i.e., to improve test results).

This data-driven regime undoubtedly made children better at passing tests but it also changed the ethos of the educational system – from pre-school to top secondary – in ways that weren't in anyone's interests. A 'tests-and-targets' mentality narrows the curriculum down to the elements that are to be tested each year, as though children learn in a mechanical, linear fashion. Since they aren't merely machines to be programmed, this isn't how children learn, and their understanding becomes increasingly patchy and superficial. The UK has been plummeting down the international league tables for the 3Rs ever since the regime began, and complaints from universities and employers about school leavers' general ability grow louder every year.

The educational journalist Warwick Mansell described the effects on schools in his 2007 book *Education by Numbers*. At primary level, teachers feel forced to concentrate on satisfying inspection demands and coaching children to the next 'level of achievement', which leads to bland, superficial, uninteresting lessons. By the time they reach their teens, many pupils are so turned off by the whole process, and so lacking in the skills they actually need, that the only way for schools to keep churning out the necessary statistics is to play the system even more cynically. The statistics that attract political attention for this age group are the results of the public examinations taken at ages 16 and 18.*

Mansell catalogues details of widespread cramming for these exams (using resources written for this purpose by examiners, aimed at getting pupils through the tests) and loosely disguised cheating, leading to steady grade inflation. It's not that teachers and pupils aren't working hard – many of them are working very hard indeed. But grinding away to produce data to satisfy politicians is an exercise in compliance, not a process of educational enlightenment. There are now attempts to undo some of the damage by slimming down the national curriculum and assessment regime, but a couple of decades of tests, targets and school league tables have changed perceptions of what education is about for parents, teachers and pupils.

Under pressure...

In 2010, the then president of the Girls' Schools Association, Gillian Low summed up these changes as a national shift 'to a perceived emphasis on examinations rather than education; on structures rather than students; inspection rather than inspiration; on specifications rather than scholarship; compliance rather than common sense, and testing rather than teaching.'

At first I was surprised to hear this remarkably succinct summary coming from Ms Low, because the independent girls' schools she represents have probably been less adversely affected by the current culture than other schools. Girls are constitutionally more capable than boys of putting up with a highly

> Girls are constitutionally more capable than boys of putting up with a highly structured regime.

* At the time of writing, the public exams at 16 are GCSEs, but these are to be replaced with the EBacc (English Baccalaureate).

structured regime, and children from wealthy middle-class homes with plenty of parental support tend to do well in tests without too much coaching – their teachers are still free to provide a broad, balanced, exciting curriculum the rest of the time. It's children from disadvantaged homes who've suffered the worst effects, with boys from disadvantaged homes at the bottom of the heap.

But then I realised that, even for the most fortunate of pupils, there's no escape from the cumulative impact of a 'test-and-targets' culture, and the perceptions it encourages in everyone involved. When pupils hit their mid-teens, they're obliged to embark on the long, hard slog through the public exam system. University admission, career choices, the entire trajectory of their life and happiness, suddenly seem to depend on their performance in a relentless succession of examinations. The pressure to achieve the right grades is particularly intense for the brightest pupils, because two decades of steady grade inflation means admission to the university of their choice often depends on a 'perfect' performance in every piece of coursework and every single exam. As Ms Low explained, the pressure is now so intense that, '*dropping one grade can blight a pupil's life*'.

For four years, at the height of angst-ridden adolescence, conscientious girls live with the knowledge that they can't afford to make a mistake. The pressure to achieve this academic perfection is exacerbated by waves of anxiety coming from their teachers (whose schools will drop down the league tables if pupils don't deliver the goods) and their parents, who are almost inevitably drawn into the general atmosphere of paranoia.* In 2011, as doctors and counselling services reported soaring demand for advice on exam-related stress, Lucie Russell, director of the charity YoungMinds, claimed that, '*we are sitting on a mental health time bomb*', especially among high-achieving youngsters.

---

* If current government plans for payment by results go ahead, teachers may also be concerned about their pay packets. In general, the more pressure teachers are under, the more pressure is passed down to the students.

Well-educated girls ...

At the beginning of this chapter I said it was only natural for loving parents to want their daughters to do well at school because they know that for a girl to take advantage of all the opportunities open to women, a good education is vital. I then proceeded to question the entire basis of the UK school system.

So, while writing this chapter, I've thought about what the phrase 'a well-educated girl' means to me. It certainly doesn't summon up a picture of an exhausted, compliant individual with little more than fistfuls of A-star exam results to show from 13 years in the education system. Instead, I imagined the sort of girl who'd develop a range of interests during childhood, including many that would lead to satisfying ways of spending her leisure time in the future. By her mid-teens, she'd have identified some academic subjects she enjoyed studying more than others, and be excited at the prospect of investigating them in more depth in the sixth form, before going on – if she wanted to – to higher education.

> An exhausted, compliant individual with little more than fistfuls of A-star exam results to show from 13 years in the education system.

By this time, she'd obviously be highly literate and numerate, and a discriminative user of information technology – exercising intelligent control of the electronic media, rather than letting it control her. She'd also probably have a few extra-curricular passions and, hopefully, a social life that didn't revolve around Facebook.

I imagined her doing her GCSEs (or EBacc) and A Levels – working hard to get the grades needed for university, but perfectly capable of recognising that her world wouldn't fall apart if she happened to drop a grade. Since she'd find academic study intellectually rewarding in itself, even if she didn't get into her university of choice, she could shrug it off and think herself into another way forward. (Mind you, her pleasure in learning would enhance her chances of scooping the grades required, so there's a good chance that that eventuality wouldn't arise.)

Then I imagined my well-educated girl moving into womanhood. She'd be well equipped to meet any challenges fate might throw at her. Throughout her life, whenever informed, rational decisions were required, she'd be unafraid to make them, and if they involved a significant change of lifestyle, she'd engage enthusiastically with the task of learning how best to deal with it. When confronted with circumstances beyond her control, even in the darkest of days, she'd have the consolations of philosophy.

During a break in writing, I read a book called *Half a Wife* by Gaby Hinsliff, who struck me as an extremely well-educated woman. In it she related her decision to leave a high-flying career as a political journalist and find new ways of earning a living that blended more comfortably with motherhood. Her first project was to look at how families and businesses can adjust the way they operate to provide a more sensible work–life balance life balance for parents, to the benefit of everyone involved. Her conclusions are a wonderful vindication of the rights of women – and men – to achieve the E-/S-type balance that underpins human well-being, both for individuals and societies.

In short, well-educated females like Hinsliff are both bright *and* balanced. If we can produce enough of them – and enough well-educated males to work alongside them – I believe they can lead us all into the broad, sunlit uplands of a brave, new, equal world.

... and under-educated boys

In the meantime, today's parents and teachers have to support girls through an education system that's apparently creating 'a mental health time bomb'. It's not easy, but I've come across many schools that still manage to find a way around the system and provide the sort of educational ethos in which girls can develop as people in their own right. With the support of parents, many more schools could join their number.

There is, however, one inhibiting factor that keeps cropping up in discussion of girls' education: boys. They need an education too, and the problems of male pupils have always been more attention grabbing than those of females. It's easy to assume that boys hog the limelight because of millennia of male supremacy, but childcare and primary education have always been dominated by women and secondary teaching becomes more feminised by the day. You'd expect women to be at least as aware of the needs of girls as they are of boys.

The reason they're not was explained to me by the psychiatrist Sami Timimi, a specialist in boys' behaviour: '*The big difference is that boys externalise their problems and it comes out as bad behaviour – girls tend to internalise it, as sadness. Boys' issues are therefore issues for others, not just themselves.*' So, when boys are under pressure, they get angry with the world and everyone knows about it. When girls are under pressure, they're more likely to think I *must try harder*. It's not until they start starving themselves, self-harming or exhibiting other serious mental health problems that anyone takes notice. And by the time that happens, their earlier educational experiences are seldom considered as a contributory factor.

> When girls are under pressure, they're more likely to think *I must try harder*.

On the other hand, the entire educational system is only too aware of boys' problems right from the beginning. Childcare workers have their hands full keeping little boys out of mischief in cramped institutionalised environments, and our early start policy means primary teachers often waste ages trying to settle them down in class. As time goes on, boys' general lack of interest in literacy determines many aspects of both educational policy and day-to-day classroom practice – tests, targets and technology are all ways of trying to keep boys on track.

By secondary school level, the presence of boys has a very obvious direct affect on the girls themselves. With teenage hormones swirling around their system, many girls now obsess about what their male classmates think of them, and begin behaving in stereotypically 'feminine' ways. Whether this involves being sweet, sassy or sexy, it usually means taking a less assertive part in lessons, and avoiding appearing particularly studious. Girls' superiority in exams means less successful boys sneer at education as 'girly', which causes problems for high achievers of both sexes.

Boys of this age are just as distracted by raging hormones as girls, and the seriously lovelorn have always covered their confusion with the teenage equivalent of pigtail-pulling: mild sexual harassment. But some 21st century boys now harass or bully female pupils in overtly sexual ways for more sinister reasons; misogyny is widely promoted as a masculine virtue in X-rated computer games and internet porn. Since in many males this is accompanied by festering resentment at women's increasing influence in all spheres of life, it can lead to some nasty experiences for female pupils *and* staff.

Like Mean Girl bullying (see page 180), boys' aggressive behaviour arises from self-esteem issues in the bully, and relies for its success on insecurity in the victim. Early adolescence is a time of emotional turmoil for all youngsters, but it's much more of a problem if they've failed to acquire the emotional resilience to cope with social friction during the course of their childhood. Sexual bullying – apparently on the increase – is also clearly exacerbated by the steady sexualisation of the entire culture (see Chapter 10).

All girls together

One obvious way to help schools tailor the best sort of support for girls is single-sex education. In some independent schools, it's now possible for girls to enter an all-female pre-prep class from the age of two or three, and then go all the way to A Level without having their education polluted by the presence of pesky males.

There are seductive arguments for an 'all girls together' approach. At pre-school level, the absence of boys leaves girls freer to behave in 'boyish' ways themselves – for instance, playing with construction equipment, or rushing around being adventurous outdoors. In the primary and secondary years, if teachers aren't preoccupied dealing with male mischief-making, there's more time to encourage girls to develop as all-rounders – not just in the classroom, but in the arts, on the sports field, and so on. Once they reach the teenage years, girls untroubled by the presence of the opposite sex don't need to waste time trying to be 'feminine'; they can be as academic as they like, speak up confidently in class, and allow themselves to excel in traditionally male subjects like maths and science. Single-sex education gives girls the opportunity to be themselves, developing self-confidence that will see them in good stead in the future.

On the other hand, that future will not be a male-free zone. In a sexually equal workplace, women have to work in partnership with men, dealing with all the petty power struggles of daily existence. And for most women, a lasting sexual relationship with a male partner is a central element of personal well-being – and if it's to be a relationship that's equal sexually, it will rely on mutual understanding. So, in terms of social development, the two sexes need as many opportunities as possible to learn how to get along together naturally while they're growing up. It doesn't help girls (or boys) to go through the pre-school and primary school years thinking of the opposite sex as another species (possibly a threatening one). To feel comfortably equal at work and at home in adulthood, they need to interact on an equal basis throughout their childhood. And it doesn't help teenagers struggling with the onset of sexuality if the opposite sex is the subject of hormone-induced fantasies, rather than real-life people whom they meet on a daily basis.

So it seems to me that single-sex education isn't the best way to prepare girls to take their place in a society that's trying, painfully, to edge its way towards true sexual equality. Men and women find each other mysterious enough as it is, without adding to their difficulties by keeping them apart during childhood and adolescence. Neither does it help parents and teachers to solve the problems today's educational orthodoxies cause for all children, irrespective of gender.

The major issues I've identified in this chapter are as potentially harmful to the development of boys as they are to the development of girls – if the boys are pesky, it's our culture that's making them that way. An education system based on developmental principles – like that in Finland – allows teachers to respond to children's individual needs during the first few years, ensuring as far as possible that

> 'Girlish' girls just learn to shut up and tick the boxes.

negative gender-stereotypical traits aren't exaggerated. On the other hand, a system based on dreary testing has the opposite effect – the 'boyish' boys get progressively more troublesome and the 'girlish' girls just learn to shut up and tick the boxes.

If children are to have the chance of lifelong well-being and socially responsible personal fulfilment (including relationships that are equal sexually), they all need opportunities to develop as many positive character traits as possible. Girls have as much to gain from developing the 'manly' virtues listed in Kipling's poem 'If', as boys have from developing the 'womanly' ones of E-type social and emotional literacy. There's no reason the two sets of virtues should be mutually exclusive, and society's long-term equality project must surely be to help both sexes recognise – and embrace – the traditional strengths of the other.

In the meantime, if we separate boys and girls as they grow up, we may simply emphasise old-fashioned stereotypes that don't do any of them (or society) any good. This was certainly the conclusion of a recent US research study, 'The Pseudoscience of Single-Sex Schooling', which claims that *sex-segregation increases gender stereotyping and legitimises institutional sexism*. The academics who produced the report describe single-sex education as *deeply misguided, and often justified by weak, cherry-picked or misconstrued scientific claims*. They then proceed to do a very thorough demolition job.

Education and the gender wars

Having just argued in favour of co-education, I should find this demolition job reassuring. But I can't help worrying about those researchers' conclusions. After all, most gender-stereotypical messages come from marketing and media, not schools, and in my experience, all-girls schools are dedicated to challenging old-fashioned female stereotypes. So I can see why some parents and teachers still think single-sex education is worth a try for girls. It's patently evident that co-education hasn't yet stemmed the tide of gender stereotyping.

In fact, 15 cherry-picking years on the research trail have convinced me that as long as the educational system pays insufficient attention to children's developmental needs, neither single-sex nor co-ed schools will make much of an impact in countering the influences of screen-based media and marketing. Indeed, until we adjust the ethical balance of UK education, all schools are in danger of exaggerating the old stereotypical negatives of 'male' and 'female' behaviour. They're also likely to endorse two recent gender stereotypes that now crop up regularly on our screens, in dramas, reality programmes and advertisements – the concept of girls as conscientious, socially responsible little worker bees and of boys as lazy, self-interested drones.

> The concept of girls as conscientious, socially responsible little worker bees and of boys as lazy, self-interested drones.

Like all stereotypes, neither of these stands up to rational scrutiny, but both operate at an emotional level to influence our behaviour. Steve Biddulph, author of the best-selling book *Raising Boys*, has been pointing out the potential ill effects of these new stereotypes on boys for many years. So far I haven't spotted any female psychologists commenting on the possible long-term consequences of an apparently 'female-friendly' stereotype on girls' self-image. In a system that values compliance over common sense, this is yet another ingredient in 'perfect girl syndrome'. The world now abounds with harassed women, conscientiously taking on far more than their fair share of responsibility (I *have to be **everything**!*), and buzzing themselves into a state of unfulfilled exhaustion.

In a culture awash with unrealistic expectations for the female sex, the last thing little girls needs is a subconscious conviction that their role in life is to keep their noses to the grindstone and shoulder every social burden that comes their way (under the impression that males are incapable of sharing it).

That message had clearly been absorbed by the girl I met in the school playground I visited a few years ago to interview some male pupils for my book *21st Century Boys*. She couldn't have been more than five years old, but she nodded wisely when I told her I'd come to find out about how boys were doing at school. 'Oh yes,' she said, 'There's a poem about that:

"Girls go to college to get more knowledge –
Boys go to Jupiter to get more stupider!"'

When I asked some of the boys at her school about the rhyme, they rolled their eyes and laughed. But it was clear that many had already opted for 'Life on Jupiter'. They had no hesitation in declaring school 'boring', while expressing great enthusiasm for computer games. One of them, a ten-year-old who was being brought up by his single mother, told me how much he enjoyed being a 21st century boy; he spent his out-of-school hours in his bedroom, watching TV, playing computer games, 'and if I get hungry, I text down to my mum and she brings me up a pizza'.

It's been depressing to note how many of the children I've interviewed over the last ten years were being reared by lone mums, struggling womanfully to combine childcare with earning a living. There's been a lot of fallout from the gender wars over the last 50 years, with many unintended consequences for women that 1960s women's libbers couldn't have begun to imagine when we started trying to even things up a bit. The impact of gender stereotyping, and other aspects of half a century of gender wars, on adult relationships is discussed in the next chapter. Suffice to say here that, so far, education hasn't been much help in furthering the cause of sexual equality in people's daily lives.

And, as described in Chapter 2, the mainstream feminist agenda was hijacked long ago by a traditionally 'male' obsession with systems and status. So most feminist academics are as blind as most female politicians to the inadequacies of an educational status quo devoted to systems and status. They inevitably become preoccupied with convoluted S-type arguments, such as whether men are marginally better at science than women or whether single-sex schools are more sexist than co-ed ones. It doesn't occur to them that E-type thinking might be just as important as the S-type variety in influencing the average schoolgirl's potential to develop a mind of her own. So they've done very little to help parents and teachers turn out well-balanced, well-educated girls.

***

If sexual equality is ever to become a reality, both girls and boys need to be 'educated' rather than well schooled to pass exams. Learning to think isn't easy – children have to *want* to do it, not just to gain extrinsic rewards or avoid punishment, but because it's fundamentally interesting. The job of adults who educate children is to nurture that intrinsic motivation, supporting their learning in the ways that work best at different stages of development. They also have to challenge those aspects of a seriously unbalanced culture that – intentionally or unintentionally – deny children the chance to develop minds of their own.

That doesn't mean schools don't need a curriculum or exams, or that children should never be expected to do anything they don't fancy. Teachers have to balance warmth and firmness just as parents do – they need authoritative control of their classrooms. This means that the E-type personal skills of teachers are as important as their capacity for S-type rational thought. If an education system is to work, it needs to involve an S/E balance, just as a society needs that balance to keep moving onwards and upwards.

Education Timeline

0–3 years

See the Play Timeline for 0–3 years, for all the activities that will help your daughter to learn to control her focus of attention, regulate her behaviour and empathise with others. They also help to develop creativity and problem-solving skills.

Avoid screen-based technology, which is likely to have the opposite effect (see page 134).

To help develop her language skills, sing songs and share rhymes as often as you can. Encourage her to sing or chant along and join in with any actions.

You can't tell or read her enough stories! They develop her language skills, feed her imagination and prepare her to read by herself one day.

Use opportunities to count in a rhythmic way. For instance, as you go up stairs (*'That's one stair, two stairs...'*), button her coat (*'That's one button, two buttons...'*), feed her spoonfuls of food, etc. And sing counting songs, like *Ten Green Bottles* and *Five Little Speckled Frogs*.

3–6 years

Again, see the Play Timeline – play is the best way for this age group to learn.

Keep up the songs, rhymes and stories (see page 188). Encourage her to learn rhymes – it's the natural way to develop auditory memory. Listening to stories will also help to develop her vocabulary and a feel for written language patterns.

When you're out and about, point out familiar words, letters and numbers that you see in the environment around you (*Open, Pay here, Stop, Playground; L for learner, H for hydrant, P for parking; house numbers, bus numbers, etc.*).

Give her plenty of opportunities for outdoor play and exploration. Encourage her to be tomboyish! And look for a nursery that lets children spend as much time as possible outdoors (see page 158).

If possible, find a primary school that resists early 'schoolification' and maintains a genuinely play-based curriculum in the early years (see page 189).

If she shows interest in the 3Rs, encourage and support her, but don't try to rush her into schoolwork at the expense of other activities. Let her enjoy her childhood first.

Encourage her to play in the real rather than the virtual world, and don't confuse play with passive entertainment (see page 133 and Media Timeline).

6–11 years

Choose a primary school by reading the prospectus, arranging a visit and chatting with other parents. For instance, does the school encourage all-round development and enthusiasm for learning, rather than concentrating on tests?

Keep a folder for the school prospectus, other information about school procedures, school reports and certificates.

Once she's picked up the basics of reading, she needs lots of practice at an appropriate reading level, so help her to find books she'll love reading. Carry on reading to her too – she'll still enjoy a bedtime story for several years.

If she gets hooked on writing (a diary, letters or emails to a pen pal, her own stories), it will also help her education.

Real-life maths (measuring, estimating, calculating, etc., for a real purpose) can help consolidate school lessons.

Encourage any hobbies, sporting interests, musical activities, etc. (see Play Timeline). But don't overload her with out-of-school activities; she also needs time for less organised play, and for just relaxing and dreaming.

Make sure she gets enough sleep every night (see page 126) and eats a balanced diet.

Always try to attend school functions and parent-teacher interviews (if you can't, ask for an appointment to meet at another time).

Involve yourself with her school as much as possible, seek out like-minded parents, and work with staff to create a 'village' that will challenge the dumbing down of girls by tween culture (see page 87).

Help your daughter to develop a disciplined approach to homework: getting it done as soon as possible, taking pride in doing a good job and completing it in the allotted time, as stated in the school homework policy. (If she regularly needs longer, let her teacher know.) Support her homework routine, but don't do her homework for her.

For technology advice, see the Media Timeline and page 197.

11 years +

Help her to adjust to secondary school by developing routines for getting her to school in the morning with minimum fuss, and dealing with homework in the evening.

Continue to encourage reading, hobbies, sport, etc., and ensure she gets enough sleep and a healthy diet.

Continue to support her in her homework routine, bearing in mind that she'll now need to schedule homework in different subjects. Once she begins studying for exams, support her in developing and sticking to a revision schedule.

Discuss her needs in terms of technology for completing homework and ensure she's adequately equipped.

Show interest in what she's studying at school and encourage her to share what she's learning with you. Ask if there are any ways you can help (e.g., by organising trips to museums).

Involve yourself with her school as much as possible, and ensure you're aware of all letters home, permission forms, homework diaries, etc. Make sure you know what's required of you as a parent.

She may need extra emotional support to cope with the conflicting demands of school and 'cool', so keep all lines of communication open. If she has problems, it helps to draw on support from other members of your 'village' who can act as adult mentors.

She'll need more emotional support when she begins sitting public examinations. While encouraging her to do her best, help her to keep a sense of proportion.

CHAPTER 10

SEX, POWER ... AND LOVE

Raising bright, balanced girls in a highly sexualised
techno-consumerist culture

'I don't know what to do!'

She was an attractive, efficient-looking head teacher, probably in her early forties, who throughout the morning had made crisp, considered contributions to my seminar about the effects of modern lifestyles on children's school performance. Then, shortly after lunch, the discussion turned to the early sexualisation of girls. Suddenly she crumpled before our eyes into a desperate, weeping mother.

Her daughter was 12, she told us, but in full make-up and Primark regalia, looked at least 16. A year or so ago, she and her friends had become obsessed with rap music. 'Horrible stuff – disgusting, misogynistic – I couldn't believe how vile it was'. Mum banned it from the house, but Ginnie just went to a girlfriend's home and listened there. They were knocking around with a crowd of older boys, and God knew what they were getting up to.

'We had terrible rows about the way she was dressing, and coming home at all hours. But lately I've been terrified she wouldn't come home at all. We've been living on a knife edge. Then yesterday I noticed a plaster on her arm – thought she'd been injecting drugs. But that wasn't it. It's a contraceptive implant. I don't know what to do!'

The rest of the group, all female senior managers in primary schools, didn't know what to do either. The seminar turned into an ad hoc support group, trying to bolster up this distraught mum with advice and reassurance in which none of us really had any confidence...

Girls growing older younger

That was several years ago, and I've no idea what happened to Ginnie. It seems likely she joined the rapidly growing band of girls engaging in underage sex, and I do hope her poor mum managed to help her deal with the emotional fallout. In 2011, for the first time ever, official UK records showed more girls than boys (27 per cent as opposed to 23 per cent) having their first sexual experience before the age of 16, with more young women than men now clocking up more than ten sexual partners by their early twenties. As in education, girls have not only caught up with boys but are now overtaking them.

I've often wondered who settled on 16 as the age at which sex becomes legal, but it's now an established social norm and also the age at which young people can legally leave home, marry and start full-time work. It might be arbitrary, but in a confused and confusing world it's helpful for both parents and children to have a socially agreed age at which young people are considered mature enough to make these important decisions for themselves. Today's teen culture is a sexual, social and emotional minefield and – whether they think so at the time or not – younger teenagers need the support of older, wiser heads to see them through.*

Certainly, in the opinion of all the women at my seminar that day (and every other grown woman with whom I've discussed this subject), a 12-year-old girl isn't emotionally equipped to deal with a sexual relationship. She may be urged constantly by commercial forces to 'grow older younger', so that she dresses and looks like a young adult, but a fashionable exterior is no guarantee of emotional maturity.

There's also a disturbing trend for girls (and, recently, boys) to

---

* Because of this I have serious doubts about health professionals doling out contraceptives to girls as young as 12. There are obviously social and medical reasons to help youngsters avoid early pregnancy, but there are also serious ethical questions about parental rights and responsibilities with which the authorities seem reluctant to engage.

begin puberty earlier than in the past, meaning many youngsters have to cope with a rush of sex hormones even before reaching their teens. The early onset of puberty hasn't yet been explained satisfactorily, although it seems to be linked to a cocktail of factors associated with modern lifestyles, such as increased body weight and poor sleeping habits (see page 123). But accelerated physiological development doesn't go hand in hand with social and emotional development, which rely on a childhood's worth of experience.

It's also impossible for children to miss the message – in adverts, pop songs, screen dramas and every aspect of celebrity culture – that sex is the ultimate adult fun activity (closely followed, of course, by drinking and drugs). Many girls well under the age of 16 now look many years older, feel as though they've been in training for adulthood for ages and assume they're ready to join in the fun, whether it's legal or not.

The problems for parents are obvious. Even a girl who's avoided the worst excesses of tween culture often finds the early teenage years difficult. There's a period of adjustment for the whole family as she comes to terms with the physical changes and mood swings that accompany the complicated process of growing up. The influence of her peer group becomes steadily stronger, surging sex hormones cause constant confusion, and the comfortable security of home and family can suddenly feel like restraint.

All loving parents can do as their daughter moves through this phase of her life is to maintain a 'warm-but-firm' stance about her behaviour (as long as she lives with them, they're entitled to assert their family values at home), while tuning in sympathetically to the trials of adolescence. When she's away from home, they have to hope that a dozen or so years of parental love and respectful discipline have been transformed at as deep a level as possible into self-love, self-respect and self-discipline.

If she's also learned to think for herself, their daughter has a very good chance of negotiating her way safely through the teenage minefield, especially if – in the event of a crisis – she knows she can turn for advice to mum, dad or another caring adult. This is another good

> Adolescent girls are at a huge advantage if they can turn to a trusted, older 'female mentor'.

reason for parents to establish a network of like-minded family friends. Adolescent girls are at a huge advantage if they can turn to a trusted, older 'female mentor' when relationships in the family are under strain. If she can't, any challenge to parental authority is likely to lead to a power struggle, and consequent communication breakdown.

What was very clear to me – as the members of our seminar group tried to help Ginnie's mum that day – was that, if parents don't establish a comfortable authoritative relationship with their daughter from the moment she's born, it becomes progressively more difficult as the years go by. So if things do go awry when sex eventually rears its head, it may turn out to be too late.

Anglo-Saxon attitudes

Despite sex education in schools and readily available contraception, the UK has long had the highest teenage birth and abortion rate in Western Europe. But the problems associated with underage sex are far greater than the possibility of pregnancy; it's also linked to sexually transmitted diseases, emotional problems and the disruption of education. Parents – especially the parents of girls – can't afford to ignore these statistics. So how can they equip their daughters to steer through the teenage minefield?

Interestingly, the European country with the lowest levels of teenage pregnancy is the Netherlands, which also came top of the UNICEF league for childhood well-being (the one in which the UK came bottom). Commentators ascribe this success in child-rearing to the fact that Dutch parents spend a lot of family time with their children, especially in their early years. Dutch teenagers' more sexually responsible attitudes are usually attributed to a more relaxed attitude about sex in the nation as a whole. Parents (and other responsible adults) are, from the very beginning, more open with children about the nature of sexual relationships.

The British, on the other hand, are famously repressed when it comes to sex. Although our culture has become increasingly sexualised, and growing girls can scarcely miss the female objectification and 'pornified' images all around them, many parents are too uptight to engage in conversation on the subject. But if we avoid talking to children about sex when they're small, it becomes increasingly difficult to do so as they grow older. Instead, they acquire their information from tween and teen magazines, celebrity gossip, TV, the internet and their peer group, so yet again marketing and media usurp the parental role.*

This doesn't mean that parents have to plunge into detailed descriptions before their daughter is ready to listen and understand. As long as mum and dad are clearly ready to discuss the issue, she'll ask for information when she's interested. But when that happens, she needs a sensitive, age-appropriate explanation, so potentially embarrassed parents might find it helps to swot one up in advance. There are plenty of books and internet articles on the subject – for instance, see the Mayo Clinic's advice about how to answer questions from toddlers and pre-schoolers.

It helps if right from the start parents encourage their daughter to feel at ease with her body (see Chapter 5) and provide the necessary vocabulary for talking about the parts of it that are connected with sex. It also helps if mum and dad are clear in their own minds about their feelings

> It helps if right from the start parents encourage their daughter to feel at ease with her body.

on the subject, particularly the knotty problem of 'morality'. Parents with a strong religious faith don't have a problem here, but for the secular majority it's become more and more difficult.

I suspect that many parents' problems in talking to children about sex are due to adult confusion around the subject of morality. Fifty years of 'sexual liberation' haven't worked out the way secular liberal thinkers hoped. As the feminist writer Natasha Walter puts in it her

---

* According to teenage interviewees, school sex education – often uncomfortably delivered by press-ganged teachers – is usually as hilarious and counterproductive as it was in my own day, more than half a century ago. This is a subject – like learning to cross the road or use the internet – for which parents can't offload responsibility onto schools.

book *Living Dolls: The Return of Sexism*, there was an expectation that once women were free '*to focus on their own desires and independence*', there'd be '*an honest acceptance of girls' sexuality*'. Instead, as she admits, the market has homed in on carefully selected female desires and transformed these into '*the narrowest kind of consumerism and self-objectification*'.

So to take an authoritative stance on sexualisation, parents have to overcome any Anglo-Saxon diffidence and tackle the question throughout their daughters' lives. I've tried in the rest of this chapter to provide them with some starting points by:

- explaining how the sexualisation of young girls in Britain now affects children across the social classes, and the way feminism has unintentionally contributed to this
- offering some suggestions about sexual manners and morality in a sexually liberated world, based on many conversations with modern girls and parents (including some admirably matter-of-fact parents from the Netherlands and Scandinavia).

But the first step is for parents to recognise how consumerist culture colours their own and their daughters' attitudes to 'girl power' from the very beginning of her life.

Cute kids

I'm not trying to put all of today's parenting problems down to market forces (although the more I research modern childhood, the more I find myself muttering '*It's the economy, stupid!*'). Neither do I think marketers are all wicked people who've set out to destroy family life, possibly taking Western civilisation with it. As far as they're concerned, they're just doing their job, which is selling as much stuff as they possibly can. Since they know the best way to hook children into a lifetime of consumption is to catch 'em young, that's what they do.

Babies aren't equipped to go shopping, so the market has to rely on caring adults to begin the process. It's not difficult. Adults of both sexes naturally find little girls physically attractive – small, sociable, vulnerable creatures bring out the tender side of human nature, and as long as we retain any vestige of empathy, we're unlikely to confuse the impulse to cuddle a child with sexual desire. Meanwhile, these small, social, vulnerable creatures have an agenda of their own. They're programmed to use the limited resources at their disposal to establish as much control over their environment as they possibly can.

With their acute social observation skills, many little girls learn at a very early age that 'flirting' with adults pays off. It isn't flirting from the little girls' point of view, of course – they know nothing about the conventions of courtship. They've merely discovered ways of behaving that make the grown-ups smile and, as they grow older, often get them their own way. It's adults who interpret children's behaviour according to adult criteria, and if a girl's parents find her flirtatiousness amusing they'll probably encourage it.

> Many little girls learn at a very early age that 'flirting' with adults pays off.

Of course, the Daily Mail would be up in arms if marketers were to label products for infants as 'flirty'. So the usual term of choice is 'cute'. This has proved a highly successful ticket for the marketing of products to little girls and the doting adults who finance their purchases (Lelli Kelly, you may remember, are 'the cutest shoes').

At first sight 'cuteness' seems innocuous enough. The synonyms in my Microsoft thesaurus are: *attractive, pretty, delightful, charming, appealing, endearing, adorable* and *sweet*. However, the 1982 edition of *Roget's Thesaurus* lists other synonyms, including: (1) *sexy, kissable, glamorous* and *winsome*; (2) *coy, twee, simpering* and *hypocritical*. Word meanings change with time to reflect the values of the age, but I'd like to bet that the lessons little girls learn when their 'cuteness' is indulged haven't changed a bit.

If a young child absorbs the message that appearing sexy, kissable, glamorous and/or winsome pays dividends, she's likely to embark upon a personal self-objectification project that leads to issues with body image and a growing preoccupation with girly pursuits like fashion, shopping and makeovers.

The other message a little girl absorbs when cuteness pays dividends is that coy, twee, simpering, hypocritical behaviour (sometimes known as 'feminine wiles') is helpful in winding mummy and/or daddy around her little finger. Any child who learns to get her own way by exercising these skills is increasingly likely to pervert her E-type strengths into emotional manipulation of those around her. The Mean Girls described on page 180 have usually been 'spoilt' in this way, as have many wealthy and attractive young women through the ages.

While it's inevitable that human beings sometimes use their capacity for empathy for selfish reasons, we are – as a species – generally disapproving of such tactics, and for good reason. If we can't trust each other's motives, the entire social fabric will begin to unravel. Parents are often disarmed by their small daughter's wide-eyed appeals to their generosity, because they realise she's not consciously trying to manipulate them – and she's just so *sweet*. But if they repeatedly succumb to her charm, they reinforce the behaviour, and she gradually discovers the advantages of feminine wiliness.

Girls who become habitually manipulative at an early age are unlikely to enjoy the benefits of real friendship, and may have real difficulties during adulthood in untangling the concepts of 'sex' and 'power'. So if you don't want your daughter to end up like the heroines of celebrity culture, I'd advise caution in colluding with cute behaviour, especially when it involves spending money.

The sexualisation of childhood

The suggestions given in Chapter 8 for dealing with commercial influences at different stages in girls' development provide plenty of opportunities for opening up conversations about sex (and power), since gender stereotyping and highly sexualised behaviour are now all-pervasive in British media and marketing campaigns. Public concern about the issue has been reflected in recent

> Gender stereotyping and highly sexualised behaviour are now all-pervasive in British media and marketing campaigns.

years in two major government reports on premature sexualisation, both of which are useful for parents who want to help steer their daughters round 21st century pitfalls.

In the first, a report published in 2010, the 'Sexualisation of Young People Review', psychologist Linda Papadopoulos states her ultimate objective very succinctly:

> I want ... all girls and boys to grow up confident about who they are and about finding and expressing their individuality and sexuality, but not through imposed gender stereotypes, or in a way that objectifies the body or commodifies their burgeoning sexuality.

She then proceeds to list the myriad social influences behind early sexualisation (a depressingly long and scary catalogue), a mass of research that would surely convince any government that Something Must Be Done, and gives a number of sensible recommendations that might at least begin to clear up some of the mess. Unfortunately, the government that commissioned her report was let off the hook because it was voted out a couple of months later. The incoming government decided to drop it and commission another, thus allowing the situation to worsen, as Moore's Law rolled through another cycle.

Interestingly, in an earlier life Dr Papadopoulos was consultant psychologist to *Big Brother*, a TV phenomenon that I believe made a significant contribution to the sexualisation of society in general. The programme and its various media offshoots seemed to exemplify and encourage the type of female objectification described in her report, for instance:

- a cumulative, drip, drip effect of hyper-sexualised images selling the idea that female value lies in looking 'hot' and 'sexy'
- a disproportionate number of hot, sexy women disporting themselves in adverts, TV, films, magazines, pop music videos and on internet sites
- the mainstreaming of the porn and sex industries, so that 'glamour modelling', lap dancing and even 'high class' prostitution have

been 'normalised' ('*lending credence to the idea that women are there to be used and that men are there to use them*')

• the influence of celebrity culture on these social phenomena.

I've already mentioned the second government report – *Letting Children be Children* – earlier in this book. Its author, Reg Bailey, the Mothers' Union's chief executive, was asked to consider the commercialisation and sexualisation of childhood alongside each other. He picked up some of the Papadopoulos recommendations and in 2012 pushed through two useful changes. The first was a proposed porn opt-out clause for handheld internet devices (see page 176). The second was Parent Port (www.parentport.org.uk), a one-stop shop where parents can register complaints about any media or marketing developments they consider damaging to children.

But while any increase in parent power is obviously welcome, it's utterly unfair to expect parents to shoulder the entire responsibility for challenging multinational companies with billion-dollar budgets and the services of highly qualified psychologists. As one contributor to Bailey's report put it: '*There is a need for such a huge cultural shift away from consumerism that I feel powerless as an individual to act.*' Eventually, there must be more support for parents, such as government recommendations on children's media use, distributed by all agencies concerned with childcare and education, and strict regulatory curbs on marketing to children.

And eventually, some powerful political force must also challenge the market's increasingly exploitative use of female flesh for raking in the cash. This is why, a few years ago, I found myself flirting with feminism (see Introduction), which at the time seemed the only recognisable movement capable of rallying public and political interest in the question of whether 'sexualisation' in general has gone too far.

Sexualisation and feminism

Ever since the 1960s, the concepts of sexual equality and sexual liberation have gone hand in hand. They were part of a general move towards liberal democracy and tolerance that typified the spirit of the age, and – to a young liberated woman like myself, who turned 18 in 1966 – it seemed a pretty good direction of travel. But, as described in Part One of this book, by the turn of the century I was beginning to have serious qualms at how it was turning out. While sexual equality had run into trouble because of the seemingly insuperable problems associated with motherhood, sexual liberation was going from strength to strength. Indeed, it seemed to have spiralled well beyond liberation into outright licentiousness.

Liberty isn't the same as anarchy, and a more liberal attitude to sexual matters doesn't necessarily mean a libidinous free-for-all. Yet, until very recently, the only people prepared to voice concerns on this subject were from religious circles, and in an increasingly secular culture their voices didn't garner much of a

> Liberty isn't the same as anarchy, a more liberal attitude to sexual matters doesn't necessarily mean a libidinous free-for-all.

following – indeed, they probably made things worse. The most vociferous critic of 'the permissive society', Mrs Mary Whitehouse, objected to almost everything, from mild swear words in TV comedies to homosexuality, and her all-embracing moral outrage allowed the media to turn her into a national figure of fun. By the time she died in 2001, this 'mediated' national attitude meant that any objection to any aspect of sexual liberation had become associated with prudishness and intolerance.

So, in the absence of any mainstream disapproval, market forces have cheerfully exploited the selling power of sex, TV stations have vied to push the boundaries for adult audiences, pop songs and videos have grown raunchier by the year, lap dancing clubs have sprung up across the land and pornography has flourished on the internet and dedicated porn channels. 'Glamour modelling' turned into an acceptable career choice when Katie Price (formerly known as

Jordan, and famous on account of her surgically enhanced breasts) apparently transformed herself into a wealthy businesswoman. A couple of best-selling books by a middle-class academic, detailing her life as a call girl under the pseudonym 'Belle de Jour', gave prostitution a similar air of respectability.

I've known for many years that I wasn't the only person to find all this unsettling. Chats with female friends of all ages revealed that they too felt that sexual liberation had gone too far. So I was deeply relieved when the feminist movement, which had always embraced greater openness about sex on the grounds that women have as much right as men to express their sexuality, suddenly rediscovered its roots and revived its interest in the objectification of women.

In 2010, Kat Banyard's *The Equality Illusion: The Truth about Women and Men Today* detailed the lives of women in the rapidly burgeoning sex industry, and linked their feelings of personal degradation to violence against women, rape and the low pay issue. A few months later, in *Living Dolls*, Natasha Walter described young working-class women queuing up in nightclubs to strip off for the delectation of baying males during 'Babes in the Bed' nights, for the chance of a shot at glamour modelling, and female Cambridge undergraduates stripping down to their thongs for photos in the college magazine. The word 'exploitation' was brought out of cold storage, and juxtaposed with the now very familiar expressions 'empowerment of women' and 'personal choice'.

Walter, who'd argued twelve years previously in *The New Feminism* that we should no longer worry about sexual matters but instead '*concentrate on pragmatic advances in terms of economic and political equality*', admitted she'd been wrong. While the feminist movement had taken its eye off this particular ball, many young women had come to believe that '*sexual confidence is the only confidence worth having*' and that sexual confidence involves looking and acting like soft porn stars.

Social class and the normalisation of porn

Not surprisingly, the vast majority of these 'sexually confident' young women are from what are politely known as 'disadvantaged' backgrounds. As I pointed out in Chapter 4, the effects of childhood toxicity are always noticeable in children from poorer neighbourhoods first, and during my research I'd seen it happening first-hand. Today's young women are yesterday's children, and the beliefs they hold are the beliefs they absorb from the adults who reared them.

In the early 2000s, a head teacher in a disadvantaged area told me how he'd unleashed considerable parental outrage by objecting to their nine-year-old daughter attending the school disco in her 'Porn Queen in Training' T-shirt. And I've lost count of the number of tales from other parts of the country of tiny girls wearing thongs, bras or high heels to school, and teachers struggling to deal with precocious sexual behaviour in the playground or obscene contributions to class discussions given in all innocence by children as young as five.

Celebrity culture and TV programmes catering to the lowest common denominator such as *The Jeremy Kyle Show*, *Big Brother* and sensational soaps are popular in disadvantaged communities, presumably because sensationalism and gossip offer an interesting escape from the miserable and mind-deadening circumstances of daily life. Children from these homes are more likely than others to spend their time indoors staring at screens because their parents are afraid to let them out. So even if mum and dad don't dress them in thongs or silly T-shirts, they'll pick up the message that 'sexual confidence' is the only confidence worth having.

Media and marketing folk pander to disadvantaged adults' escapist tendencies under the guise of reflecting social trends, and children who soak up the stuff throughout their childhood assume they're watching normal adult behaviour. So, as soon as they're able to dress and behave like adults, they follow suit and dress and behave in a similar way. And the 'sexual confidence' this suggests is at the most skin deep – these children and young women have simply been brainwashed into increasingly sexualised behaviour. The mainstreaming of pornography and fierce competition between media outlets means the sexual content of TV programming is ratcheted up on a regular basis, so 'normal' sexual activities become more 'pornified' with every passing year.

> Well-educated political campaigners don't generally spend much time in disadvantaged neighbourhoods.

The reason it took so long for middle-class feminists to notice these developments is probably a mixture of ignorance and unconscious snobbery. Well-educated political campaigners don't generally spend much time in disadvantaged neighbourhoods, so they aren't aware of the day-to-day reality of life on Britain's meanest streets. It's therefore easy to assume that poor people are a different breed – that they're born coarser, more vulgar, less educable than the middle class. I remember once having a heated argument about this with a left-wing professor of education when I was anthologising poetry for primary schools. I wanted to include Blake's poem 'The Tiger' and he accused me of 'cultural imperialism'.

Phil Edgar-Jones, creative director of *Big Brother*, which is dedicated to 'reflecting social trends', would probably agree with his assessment. When asked in an interview with Natasha Walter whether he'd like his own daughter to become a glamour model, Edgar-Jones replied: '*I would hope she would have different aspirations. I encourage her to read books. Other people have different backgrounds.*'

Many of those teachers I meet in disadvantaged areas strive constantly to help children rise above the social trends *Big Brother* 'reflects', but the influence of the electronic media is so great that it's usually a losing battle. And, thanks to the democratising power of the internet, the popular culture adored by the uneducated masses is now available 24 hours a day to children of every social class.

Since the essence of consumerism is choice, and educated adults tend to avoid anything they find distasteful, I suspect most middle-class adults are unaware of the depths to which popular culture has sunk. So it's my guess that you, dear reader, are blissfully ignorant about gonzo porn, the lyrics of misogynist gangsta rap, Nuts magazine's 'Assess My Breasts' website, a recent dance craze called 'daggering' and the increasing demand for labiaplasty by young women who want their private parts to measure up to those on the internet.

But if you've got teenage children, I bet they know about all of them. It's not cool to be ignorant about the latest trend. And all they have to do is google them.

Sex, freedom and exploitation

Does all this matter? Men have always objectified women, women have always taken pleasure in objectifying themselves, and sex has always had a dark side. Children have always been curious about sex and enjoyed sniggering over shreds of information from the adult world. Am I just a withered sexagenarian, confronted with a new generation's sexual mores and fretting unnecessarily about the implications for girls? While writing the last two chapters, I kept remembering my chum's comment in the restaurant (page 2): '*I dare say older women in the 1960s used to worry themselves sick about us, with our miniskirts, panda eyes and prescriptions for the Pill.*'

And I can't disagree with all those marketing messages: for most of us, sex is the ultimate adult fun. Well, it has to be, doesn't it? Human beings are programmed, like other animals, to enjoy the whole biological process, from display and courtship rituals to the act itself. It's a sort of grown-up 'play', as indicated by the language we use to describe it – men and women *play* the field to find a mate, *toy* flirtatiously with each other's emotions, then engage in *foreplay* and *sex games* to prolong and enhance the physical experience.

But social play is a demanding business, requiring a degree of compromise. For most adults (especially female), sex is most satisfying in an exclusive relationship where they can enjoy emotional as well as physical intimacy. If the emphasis in the early stages of a sexual relationship is on display rather than the more rounded process of 'courtship', the chances of making an emotional connection are reduced considerably. Both parties are too busy concentrating on appearance and technique to give each other's

> Adult play, like children's play, is being converted by commercial forces into a 'junk' version of the real thing.

feelings much thought. And the current definition of 'fun' – as mediated by the omnipresent screens – is rapidly losing sight of the fact that human beings have any emotional needs at all. Adult play, like children's play, is being converted by commercial forces into a 'junk' version of the real thing.

I think the problem for 21st century girls boils down to one question: *in terms of objectification, how far is it okay to go?* In recreational sex, men and women are probably in accord that playful 'toying' with affections is fun up to a point, but most of us don't enjoy being toyed with beyond a certain stage in the proceedings (i.e., being treated as an object, rather than a person). It's very pleasant for any adult to feel like an object of desire, but if the emotional side of human nature is taken into account, a sexual partner also needs to be treated as a person. There can't be many people, male or female, who'd take pleasure in being treated as an anonymous lump of flesh.

Men, being the less naturally empathetic sex, are more likely than women to see sexual playmates as objects rather than people and, without some sort of guidance, may find it difficult to work out when the objectification needs to stop. Women, naturally empathetic and anxious to please, may follow their sexual partner's lead further than is in their personal interests. If a girl doesn't have a mind of her own, a good helping of self-respect and the courage to get out of an unsatisfactory relationship, recreational sex may turn into a destructive assault on her emotional core.

Equality was supposed to challenge, and hopefully put an end to the idea that '*women are there to be used and that men are there to use them*'. In fact, due to a politically correct conspiracy of silence on the subject, the reverse has happened. As the Papadopoulos report pointed out, many aspects of popular culture now actively promote exploitative sex – and the uses to which women's bodies are put in internet pornography involve a degree of physical and psychological humiliation that's seriously misogynistic. Since the average age at which boys first view this kind of material is now 11, it's bound to have an effect on their expectations of sexual relationships. So time is running out.

Looking back, I realise that my growing disillusion about 'licentiousness' in the adult world co-existed with my developing concern about the commercialisation of childhood. (Duh! *It's the economy, stupid!*) Our capacity to make free, informed choices about our sexual activities as adults is hugely influenced by our experiences as children, and when children are regularly exploited by market forces, they're distracted from the mind-expanding, resilience-building 'real play' described in previous chapters. A commodified childhood is likely to lead to a commodified sex life, based on '*the narrowest kind of consumerism and objectification*'. And a 'pornified' version of sex, dreamt up by money-grubbers and ruthlessly promoted via the electronic media, is dehumanising for both men and women.

It's a great a tribute to the S-type skills of media and marketing that, over the last few decades, they've managed to convince large sections of the populace that exploitative practices are enormous fun for all concerned. But if an increasingly sexualised popular culture continues to 'reflect' current buying habits to an increasingly immature audience, I fear the only choice available to a growing number of 21st century girls will be in which aspect of the dark side of sex to specialise.

> I fear the only choice available to a growing number of 21st century girls will be which aspect of the dark side of sex to specialise in.

Sex, love and power

Still, we mustn't despair! There is still one highly desirable entity that, so far, multinational corporations haven't found a way to sell. Indeed, I don't think it's unduly optimistic to claim that they never will. It is, of course, love.

Love matters a great deal to human beings. We're born craving it because it's vital to our survival – the drive to 'attach' to another human being is as powerful in every newborn child as the drive to play. We therefore seek emotional connection all our lives, which is why 'satisfying relationships' are a critical factor in human well-being. But once we reach adulthood, sexual love has a special significance. Part of our interest in playing the field is a deep yearning to find a special person who's just right for us – not just a playmate, but a real mate.

That's why most of us know that sex isn't merely the fulfilment of a physical need like eating or drinking. And it's why, if we're lucky enough to find that special person, sex is an extraordinarily joyous experience – consciousness enhancing, life affirming, sometimes even transcendent. Michèle Roberts, feminist writer and advocate of free love, described it beautifully: '*Your lover knows you, satisfies that deep desire you have to be truly known, and you do the same for him.*' Even though we know the likelihood of these amazing feelings lasting forever is wildly against the odds, we still believe they might.

And, in a way they do because, thanks to the wonders of biology, love begets love. Despite being free to indulge in all the recreational sex they desire, even 21st century adults find that the potent combination of love and sex kindles an interest in procreation. Loving sexual relationships tend to result in offspring, so even if romantic love eventually dims,* parental love takes its place. And the E-type message can be passed to another generation.

This is the truly bright side of sex. A loving sexual relationship is possible for all adults (male and female) who've experienced the emotional fulfilment of attachment during infancy. It's more difficult to recognise love in a culture awash with messages suggesting that sex isn't about attachment but exploitation, so children need plenty of frank, intergenerational chats with adults who know that love matters. For parents seeking starting points for these chats, there are plenty of openings in the sexual shenanigans of characters

---

* Sadly, neuroscientists have found that the chemical cocktail underpinning 'romantic love' has a maximum life span of about three years. There do, however, appear to be some couples who continue to feel the same level of attachment for their partners throughout life, even after the intense hormonal activity associated with 'romantic love' dies down. Current estimates are that around 10 per cent of sexual partners might be 'in love' for life.

on TV and the constant news bulletins from Planet Celebrity.

However, it's not just marketing and the media that communicate the message that sex is often about the abuse of power. Half a century of S-type feminism has also helped erode belief in the possibility of reciprocal loving relationships between men and women. In failing to recognise the significance of E-type thought, my generation didn't just underestimate the contribution of our foremothers to human well-being and progress. We also underestimated the contribution of well-balanced men.

A man-made world is inevitably founded on the idea of power re-lationships. But E-type thought still informed many men's thinking (thanks to their mothers and other loving adults) and they gallantly tried to integrate emotional intelligence into the way civilisations de-veloped. Perhaps if the sisterhood had noticed these attempts to sys-temise empathy and had built on them, things would have worked out better over the last 50 years. Like all S-type attempts to systemise E-type thinking, they only work up to a point. Still, they're the best shots anyone's had at the problem so far, so it seems foolish to dis-miss them out of hand.

I believe the two most useful of these E-type systemisations are 'manners' and 'morals'. Manners are ways of behaving respectfully to others on a face-to-face basis. Morals (from the Latin *mores*, meaning 'customs') are socially accepted conventions for respectful behaviour in the public realm.

Manners maketh man

Since men are renownedly keen for power, the 20th century 'gender wars' focused attention on power struggles between the sexes. How-ever, in personal relationships, balanced men have always recom-mended ways of behaving based on E-type thought, such as kindness, consideration for other people's feelings and respect for a compan-ion's point of view. The 14th century bishop William of Wykeham summed up the importance of this emotionally intelligent behaviour in the aphorism 'Manners maketh man', which (like 'love your

> 'Manners maketh man',
> which is such a good motto
> that it's resonated down
> through the centuries.

neighbour as yourself') is such a good motto that it's resonated down through the centuries.

It's the motto of, among other places, New College, Oxford, which Wykeham founded. The reason I love it so much is explained in the Wikipedia entry for New College, which I like to imagine being penned by some ageing don. He tells us that the saying was 'revolutionary' because:

> ... it makes a social statement. While it might initially seem to be suggesting that it is beneficial to have good manners, this does not really capture its full scope. What it really means is that it is not by birth, money or property that an individual is defined, but by how he (or she) behaves towards other people.

E-type skills may not come as naturally to boys as to girls, but the importance of kindness, consideration for other people's feelings and respect for their point of view can be taught, through reason and example, to just about anyone. So the exercise of 'good manners' became the decent male answer to the potential imbalance of power in any personal relationship.

In Wykeham's day, a man who understood this principle was known as a gentleman. Gentleness rather than roughness in personal relationships indicated that he valued his own humanity and that of others. In his relationships with women, it showed he had the potential to love and to be loved. But for a man to show gentleness is also an act of courage because it makes him emotionally vulnerable, and displays of emotional vulnerability don't come easily to a testosterone-driven male. So, in male–female relationships, women were expected to be gentle too. According to medieval mores, their job was to act with grace, i.e., recognising a gentle man's mannerliness in a ladylike way.

As I said earlier, all S-type attempts to systemise E-type thought only work up to a point. It's extremely easy for ruthless or dim individuals to interpret 'manners' with stupefying superficiality. During Wykeham's time, Chaucer pointed out how the idea was abused in The Canterbury Tales. Since then, over the centuries, good manners have been systemised as etiquette, 'gentleman' and 'lady' turned into sou-briquets for members of the moneyed classes, and a great common-sense idea trivialised into snobbery. But men and women who valued E-type thought nevertheless hung on to the idea of good manners, as a gentle, graceful way of demonstrating their good intent.

That's why I think it was so unfortunate that 20th century feminists chose to sneer at manifestations of male good manners. Behaviour such as opening doors, carrying bags and giving up one's seat to a 'lady' may seem sexist to someone who's perfectly capable of look-ing after herself, and if the men who perform them are merely abid-ing by the rules of etiquette their actions are as worthless as they've ever been. But for many men these were small gestures that showed kindness, consideration and respect, and when 20th century women gracelessly rejected them, they added to the communication gap be-tween the sexes.

However, there's one area of life in which Wykeham's revolu-tionary idea still has currency: child-rearing. Caring parents still raise their children to be well mannered, and in families with a strong E-type streak this isn't just a matter of saying 'Please' and 'Thank you' but an at-titude of mind, requiring conscious control of one's emotions. Children learn by paren-tal example to be sensitive to other people's feelings, and to take them into account in their personal interactions.

> Children learn by parental example to be sensitive to other people's feelings.

A girl who's been brought up by loving adults is likely to under-stand the importance of manners in sexual relationships. When she's old enough to start dating, her boyfriend's general behaviour towards others will tell her a lot. A 'gentle' young man who demonstrates so-cial sensitivity is likely to understand the importance of 'courtship'. He'd probably therefore make a considerate sexual partner and, if the chemistry is right, he'll be more open to the possibility of mutual fun turning into love.

Nevertheless, it takes a lot of E-type experience to recognise the difference between genuine and assumed good manners, so girls also need to know the importance of distrusting charm. It's an extremely attractive quality in either sex but, when not accompanied by a decent value system, usually leads to exploitation. Today it's known as 'psychological manipulation' and you can find websites giving tips on how to do it.

In a world where recreational sex is the norm, boys and girls need to know that 'gentleness' towards the opposite sex is still a marker of emotional courage. Being open to emotional connection may make them vulnerable, but it also empowers them to feel love. And the glory of love is that it releases us from the mundane and material, connects us with something beyond ourselves and our beloved, and reminds us of wonder. If we cut off our access to love, we lose everything that's precious about being human.

O tempora! O mores!

This brings us to morality. Oh dear!

Times change, and we're all children of our times. Customs change, and we're all enmeshed within the customs of our culture. In the mid-20th century, when I was born, it was clear that the human race had reached a critical point in its development. The bloodbaths of two world wars, culminating in the invention of weapons of mass destruction, suggested we were perilously close to annihilating our own species. The sexual revolution was part of a general re-evaluation of our collective thought processes.

If, at the time, we'd had any inkling of the significance of E-type thought, perhaps educated women could have made a significant contribution to this re-evaluation. Perhaps we'd have recognised the importance of raising emotionally intelligent children, and convinced men that this is as important a human task as making money and shaping the world. As it was, most educated women were as unaware of the contribution of empathy to human well-being and progress as educated men. So it was left to systemisers of both sexes to sort out a new world order, and they chose to trust in competitive consumerism as the means of achieving global peace.

And so, sadly, we missed the chance to build on another gallant male attempt to systemise E-type thought: the idea of moral standards. I suspect that, in the UK at least, this was partly due to growing disillusion with religion, which has dictated morality in the past. But probably the most important factor was the apparent incompatibility of any E-informed philosophy with an economic world view that depends on selfish individualism. So instead of any identifiable standards of moral behaviour, we ended up with a vague moral relativism, loosely based on ideas of individual freedom and tolerance of a variety of views.

We've now been muddling along with this for more than half a century, during which the words 'freedom' and 'tolerance' have acquired a very hollow ring. In terms of sexual behaviour, it's led to the exploitative free-for-all described earlier in this chapter. As for general standards of behaviour, scarcely a week goes by without news of financial scandals, bullying, cheating or corruption in public, professional or corporate life. In a moral climate based on the premise that

> The words 'freedom' and 'tolerance' have acquired a very hollow ring.

'money maketh man', we can't be surprised if ruthless, self-serving individuals rise to the top of the heap, and then find endless ways of exploiting liberal ideals for their own ends.

We've thus learned the hard way that an economic system designed to support selfish individualism doesn't encourage socially responsible behaviour. Moral relativism doesn't work. We need a non-commercial source of authority to reassert the importance of E-type thought – one that's strong enough to challenge the interests of global corporations and reassert the power of the personal.

I know I'm far from alone in these opinions, and will return to the subject of morality in the Conclusion. In the meantime, the best advice I can offer the parents of girls in an age of moral relativity is to make sure that their daughters know three things.

- Women who allow themselves to be used sexually, or who model their own sex lives on those of men behaving badly through the ages, deny their own humanity – sexual exploitation is sexual exploitation, no matter who does what to whom

- There is nothing wrong with wanting to be desired, but women who turn themselves into little more than an object of desire also deny their humanity – objectification is objectification, even if you choose to objectify yourself.

- There's no recipe for a happy sex life, no way of avoiding pain if things go wrong, no guarantee that you'll ever find The One. But there is one eternal truth: *love matters*. In the absence of a widely accepted moral code, hold fast to that.

However, any parents who would agree these messages are important for their own daughters must inevitably recognise that they're important for all children (male and female) everywhere. So I believe that the grown-ups among us, who know love matters, have a social responsibility to challenge the normalisation, by media and marketing, of frankly immoral behaviour that exploits the dark side of sex for financial gain.

> Love matters, manners matter, morality matters, and I'm going to stick up for all of them.

There – I've said it. Love matters, manners matter, morality matters, and I'm going to stick up for all of them. Now, call me Mrs Mary Whitehouse and throw me to the lions.

***

Perhaps by now you've googled the information I listed a few pages ago. If so, you'll know how important it is for 21st century girls to be self-confident, resilient, assertive and able to think for themselves. Once pornography and the sex industry went mainstream, sexual exploitation moved into new realms. However, a girl who's had a good enough childhood should be able to make sensible decisions about the way she conducts her sex life.

But being self-confident, resilient, assertive and able to think for oneself isn't enough. To preserve their own vital emotional core, today's girls (and boys) also need to know about the importance of

E-type thought, and to value it in themselves and others. Above all, they need to know that being empathetic is *not* the same as being a pushover.

If a girl doesn't understand all this, she may end up like poor Ginnie, convinced that the lyrics of gangsta rap are worth listening to, and that brutality is an attractive quality in a male. Or she might choose the same route as three attractive, articulate teenage girls interviewed by Natasha Walter. They'd been running their sex lives for several years along thoroughly S-type male lines and were deeply scornful of boys who got '*soppy ... emotional and wimpy*'. Their 'sexual self-confidence' depended on ruthless exploitation of male totty.

Walter's concern about these girls and other casualties of 'growing up in a material world' really raised my hopes for 21st century feminism. But within a few chapters she'd joined in with the demolition job on Simon Baron-Cohen's S- and E-type theories, raging on behalf of womankind at the suggestion that we might be a teeny bit less good on the S-type front, and showing not the slightest interest in women's slight superiority in empathising. Perhaps one day, the sisterhood will spot that gender stereotyping, the objectification of women and the commercialisation of sex are, like so many social ills, the result of the profound S/E imbalance in society. But, until then, I fear that raging against the sexualisation of girls and young women will just take them round in ever-decreasing circles.

Sex and Relationships Timeline

1–6 years

Spend as much time as you can with your daughter. The quality of the 'dance of communication' with you (and your partner) will underpin the quality of her relationships throughout life.

Enjoy physical closeness and touch (e.g., try an infant massage course with your baby).

Use the correct vocabulary when talking about her private parts from the beginning (i.e., before she can talk), and prepare to be matter-of-fact about conversations related to sex.

When the occasion arises, talk about what's okay in private but not in public. For instance, toddlers often masturbate – if she does, don't tell her off, but explain it's very private behaviour.

On other occasions, use the private/public topic to ensure she knows not to let anyone touch her in 'private' ways without permission. And tell her always to tell you if she's worried.

When she asks questions about sex, give direct, age-appropriate responses. If you can't think of a good reply offhand, say, *'That's a very good question – we'll talk about it later'* ... and do so!

Buy a book on sex and relationships or consult websites such as BBC Health (www.bbc.co.uk/health) or the Mayo Clinic (www.mayoclinic.com), so that you'll be armed with good answers in advance.

The more time she spends with her father (and the more loving and open their relationship), the more confident she'll be in the future – both in herself and in her relationships with the opposite sex.

6–11 years

Maintain a strong emotional bond with your daughter, by spending time with her, enjoying her company and giving her lots of physical affection. Let her know that both her parents are always there for her and are always ready to answer her questions.

Always answer questions about sex frankly (without going into more detail than necessary for her age), and use everyday opportunities, such as something in the news or a TV programme, to open up conversations yourself.

Use everyday opportunities to talk about relationships too, and the importance of love, trust and respect. Help her to see the emotional consequences of manipulation and exploitation (TV and celebrity culture are a rich source for discussion here).

If it hasn't already cropped up by the time she's about eight (such as when you see an ad for tampons), explain about periods and the other bodily changes she can expect at puberty.

Remember that she'll be hearing about sex from her friends too, and their conversations will be informed by contemporary culture. So explain the difference between porn and sex, and reassure her that the sex in 'pornland' is not normal sex.

As she gets older make sure she knows about the dangers of sex (e.g., unwanted pregnancy, sexually transmitted diseases and the consequences for girls of allowing people to 'objectify' them). But make sure she also knows that in a committed relationship sex is the ultimate, and wonderful, expression of love between adults.

Get her an up-to-date, age-appropriate 'facts of life' book so that she can read up on the subject herself. But don't use a book as a substitute for listening and talking to her about sex and relationships.

11–16 years

Find out about the sex education policy at your daughter's secondary school. Make sure you know what it covers so you can fill in any gaps.

From now on, conversations about sex are even more important; today's teenage girls need to feel confident about resisting 'peer pressure' and making decisions that are right for them.

If you've always been open about sex, there'll probably be no difficulty in maintaining openness as she grows older, but some conversations may be difficult so prepare yourself in advance (the Mayo Clinic advice is very helpful).

Struggling with many physical and social changes, adolescent girls find it difficult to talk about some issues, so make sure age-appropriate information is available whenever she needs it (e.g., the Family Planning Association's 4Girls booklet from the FPA website (www.fpa.org.uk).

If she does withdraw from you, ask a trusted female adult friend to help by offering a listening ear and acting as a 'mentor'. Girls need access to wise adult advice about dating and sexual health.

Welcome boyfriends as well as girlfriends into your home. Don't pry into her relationships – she's entitled to privacy about her personal life – but let her know you're there if she needs to talk.

Keep an eye open for signs of emotional upset, and offer comfort. But unless you're really worried, wait for her to open up to you.

If she starts a serious relationship, discuss the implications of sexual involvement – this may be a tricky conversation, so think it through in advance. Be 'warm but firm' about your views, but take her feelings into account too. In the final analysis, the most important things are her safety and maintaining your relationship.

16 years +

At 16, she's legally entitled to have sex so it's no longer your responsibility. But if you think she's making a mistake, you're still her parent and are entitled to an opinion. Always keep lines of communication open, and give her support if anything goes wrong.

CONCLUSION

My interview with Simon Baron-Cohen was memorable. I read his book *The Essential Difference: Men, Women and the Extreme Male Brain* shortly after finishing *Toxic Childhood*, when my head was buzzing with research and expert advice on child-rearing, and I was keen to find out more about the developmental differences between boys and girls. His S- and E-type division fitted really well with what I'd already found out about two things:

- the inborn drives for attachment and play which, on the whole, seemed to take girls down a more social path and boys towards exploration of the material world
- the hugely different marketing strategies aimed at boys and girls, men and women.

He was kind enough to grant me an interview, and I turned up in Cambridge at five to ten on the appointed day, and knocked on his office door. There was no one there, so I sat on the stone steps of the huge draughty college building and waited. And waited.

After almost an hour a man appeared on the stairs. I could tell it was Professor Baron-Cohen, because there was a slight family resemblance to his cousin Sacha (who at the time was better known as Borat). The poor man was mortified at forgetting the appointment, and didn't want to send me all the way back to Edinburgh without my interview, but he had a tutorial booked for eleven which he couldn't possibly postpone. It was with a brilliant student, who was also severely autistic so would be extremely upset if her routine were disrupted.

We agreed to attempt a compromise. When the student arrived he explained the situation and asked if she'd mind listening in for a while. She took out a handheld computer and immersed herself in a game, but every so often made angry noises which were definitely directed at me.

It was an extremely tense half-hour, but I managed to ask a few questions about early brain development and on one occasion the student furnished some facts her professor wasn't sure about. There was, however, no way just to get him talking, which is what I'd really come for. You can find out people's theories from their books – interviews are for chatting round the theories, to try and make an E-type connection. And there was something I specially wanted to chat about.

In his book, Baron-Cohen describes a number of people with extreme male brains: men who are intellectually brilliant (usually within a very limited field) but completely hopeless in terms of social interaction. Great at systemising, rubbish at empathising. Then he points out that, although we know what an outstanding systemiser looks like (we call them geniuses), there's as yet no agreement on what constitutes outstanding empathisers. Might they, for instance, be people with 'extra-sensory perception'?

So eventually I brought up the subject of great empathisers. The professor sighed. Apparently, people are always writing to him with theories about that. A few are interesting, most are cranky.

It didn't bode well, but I decided to press on. 'I've got a theory,' I volunteered.

He sighed again and picked up some papers from his desk. 'Uh huh?'

'Yes. I think the great empathisers of history have been good mothers.'

In The Essential Difference, there's an empathy test – you have to look at pictures of people's eyes and decide which of four emotions they convey. (As I expected, my score was average.) While blurting out my 'theory', I couldn't see Professor Baron-Cohen's eyes because he was studiously inspecting the papers, but his body language was eloquent.

'I mean *good* mothers,' I added hastily. 'Not possessive ...um... not mothers who don't know when to back off... '

He granted me a brief look. Quizzical? Impatient? Bored? Pitying? I haven't the faintest idea.

Spread a little empathy

Fortunately, before I could dig myself in any deeper, the brilliant autistic student indicated – very loudly indeed – that my time was up. I escaped down the echoing staircase, feeling rattled. What *had* I been thinking of? *Good mothers*, for goodness sake! It wasn't till the words left my lips that I realised how vague, sexist and judgemental they sounded.

I've since decided that instead of 'mothers' I should have said 'primary attachment figures' – i.e. people who care for babies in the few years of life. It's in the early years that mothering – as opposed to parenting – really matters. Also, it sounds less sexist and more scientific. Instead of 'good mothers' I could have expanded it to something like 'primary attachment figures who are really skilled at tuning in to o- to 3-year-olds in order to support their developmental needs'. It isn't very snappy, but more precise, and without the judgemental overtone.

It also puts the focus on the importance of empathy in mothering. The greater a mother's capacity for empathy, the more responsive she's likely to be – not only to the child's physical needs, but to emotional, social and cognitive needs as well.

Every woman starts her mothering career with a huge E-type boost, because of the physical and emotional bonds forged by pregnancy, childbirth and breastfeeding. But as time goes on, a mum like me with only average E-type skills can be easily distracted. I love my daughter beyond all measure, but I'm not naturally skilled at empathising so I didn't know exactly how to apply my love – that's why I encouraged her to tune in to a video, rather than tuning in to her myself. I suspect contemporary phenomena such as helicopter mothering and the sub-stitution of presents for presence are variations on the same theme.

In recent years, I've had opportunities to watch talented E-typers interacting with small children that aren't vouchsafed to many women these days. My work has brought me into contact with many mothers and other people who spend time with small children – nursery nurses, early years teachers, childminders, fosterers and health service workers – and among them there have been some highly gifted empathisers. Their ability to read infant minds (and provide exactly the sort of response and/or support they need at the time) is extraordinarily impressive. Children adore them, and colleagues appreciate that they're special and learn from watching them.

The 'theory' I developed as a result of this experience is that tal-ented E-type mothers have probably always acted as role models to other mums. In close-knit communities, where women shared do-mestic duties, less naturally empathetic mothers (like me) would notice a gifted E-typer in their midst, see the advantages of copying her behaviour, and thus improve their own interactions with their off-spring. Girls growing up in the neighbourhood would learn from her too, and put the lessons into practice when they had babies of their own. Older women could incorporate the insights of good mothers into the child-rearing lore they passed around the community. Over time, the value that women placed on 'good mothering' would help more mothers develop the skills of E-type thought.

But then, in the mid-20th century, everything changed. Efficient contraception meant women spent less of their lives child-rearing; increasing wealth and geographical mobility led to the disintegration of traditional communities; the sexual revolution focused women's attention away from the home and on to competing with men in the workplace. The collaborative element of child-rearing – including the influence of 'good mothers'– rapidly disappeared, and there was no one left to value the significance of early E-type input in helping turn little children into well-balanced, responsible citizens.

Why motherhood matters

The 1960s feminists defined sexual equality mainly in terms of economic independence, so women's status has ever since been based, like men's, on the type of job they do and their earning power. Motherhood is irrelevant to this public identity, and having a baby is widely treated as little more than an inconvenient interruption to women's working lives. Over time the very idea of motherhood has been subsumed into the gender-neutral concept of 'parenting', while childcare is regarded as something to be fitted around parents' jobs, or farmed out to low-paid, carers.

It's increasingly apparent, however, that in the first couple of years of children's lives, motherhood matters. First and foremost, it matters to the children. Babies need someone to care for them, someone who loves them unconditionally, and is therefore prepared to be there twenty-four hours a day, tending to all of their physical and emotional needs. While anyone can fulfil this role, the most obvious candidate is the child's mother, who already (as a result of pregnancy and childbirth) has a close physical and emotional connection to her baby. So mothers are overwhelmingly the most likely people to become the child's primary attachment figure.

Motherhood also matters to society. In her book *The Selfish Society: How We All Forgot To Love One Other and Made Money Instead* the psychologist Sue Gerhardt explains how influential primary attachment figures are in terms of each generation's social development:

> The moral and emotional issues that we have to deal with as a society are the same as those we begin to grasp in the cradle: how we learn to pay attention to others and their feelings, how we manage conflict and how we balance our own needs with those of others. Morality is about the way we manage the interface between self and society, an interface that starts in babyhood and is learned from the actual practice of early relating. This gives early child-rearing a prime place in our cultural life.

She argues cogently that lack of attention to early attachment over several decades is implicated in many contemporary social ills, not least the growth of selfish individualism, increasingly fragile personal relationships, and the widening gap between rich and poor.

Finally, and unsurprisingly, motherhood matters to mothers. Pregnancy and childbirth are significant emotional experiences in a woman's life, as is the rush of mother-love with which nature prepares her to care for her infant. Most new mothers soon realise they want (even *need*) to take on this caring role, despite the problems involved in a career break and the implications of a period of financial dependency. Yet our cultural concept of motherhood is so wrapped up in negative attitudes to traditional women's work that many women (particularly well-educated ones with reasonably high-status jobs) find the sudden transition to the low-status occupation of child-carer triggers a serious identity crisis. Stopping work to be stay-at-home mums for a year or so results in what Naomi Wolf has described as 'acute social demotion'.

With hindsight it's obvious that underestimating the significance of motherhood would eventually lead the sexual equality project into serious difficulties. When they failed to take this critical biological factor into account in the definition of sexual equality, those 1960s feminists unintentionally created the conditions for a new version of female 'victimhood'. Any woman who judges her worth in terms of the ability to compete on male terms in the workplace is bound to feel wanting when biology tugs her so decisively in another direction: Wolf's 'social demotion' is in the mother's own eyes as much as anyone else's. A great female strength – the capacity to care for her babies – has been turned into a social liability.

Genuine equality obviously depends on men and women sharing the rewards and responsibilities of parenthood, and after the first couple of years of their baby's life, this should be perfectly possible, with both parents organising their working lives to accommodate childcare in the way that works best for them. But if every baby's birth is accompanied by an emotional, practical and/or financial dilemma for the mother (leaving her feeling put-upon, socially devalued and exhausted) it's not surprising that the majority of men haven't yet seen the rewards of hands-on care as worth sharing at all.

Now that science is proving the huge social importance of the primary attachment figure, there's an opportunity to re-evaluate the significance of mothers' contribution to society, and in doing so, to change the cultural concept of care. If the feminist movement were to take it, we could start to unpick some of the damage wrought by the socio-cultural storm of the last few decades. It does, however, depend on women rediscovering the personal rewards of motherhood.

What do 'good mothers' do?

Sadly, most new mothers are now seriously unprepared for the role of primary attachment figure. Education has equipped them for the fast-paced, S-type world of the workplace, not the slow, baby-centric world of motherhood. Most modern mums have had little to do with babies before meeting their own so – despite the heady rush of mother-love – they feel anxious, inadequate and insecure about how to proceed. Few can expect support from an extended family or a close-knit community, so they often find themselves socially isolated for long tracts of time. And the only role models on offer are the celebrity yummy mummies on all-day TV and the smiling Stepford Wives in the advertisements ... all of whom focus mums' attention on appearances and acquisitions, rather than on tuning in to their babies' minds.

This is why I became so interested in the 'good mothers' I met on my travels. They clearly found their interactions with babies and toddlers extremely rewarding, and the children were similarly delighted to spend time interacting with them. What was it that made these women (they *were* all women) so keen on a mothering role? If their enjoyment could be bottled in some way, perhaps it would be possible to reinvigorate the concept of maternal care?

Over the last decade, I've had many conversations on the subject, with mothers, developmental psychologists and caring professionals. My conclusion is that, right from the beginning, talented E-type mums see their babies as unique personalities with minds of their own. This means they're just as interested in communicating with them as in keeping them safe, well fed and comfortable. During every interaction (feeding, nappy-changing, dressing, bath-time, etc.) they look for emotional rewards by making emotional connections.

Their E-type skills mean they swiftly recognise behaviour that encourages these connections (cuddling, stroking, rocking, singing, exaggerating their facial expressions and talking in the sing-song, rhythmic, often nonsensical language of 'motherese') so they engage in the time-honoured dance of communication whatever they're doing and as often as possible. All of this attention and responsiveness is emotionally rewarding to the babies, who then respond in kind. And the mutual meeting of minds keeps 'good mothers' joyfully focused on their babies' feelings and intentions ... and safe from 21st century distractions.

Because they're constantly trying to see the world from their child's perspective, rather than their own adult one, they tend to talk about what they intuit is going on in the baby's mind. This provides a sort of running commentary about what he or she is doing (*'Oh, you like splashing the water!'*), experiencing (*'It's nice and soft, isn't it?'*) or attending to (*'Yes – it's a doggy!'*) which must, over time, have an impact on the child's language development. But they're not consciously trying to 'teach' – they're just enjoying a shared experience. As is the baby.

The importance of taking a 'child's eye view' is particularly stressed by specialists in early years education, who tell me that gifted practitioners *watch* little children play, while trying to divine what's going on in their minds. This respectful, insightful observation helps them support play in ways that encourage learning while being fun for all concerned. A talented E-type mother is also natural child-watcher, so for her enjoyable play is a feature of the communicatory dance. As it's enormously satisfying to share infant wonderment at the tiny details of everyday life we jaded adults take for granted, the mutual rewards continue to flow.

All these real-life observations and conversations seemed to fit neatly with the developmental literature I've come across over the last decade, including a 2004 research paper about 'maternal mind-mindedness', saying that some mothers appear to predict their infants' intentions, apparently by 'reading their minds'. As the years went by the word 'attunement' began to crop up in conversations with psychologists and literature about adult-child interactions and that helped a lot. Now there was a word for what I'd seen – 'tuning in to' another mind is a great way of summing up the process of E-type engagement. While it's relatively easy if the other mind belongs to someone with similar experiences to one's own, tuning in to a tiny baby's thought processes requires a level of E-type talent far above the average. These mind-reading mothers have something to teach the rest of us.

Tuning in to children

In 2012, as I was finishing this book, I heard Dr Elizabeth Meins – one of the psychologists behind the 'maternal mind-mindedness' paper – say on a radio programme that she and her colleagues at the University of Durham have completed a long-term study showing that highly attuned mothers tend to raise more securely attached children. It seems that science is finally catching up with what's come naturally to 'good mothers' through the ages. Perhaps we're on the verge of finding effective 21st century ways of reintroducing positive role models of motherhood.

It's impossible to give a recipe for maternal attunement, because it's entirely context-dependent, rooted in real-life interactions in real time and space. However, there's now video footage showing highly-attuned mothers interacting with babies and toddlers (e.g. see the trailer for Dr Suzanne Zeedyk's DVD of *The Connected Baby*). There's also a fascinating YouTube clip, showing what happens when a tuned-in mum ceases to connect with her baby (see Dr Edward Tronick's *Still Face Experiment*), which I've watched make a notable impact on a range of audiences. Combined with information about child development, this sort of visual information about effective mothering could be a starting point for educating all potential parents in the need for E-type input in child-rearing.

It would be wonderful if every 21st century girl could learn about the importance of tuning in to babies. Not only could it help develop her own mothering skills for the future, it would celebrate her foremothers' contribution to society, and illustrate the significance of E-type thought in the nurturing of relationships. Even girls who don't eventually choose to have children themselves would be brighter and more balanced women for appreciating what mothering is all about (and less likely to see career breaks for motherhood in a negative light).

Of course, 21st century boys would benefit from learning about attunement too. Men may be less likely to find themselves acting as primary attachment figures, but fathers are the most significant secondary attachment figures for both sons and daughters. The more attuned dads are to their offspring from the start, the sooner they'll discover the rewards of hands-on involvement, and the more inclined they'll be to collaborate with their partners in genuinely shared, tuned in, authoritative parenting once the intensive mothering phase is over. (Authoritative parenting also involves attunement: it's a key aspect of 'warmth' in warm-but-firm parental behaviour.)

The obvious way to start would be by giving E-type thought a valued place in the education system. The *Roots of Empathy* programme from Canada, in which mothers and babies are invited into primary classrooms, has a long track record for developing young children's social and emotional intelligence. A follow-up course about child development at secondary level, including the sort of video footage mentioned above, would help stress the value of care, as would the inclusion of practical community-based projects for all young people from the age of 14 (as I describe in *21st Century Boys*). Sadly, there's little chance of UK education systems making these sorts of adaptations in the near future so the best we can hope is that information about the significance of attachment and attunement will soon be included in antenatal courses.

My advice to the parents of 21st century girls is to include discussion of motherhood in the on-going dialogue with their daughter about sex and relationships, to ensure she has plenty of opportunities to mix with mothers and babies as she grows up and, by finding the time to tune into her feelings throughout her childhood, model the 'female' strength of E-type thought.

O tempora! O mores! (reprise)

Unfortunately, as the sexual revolution temporarily blinded us all to the importance of E-type input in child-rearing, the impact of the two other great cultural fronts behind the perfect storm has added to the problem of reviving its popularity. The screen-based technology that now allows us to tune in to videos of attunement has also provided innumerable alternative diversions. Thus, technology constantly distracts adults and children from real-life interaction of any kind. And in family homes saturated with electronic media, there's no shortage of consumerist marketing messages, promoting exciting new products to distract us even further.

We certainly live in interesting times – especially for parents. It's obvious that the techno-consumerist values infecting society at large are now completely at odds with the human values underpinning attuned mothering, authoritative parenting and – in the long run – all successful human relationships. In any society where money and status are valued far above love and care, responsible loving parents inevitably feel like a besieged moral minority.

In my newfound role as a moraliser, I regularly find myself supporting calls for government to help parents fulfil their vital social role, such as

- banning any type of marketing to children under the age of 12
- introducing a statutory opt-in requirement for 'adult' content on the internet, making it much more difficult for under-18s to access pornography
- requiring manufacturers to conduct rigorous research before marketing new products for children, if there are any grounds to suspect they could be developmentally harmful (as is required of the pharmaceutical industry before marketing a new drug).

These seem to me fairly mild suggestions for protecting the next generation from the rampant commercialisation and sexualisation of childhood. Sadly, whatever party is in power, these days economic considerations always trump ethical ones for politicians, so there's no political appetite for reining in corporate greed. This means it's left to parents to police the global marketplace, protect their children from the dark side of the internet and personally decide when to exercise the precautionary principle in a world where new products hit the shelves almost hourly.

It's just as well there are also intense joys in child-rearing! Fortunately, when mothers and fathers tune in to their children rather than the perfect storm raging outside their family home, they immediately remember what is truly valuable about human existence. From the moment they're born, children remind us about the value of human life, the importance of love as opposed to money, and the immense power of the personal, even in a depersonalised hyper-systemised culture.

Parental love is probably the greatest force on the planet, and has seen humanity through many other dark ages – in the end, I'm sure it'll help humankind find a way through this particular storm. But just now, for many parents love for their children is the only guiding light in a bewildering moral maelstrom. If they don't have a religious faith or allegiance to some other ethically based value system, they really are on their own... unless they can find some moral support.

It takes a village... (reprise)

At the end of Part One of this book, I recommended that parents seek out a 'village' of like-minded adults to help raise their children because:

- it would provide peer support in resisting commercial pressures
- authoritative parenting is much easier in the context of an authoritative community with shared values and approaches.

In fact, you can't start looking for moral support too soon. The moment any young woman decides to have a baby, I'd advise her and her partner to start building a real-life social network of other young parents and/or parents-to-be. The social isolation that all too often attends the transition from working woman to stay-at-home mum isn't good for either her or her baby, so she needs a ready-made sympathetic social circle, such as other mothers in her local neighbourhood, and new mums met at an antenatal course or via organisations like MAMA (Meet A Mum Association).

Many mothers have told me that friendships forged in these circumstances have been among the strongest and most sustaining of their lives, so they're the ideal basis for moral support in child-rearing. There are opportunities to find further villagers at every stage of a child's life – clubs and activities for new mums; fellow parents at nursery, primary or secondary school; the parents of one's offspring's friends, and so on. At the very least, these are people to talk to about parenting dilemmas; at the most, they could help to change the world.

Working together with other people is an opportunity to value the power of personal relationships over systems and spending power. For busy parents, there could be advantages in branching out into more practical mutual support, such as:

- shared arrangements for babysitting and after-school care
- shared organisation of the school run, and delivery of children to clubs, etc.
- pairs or groups of parents taking turns to supervise children's outdoor play, in the local neighbourhood or park (from messing about for an hour or so after school, to organised expeditions, games of football, etc.)
- emergency childcare, from known and trusted sources
- shared birthday parties and other celebrations, such as Hallowe'en and Bonfire Night (including agreed limits on expenditure, to prevent 'birthday party competition')
- communal outings and trips (or even holidays) where children can play and parents relax together.

This sort of co-operation between families could solve many difficulties for working parents. Indeed, mums already often help each other out in one or more of the ways listed, following in a long female tradition of collaboration in the process of care. In a modern 'village', connected by social networking sites and instant messaging, it would be relatively easy to extend the collaborative ethos, to everyone's advantage.

It might also be a way of encouraging shared parenting. My advice to any mums who decide to collaborate over aspects of childcare is to involve their male partners as soon as possible in enjoyable social events. Without wishing to stereotype, I've noticed that men are often particularly good at setting up and supervising outdoor activities for children and enjoy organising aspects of outdoor social gatherings. Since getting 21st century children outdoors is a child-rearing priority, they obviously have an important role to play.

Working together on family-based projects of this kind would give fathers the opportunity to strike up male relationships based around their children's welfare, rather than work. These could then be developed to keep the village ethos sexually equal, which is, of course, an important aim for the fathers of girls.

We've spent 50 years pursuing sexual equality along traditionally 'male' competitive lines, with the focus on working life. It hasn't worked out particularly well. So it seems appropriate to end a book about raising bright, balanced girls with a suggestion for drawing on the two traditionally 'female' strengths of care and collaboration to help parents of both sexes redress the balance of their lives.

***

It's impossible to imagine the world our girls will inhabit when they reach adulthood. As our culture evolves at an ever-crazier pace, the opportunities, choices and challenges they'll encounter will be very different from those women face today. But the social, emotional and intellectual strengths they'll need to face them will be the same, and so will the human nature from which those strengths emerge.

The more attuned parents are to their daughter as a unique individual, the greater the chances of her maximising those strengths. Their empathetic interest will help her grow up self-aware and self-confident, ready to make the most of all her opportunities. If they also maintain a warm-but-firm authoritative balance (veering neither to over-control nor over-indulgence) she'll also acquire the self-discipline needed to steer through the minefield of 21st century girl-hood. Add in the personal skills she learns through 'real play', and she's ready to choose her own personal path to fulfilment ... and to face any challenges fate throws in her way with realism and resilience.

This bright, balanced 21st century girl isn't likely to be distracted from her personal route to fulfilment by impossible dreams of perfection. She'll recognise that systems have their limitations, that human well-being can't be bought in the shops, and that the 20th century feminist dream of 'Having It All' has merely led to disillusion and new versions of 'female victimhood'.

Instead (if she chooses to become a mother) she can value those two 'female' strengths – care and collaboration – and help move the great sexual equality project on to the next level. Working with other enlightened 21st century men and women, she can seek out sustainable, personally fulfilling ways of Sharing It All.

NOTES AND REFERENCES

Introduction

The erosion of childhood

'Fascinating voyage of discovery' – see Palmer, 2006, 2007, 2009 and Chapter 4 of this book.

The erosion of childhood – see House et al, 2011. Also the 'Save Childhood' movement, launched in 2012 (www.savechildhood.net).

Theory of American essayist Neil Postman – see Postman 1994.

Recent campaigns to save childhood – e.g. see Save Childhood (above), www.allianceforchildhood.org , www.earlychildhoodaction.com.

Mind the gender gap

Young girls losing virginity before boys – NHS's Health Survey for England, 2010 (www.ic.nhs.uk/webfiles/publications/003_Health_Lifestyles/ HSE2010_REPORT/HSE2010_Ch6_Sexual_health.pdf).

On body image problems in girls as young as five – see the All Party Parliamentary Group on Body Image's 2012 report, *Reflections on Body Image* (http://issuu.com/bodyimage/docs/reflections_on_body_image?mode= window&backgroundColor=%23222222).

Outbreak of feminist literature – see Banyard, 2010, Fine, 2010, Walter, 2010, Asher, 2011.

PART ONE

Chapter 1: Material Girls

Sophisticated toys can stunt children's long-term development – see Linn 2008, Goddard Blythe, 2008.

The plague of pink

Boys' and girls' gendered play – e.g. Moir and Moir, 1999.

Children as a lucrative market for parental 'guilt money' – see Schor, 2005.

Biological development and children's interest in the peer group– see Richard A. Lippa's book *Gender, Nature and Nurture, second ed.* (Taylor & Francis, 2009).

About 'pinkification' of girls and gender stereotypes – e.g. 'Pink makes me see red! A leading child development author attacks the marketing firms who target little girls' (22 January 2009).

Pink Stinks pressure group, 2009 – www.pinkstinks.co.uk.

Girls on top

Girls' educational attainment (at time of writing) – for girls' head start, see Department for Education figures (www.education.gov.uk/cgi-bin/rsgateway/search.pl?keyw=184&q2=Search and www.education.gov.uk/cgi-bin/rsgateway/search.pl?keyw=066&q2=Search) and for their superiority in later educational achievement, see Paton, Graeme: 'David Willetts warns about "striking" university gender gap', *Daily Telegraph*, 6 11 2011. www.telegraph.co.uk/education/universityeducation/8873031/David-Willetts-warns-over-striking-university-gender-gap.html. For information on gender gap in Special Educational Needs, see Palmer 2009

'Statistics suggest girls only half as likely to suffer from emotional, behavioural and mental health problems' – British Medical Association *Child and Adolescent Mental Health: A Guide for Healthcare Professionals* (2006). However, psychologists I've spoken to suggest this may be because mental health and emotional problems manifest themselves differently in boys – see Chapter 9 **...and under-educated boys**.

Women don't fulfil their early promise and men still dominate upper echelons – see Banyard, 2010.

On single and stay-at-home mothers – see Banyard, 2010 and Asher, 2011.

From pink to precocity

Government reports on 'the sexualisation of children' – Papadopoulous Review, *The Sexualisation of Young People* 2010, Bailey Review, *Letting Children Be Children*, 2011.

Kids Are Getting Older Younger marketing strategies– see Lindstrom 2003, Linn, 2005, Shor, 2005.

Coda

Well-being more important than material excess – see, e.g. Layard, 2005; potential for happiness laid down in childhood – see, e.g. Martin, 2005.

Chapter 2: Stone Age Girls

Genes and gender

Theories of evolutionary biologists. The major text on sex differences and evolutionary biology is Geary (1998). Debate still rages and will probably continue to rage on the subject, but it's now widely accepted that differences exist. My summary is taken from Geary, 1998 and Stephen Pinker's case in the Harvard Mind/Brain/Behaviour debate on 22 April 2008. (*The Science of Gender and Science: Pinker v Spelke – a debate*: The Edge: The Third Culture www.edge.org/3rd_culture/debate05/debate05_index.html.)

Humans and machines

'helped spark a furore in scholarly circles' – see the Harvard Mind/Brain/Behaviour debate, above (in 2006, Professor Lawrence Summers was forced to resign his post as President of Harvard University for suggesting that the evolutionary theory might contribute to the gender imbalance in some academic disciplines). Baron-Cohen's research has since been dismissed by female authorities (e.g. Eliot, 2010, Walter, 2010, Fine, 2010).

The significance of empathy in the modern world: see De Waal, 2007, Rifkin, 2009. There is an excellent RSAnimate video summing up Rifkin's theory at www.thersa.org/events/rsaanimate/animate/rsa-animate-the-empathic-civilisation.

The dance of communication

I first heard the expression 'the dance of communication' in a personal interview with Professor Colwyn Trevarthen, during research for *Toxic Childhood* in 2005. Since then I've encountered debate among psychologists about the phrase's origins. However, the image is widely used, as in a paper on *Helpful Parenting* from the Royal College of Paediatrics and Child Health, 2002, which describe attachment as a 'reciprocal relationship', developing into 'attentive parenting in which children and parents follow each other's rhythms, rather like dancers'.

From Stone Age to stereotypes

'falling levels of empathy in young people' – see Konrath, Sara H., O'Brien, Edward H. and Hsing, Courtney, 'Changes in Dispositional Empathy in American College Students Over Time: A Meta-Analysis', *Personality and Social Psychology Review*, 15(2): 180–198. Available from: www.ipearlab. org/media/publications/Changes_in_Dispositional_Empathy_-_Sara_ Konrath.pdf See also Twenge, 2006, Twenge and Campbell, 2009, Gerhardt, 2010.

The S/E balancing act

Susan Pinker's findings on talented female S-brainers: see Pinker, 2008.
The key ingredients of human well-being were taken from Professor Felicia Huppert's address to Baroness Greenfield's all-party House of Lords committee: *Well-being in the classroom*, Portcullis House, 23 October 2008

Redressing the balance

'mountain of evidence' about the importance of responsive, empathetic care in early life – see Gerhardt, 2004, Sunderland, 2006, and the outpourings of Harvard University's Centre for the Developing Child (www.developingchild.harvard.edu).
the reasons behind the loss of care in contemporary culture are powerfully argued in Sue Gerhardt's 2010 book *The Selfish Society*.
'childcare in modern Britain isn't focused on responsiveness and empathy' – See the manifesto from the Daycare Trust, defining 'quality' early years education and care as 'highly trained staff, with a low staff-to-child ratio, good facilities and strong management'. www.daycaretrust.org.uk/ data/files/Research/daycare_trusts_childcare_charter.pdf and Bowlby, Richard, 'Babies and toddlers in non-parental daycare can avoid stress and anxiety if they develop a lasting secondary attachment bond with one carer who is consistently accessible to them.' *Attachment in Human Development*, December 2007; 9(4).

Chapter 3: Mothers, daughters and child development

The eyes have it

For more information on newborn babies gazing at human faces and their imitative capacities, see Zeedyk 2012, paper by Professor Lynn Murray or the National Childbirth Trust: *Can newborn babies imitate?* www.nct.org.uk/ sites/default/files/related_documents/Bollen%20Can%20newborn%20 babies%20imitate%20p14-5%20Dec11.pdf and Gallese *et al*'s paper on the potential role of mirror neurons (www.informatik.uni-hamburg.de/ WTM/projects/nestcom/papers/Gallese-Eagle-Migone2007.pdf).

Here's looking at you, kid

On the significance of eye contact – see Hobson, 2002.

On girls' developing potential to make eye contact – see Leeb and Gillian 'Here's looking at you, kid! A longitudinal study of perceived gender differences in mutual gaze behaviour in young infants', in *Sex Roles*, 50: 1–14 (2004).

Girls being 'more interested and sociable' and boys 'more excitable' or 'fussy' – see Eliot, 2010.

Girls' imitation of friendly facial expressions at six months, earlier language skills and social gesturing – see Eliot, 2010.

Girls' lower incidence of speech and language problems – see Karmiloff and Karmiloff-Smith, 2001, 'Atypical language development.' in *Pathways to Language: From Fetus to Adolescent* (MIT Press) See also Burman, Douglas D., Bitan, Tali and Booth, James R., 'Sex differences in neural processing of language among children.' *Neuropsychologia*, 46: 1349–1362 (2008) (www. ncbi.nlm.nih.gov/pmc/articles/PMC2478638/).

On girls' higher achievement scores at commencement of school and beyond – see Department for Education figures (www.education.gov.uk/ cgi-bin/rsgateway/search.pl?keyw=184&q2=Search and www.education. gov.uk/cgi-bin/rsgateway/search.pl?keyw=066&q2=Search).

The stronger sex?

The effects of exposure to testosterone in the womb – see Baron-Cohen, 2004, Brizendine, 2006 and Eliot, 2010.

A summary of Sebastian Kraemer's research can be found in 'The Fragile Male', *British Medical Journal*, 321, December 2000. The Duracell battery quote – personal correspondence, 2008.

An essential difference

Slope-crawling experiment: Mondschein, Emily R., Adolph, Karen E. and Tamis-LeMonda, Catherine S., 'Gender bias in mothers' expectations about infant crawling', *Journal of Experimental Child Psychology*, 77: 304–16 (2000).

12-month-old girls four times as likely to check for maternal approval – see Leeb and Gillian, 'Here's looking at you, kid! A longitudinal study of perceived gender differences in mutual gaze behaviour in young infants', in *Sex Roles*, 50: 1–14 (2004).

The drive to learn

Variation in behaviour between gender categories – see Diane F. Halpern's book, *Sex Differences in Cognitive Abilities*, 4th edition (Psychology Press, 2011).

The 'two great cognitive quests' – see Gopnik, Meltzoff and Kuhl 2001.

The development of 'thought' – see Hobson, 2002.

The influence of the unconscious mind on perceptions of gender – see Fine, 2006 and 2010.

Little princess syndrome

Elizabeth Spelke's quote comes from the Harvard Mind/Brain/Behaviour debate on April 2008. (*The Science of Gender and Science: Pinker v Spelke – a debate*: The Edge: The Third Culture www.edge.org/3rd_culture/debate05/debate05_index.html).

For a range of evidence on the lasting impression of children's experiences in the first few years of life, see Harvard University's Centre for the Developing Child (www.developingchild.harvard.edu).

Little Miss Perfect

On 'flow' as the route to long-term well-being – see Mihaly Csikszentmihalyi's 2004 talk, 'Flow, the secret to happiness' (www.ted.com/talks/mihaly_csikszentmihalyi_on_flow.html).

Female fragility and female strength

Fifty years of research projects on gender stereotyping, e.g. Haviland, J.J. and Malatesta, C.Z., 1981, 'The development of sex differences in non-verbal signals: fallacies, facts and fantasies', in *Gender and Non-Verbal Behaviour* (eds Mayo, C. and Henley, N.M.); Stern, M. and Karraker, K.H., 1989, 'Sex stereotyping of infants: a review of gender labelling studies', in *Sex Roles*, 20:501-22.

On unconscious gender-stereotyping or 'neurosexism' – see Fine, 2010.

Tuning in to 21st century girls

Quote from report of the White House conference – Shonkoff and Phillips (eds), 2000.

Who cares?

On the controversy about institutionalised versus personal care for babies, see summary in Chapter 6, Palmer, 2006, Biddulph, 2006, Sunderland, 2006, James, 2010.

Mum's the word

Camille Paglia describes the problem of modern motherhood rather well in a 2012 article 'Motherhood gets a raw deal from the feminists': www.theglobeandmail.com/commentary/motherhood-gets-a-raw-deal-from-feminists/article4592703/.

The best mother-substitutes for early childcare – see James, 2010.

Chapter 4: Toxic Childhood

Dr Sally Ward's research is summarised in her book *Babytalk* (2000).

Nature, nurture and culture

Nursery rhyme knowledge correlated with success at school – research by Bryant and Bradley in the 1980s (see their 1985 book *Children's Reading Difficulties*).

The special needs explosion

See Chapter 1 of *Toxic Childhood* for discussion of this issue.

Ballooning children

As a result of the meeting with Sally Ward, I helped start a project with the National Literacy Trust called *Talk to Your Baby*. TTYB investigated the pushchair issue, resulting in a 2008 research study for the NLT by Dr Suzanne Zeedyk of Dundee University: 'What's life in a baby buggy like? The impact of buggy orientation on parent-child interaction and infant stress'. www.literacytrust.org.uk/talk_to_your_baby/resources/1555_whats _life_in_a_baby_buggy_like .

On the obesity explosion, especially in poor areas – e.g. see the Social Issues Research Centre article (www.sirc.org/articles/poverty_and_obesity.shtml)

and the NHS's 2011 *National Child Measurement Programme* (www.ic.nhs.
uk/webfiles/publications/003_Health_Lifestyles/ncmp%202010-11/
NCMP_2010_11_Report.pdf).

Toxic childhood syndrome

UNICEF report (2007): UNICEF Innocenti Research Centre: *An overview of
child well-being in rich countries: a comprehensive assessment of the lives and well-
being of children and adolescents in the economically advanced nations* (www.
unicef.org/media/files/ChildPovertyReport.pdf).

The Good Childhood Enquiry (2009) – see Layard and Dunn, 2009, www.
childrenssociety.org.uk/sites/default/files/tcs/good_childhood_re-
port_2012_final_0.pdf.

Cambridge Primary Review by Robin Alexander *et al* (2009) – for a summary,
see   www.primaryreview.org.uk/Downloads/Finalreport/CPR-booklet_low-
res.pdf.

Teenage misbehaviour – see the Institute of Public Policy Research's 2006
report *Freedom's Orphans: Raising Youth in a Changing World* (www.ippr.org/
publication/55/1538/freedoms-orphans-raising-youth-in-a-changing-
world).

Spinning along with Moore's Law

On Moore's Law – see www.intel.com/content/www/us/en/silicon-innova-
tions/moores-law-technology.html.

Daniel Anderson quoted in Strasburger, Victor (2006) 'First do no harm:
Why have parents and paediatricians missed the boat on children and the
media?' *Journal of Paediatrics*, 151(54). See also the UK psychologist Aric
Sigman, e.g. 'Visual Voodoo: the biological impact of watching TV',
Biologist, Vol. 54/1 (2007).

Susan Greenfield quote: *Scotsman* (14 September 2006) (www.scotsman.
com/news/health/the-trouble-with-childhood-1-1139872).

All-consuming

For an in-depth description of the rise of consumerism, see Lawson, 2009;
for information on marketing to children, see Schor, 2005, Linn, 2005,
Thomas, 2007.

Quote on contemporary advertising techniques – see Linn, 2005.

Parents' voices not being heard regarding sexualisation and commercialisation – see Reg Bailey's report, *Letting Children be Children: Independent Review of the Commercialisation and Sexualisation of Childhood* (Crown, 2011),

and the 2012 update: www.education.gov.uk/childrenandyoungpeople/ healthandwellbeing/b0074315/bailey-review.

Mum is the word (reprise)

Focus on mothers' rights in the workplace – see Banyard, 2010, Asher, 2011
On the marketing of gender stereotypes and women's bodies – see Dines, 2010 and Walters, 2010.

Chapter 5: Growing Girls

Five-finger exercise

On human development research in psychology and neuroscience – e.g. Shonkoff and Phillips, 2000, Herschkowitz and Herschkowitz, 2004 and the National Scientific Council on the Developing Child (www.developingchild.harvard.edu).

Urie Bronfenbrenner's quote about the importance of love – National Scientific Council on the Developing Child, 2004, *Young Children Develop in an Environment of Relationships: Working Paper No. 1.* (www.developingchild.harvard.edu).

The developmental tangle

On the complex interplay of physical, emotional, social and cognitive development – see Herschkowitz and Herschkowitz, 2004.

Roots to grow and wings to fly

Research over many decades about authoritative parenting – see e.g. Martin, 2005, Lee and Lee, 2009 and Dr Gwen Dewar's 2010 article 'The authoritative parenting style: Warmth, rationality, and high standards: A guide for the science-minded parent' (www.parentingscience.com/authoritative-parenting-style.html). See also *Authoritative Parenting: Synthesizing Nurturance and Discipline for Optimal Child Development* (2012) by Robert E. Larzelere, Amanda Sheffield Morris and Amanda W. Harrist.

The missing ingredient

The problem of 'over-parenting' – see Honore, 2008.
The importance of outdoor play – see Louv, 2005, Gill, 2007 and websites including Learning Through Landscapes (LTL): www.ltl.org.uk and the four UK national play organisations: www.playengland.org.uk, www.playscotland.org, www.playwales.org.uk and in N. Ireland www.playboard.org.

It takes a village ...

'authoritative parenting possibly only achievable within an authoritative community' see 2003 review by the Commission on Children at Risk, *Hardwired to Connect: The New Scientific Case for Authoritative Communities.*

Build your own village

The importance of community in child-rearing – see Smith and Dewar, 2009.
The Mumsnet.com *Let Girls Be Girls* campaign: www.mumsnet.com/campaigns/let-girls-be-girls.
www.netmums.com Netmums seems to me more practically and locally-based than mumsnet.

PART TWO

Chapter 6: She is what you feed her

80 per cent of women dissatisfied with their body shape: *Mirror Mirror: A Summary of Research Findings on Body Image* by Kate Fox for the Social Issues Research Centre, Oxford 1997; same proportion reported in 2001 survey on http://news.bbc.co.uk/1/hi/health/1180855.stm.

Emotion and reason

Advice about establishing healthy eating habits in children – see Richardson, 2006 and the NHS's Healthy Start resources: www.healthystart.nhs.uk/food-and-health-tips/healthy-eating-eatwell-plate/

Body image and images of bodies

Orbach, Susie, *Fat is a Feminist Issue* (Arrow Books, 1978 and 1982, or the new combined edition Arrow Books, 2006) and see also Orbach, 2010.
Teenage girl in 1990s saw more images of conventionally beautiful women... see *Mirror Mirror: A Summary of Research Findings on Body Image* by Kate Fox for the Social Issues Research Centre, Oxford 1997; same proportion reported in 2001 survey.
Eating disorders such as obesity and self-starvation are linked to genetics – see 'Obesity: Genetic, molecular, and environmental aspects' by Barness, L.A., Opitz, J.M., Gilbert-Barness, E. in the *American Journal of Medical Genetics Part A*, 143A(24), 3016–3034 and Dr Ulrike Schmidt's 2003 paper, 'Aetiology of eating disorders in the 21st century: New answers to old questions', in *European Child & Adolescent Psychiatry*, 12:30–37.
On historical expectations of female beauty and modern women's relentless pursuit of a physical beauty unattainable for 95 per cent of women – see

Naomi Wolf's book *The Beauty Myth: How Images of Beauty are Used Against Women* (Vintage, 1991).

Young girls are developing eating disorders at ever-earlier ages – see for example http://edition.cnn.com/2011/HEALTH/08/08/tweens.anorexia.parenting/index.html.

The BBC and Open University's *Child of Our Time* documentary series www.open.edu/openlearn/profiles/guest-256.

Quote from Susie Orbach from an interview with Janice Turner published 24 January 2009 in *The Times*:www.thetimes.co.uk/tto/health/article1964231.ece.

A developmental reality check

The International Association of Infant Massage's UK chapter: www.iaim.org.uk.

Naomi Wolf's *The Beauty Myth*, 199.

Benefits of having positive relationships with her father on a girl's self-esteem – see Lynn Neilsen's *Father-Daughter Relationships: Contemporary Research and Issues* (Routledge, 2012).

Female mentors for adolescent girls, see Dines 2010 and Steve Biddulph's *Raising Girls* (2013).

Connections between physical, hands-on learning and cognitive development – see Edward F. Zigler and Sandra J. Bishop-Josef's 2009 article, 'Play under Siege: A Historical Overview' in *Zero to Three*, 30 (1), 4–11.

'Nothing tastes as good as skinny feels' quote by Kate Moss – interview available at www.wwd.com/beauty-industry-news/beauty-features/kate-moss-the-waif-that-roared-2367932.

The dance of nutrition

Breastfeeding linked to greater physical and emotional health – see NHS advice on breastfeeding La Leche League website http://www.laleche.org.uk/.

Rebecca Asher's experience – Asher, 2011.

Attachment to junk

Information on the effects of the junk food industry's marketing techniques – see the Ofcom report: *Childhood Obesity – Food Advertising in Context: Children's Food Choices, Parents' Understanding and Influence and the Role of Food Promotions*, UK, July 2004, and updates by the Children's Food Campaign run by the charity *Sustain*, www.sustainweb.org/childrensfoodcampaign/.

Marketing products to infants and toddlers – see Linn, 2005, Schor, 2005, Thomas 2007.

Quote from Martin Lindstrom – Lindstrom, 2003.

Evidence of junk food being addictive – see Deanne Jade, psychologist and founder of the UK Centre for Eating Disorders, reported by Rachel New-combe, 'Is Junk Food Addictive?', BUPA *Investigative News*, 19 July 2003. The phrase 'psychological addiction' came from a personal interview with nutritionist Dr Susan Jebb, Head of Nutrition and Health Research at the Medical Research Council in 2004.

Quote about UK food product marketing on children – Ofcom report, 2004 (see above).

Social eating

Family meals associated with childhood well-being and teenage mental health – see Maria E. Eisenberg *et al.*, 'Correlations Between Family Life and Psychological Well-Being Among Adolescents', *Archives of Pediatrics and Adolescent Medicine*, Vol. 158, August 2004.

Quote from chef Raymond Blanc –'Let's eat en famille! From a French celeb-rity chef, a plea from the heart...' *Daily Mail*, 4 January 2007.

Psychologist and nutritionist Ellyn Satter's rule of thumb and a lot more helpful advice– see www.ellynsatter.com.

Time to digest

American adults in Philadelphia eat a McDonald's meal in an average of 14 minutes – see Rozin, P. *et al.*, 'The ecology of eating: smaller portion sizes in France Than in the United States help explain the French paradox', *Psychological Science*, September 2003, 14(5): 450-4.

Clotaire Rapaille quote is from his book *The Culture Code* (Broadway Books, 2006), quoted in Jackson 2008.

Fast food ingredients designed to affect neurotransmitters – see Dr Vyvyan Howard, toxico-pathologist, Liverpool University, quoted by Tim Utton, 'Children's Drinks are a Chemical Cocktail', *Daily Mail*, 11 May 2004and Patrick Holford, nutritionist in *Food on the Brain*, Independent TV, UK, 29 April 2005.

The appliance of science

Marketers promoting junk food as 'healthy' – see ,for example, the report by Felicity Lawrence, consumer affairs correspondent, 'Revealed: How Food Firms Target Children', *Guardian*, 27 May 2004 about Kellogg's Real Fruit Winders snack (which is one-third sugar).

Chapter 7: Home and away, safety and play

The rise of the electronic bedsit

80 per cent of under-12s and 40 per cent of under-5s had a TV in their room by 2004 – see Close, Robin *Television and Language Development in the Early Years: A Review of the Literature* (National Literacy Trust, 2004). Since 2007, updates by Ofcom have shown a decline in TVs in children's bedrooms – possibly due to a rise parental awareness of the dangers, but probably also influenced by young people's preference for accessing entertainment (including TV) on mobile internet devices, such as smartphones and iPads, http://stakeholders.ofcom.org.uk/binaries/research/media-literacy/oct2012/main.pdf .

Why girls need a good night's sleep

Research on sleep and the negative effects of adults' accumulating 'sleep debt' – see Paul Martin's book *Counting Sheep: The Science and Pleasures of Sleep and Dreams* (Flamingo, 2003) and also the US National Sleep Foundation: www.sleepfoundation.org.

On healthy sleep patterns being set during childhood – see Weissbluth, 1998 and Sunderland, 2006.

Link between obesity, poor sleep habits and and possible link to early onset of puberty, see Sigman, A. 'Visual Voodoo: the biological impact of watching TV' in *The Biologist* 54:1, 2007.

On the importance of shallow and deep sleep for transfer of different types of learning to long-term memory – thanks to sleep researchers Dr Jan Born; see also Maquet P. *et al*, 'Experience-dependent changes in cerebral activation during human REM sleep', *Nature Neuroscience* (2000) and Huber *et al*., 'Local Sleep and Learning' *Nature*, Vol. 430 (2004).

For findings about the effects of too little sleep on school performance and IQ – see Sadeh, A., Gruber, R. and Raviv, A., 'The Effects of Sleep Restriction and Extension on School-Age Children: What A Difference An Hour Makes', *Child Development*, 74/2 (2003).

Hush, little baby, don't you cry

Elizabeth Pantley's book, *The No-Cry Sleep Solution: Gentle Ways to Help Your Baby Sleep Through the Night* (McGraw-Hill, 2002).

Sarah Woodhouse's book, *Sound Sleep: Calming and Helping Your Baby or Child to Sleep* (Hawthorn Press, 2004) and her foundation's website www.right-from-the-start.org.

'Bednests' that attach to the family bed to allow safe co-sleepingwww.bed-nest.com.

Goodnight, sleep tight

Appropriate amounts of sleep for children at different ages – National Sleep Foundation.

Mumsnet tips on sleep – www.mumsnet.com/babies/sleep-training-and-controlled-crying.

Sleep needs during the teenage years – see www.sleepfoundation.org/article/sleep-topics/teens-and-sleep.

On recommendations about bathing and childhood eczema – see www.nhs.uk/Livewell/Allergies/Pages/Stopthescratching.aspx.

Sleeping with strangers

The American Academy of Pediatricians recommendation for no television for children under the age of two years – see www.aap.org/en-us/advocacy-and-policy/aap-health-initiatives/Pages/Media-and-Children.aspx?nfstatus=401&nftoken=00000000-0000-0000-0000-000000000000&nfstatusdescription=ERROR%3a+No+local+token.

No one should sleep with the TV on: see Sleep Foundation: www.sleepfoundation.org/sleep-facts-information/myths-and-facts.

TV and children's sleep – see Sigman, A., 'Visual Voodoo: the biological impact of watching TV', in *Biologist* 54:1, 2007 and 'TV, devices in kids' bedrooms linked to poor sleep, obesity' in *Science News* 12 October 2012.

Electronic socialising and sleep – Leuven Study on Media and Adolescent Health, August 2009, reported in 'Teens, Texting and the Sleep Connection' by Jackie Burrell, *Phys.Org News*, 23 September 2009.

Reg Bailey's report, *Letting Children be Children: Independent Review of the Commercialisation and Sexualisation of Childhood* (Crown, 2011) and the 2012 update: www.education.gov.uk/childrenandyoungpeople/healthandwellbeing/b0074315/bailey-review.

Playing with strangers

Interview with Daniel Anderson in Jackson 2008, Chapter 3 – see also Richards, John E. and Anderson, Daniel R.(2004) 'Attentional inertia in children's extended looking at television', *Advances in Child Development and Behavior*, 32, 163–212.

Children focus less on their play and adults interact less with children when television is on – see Schmidt, M.E.,Pempek, T.A., Kirkorian, H.L., Frankenfield Lund, A. and Anderson, D.R. (2008) 'The Effects of Background Television on the Toy Play Behavior of Very Young Children', *Child Development*, 79 (4), 1137–1151 and Kirkorian, HL, Pempek, TA., Murphy, LA, Schmidt, M.E., and Anderson, D.R. (2009) 'The Impact of Background Television on Parent–Child Interaction', *Child Development*, 80 (5), 1350–1359.

'Real play' learners or 'junk play' junkies?

Quote defining 'real play' – widely accepted by play workers, the first record I have for it is in 'Best Play: What Play Provision Should Do for Children' (Department for Culture, Media and Sport2000), where it's described as drawing heavily on the work of play theorists Bob Hughes and Frank King.

The American Academy of Pediatricians recommendation of no more than two hours a day TV for children over two – see www.aap.org/en-us/advocacy-and-policy/aap-health-initiatives/Pages/Media-and-Children.aspx? nfstatus=401&nftoken=00000000-0000-0000-0000-000000000000&nfs tatusdescription=ERROR%3a+No+local+token

'rewarding children every seven seconds' – conversation with IT expert Ian Jukes, 2007; conversation with Suzanne Zeedyk, 2011.

See also Aric Sigman's review of the literature 'Time for a View on Screen-time' published in *Archives of Disease in Childhood* 97:11 (2012) and on http:// press.psprings.co.uk/adc/september/adc302196.pdf.

Something to play with

Howard Chudacoff quote on the demise of 'real play' reported in 'Old-Fashioned Play Builds Serious Skills', by Alix Spiegel on US National Public Radio 21.2.2008 (www.npr.org/templates/story/story. php?storyId=19212514).

A great leap backwards

Developmental psychologist Laura Berk's quote is from the NPR broadcast above. See also her work on children's development of self-regulation – Berk L.E., Mann T.D., and Ogan A.T. 'Make-Believe Play: Wellspring for Development of Self-Regulation' in *Play Equals Learning: how play motivates and enhances Children's Cognitive and Social-Emotional Growth*, Golinkoff R.M., Hirsh-Pasek, K. (Oxford University Press).

Medical recommendations for children's early development 'Start Active, Stay Active' (2011) www.dh.gov.uk/prod_consum_dh/groups/dh_digitalassets/documents/digitalasset/dh_128210.pdf.

Lady Allen of Hurtwood (1897 – 1976), advocate of adventure playgrounds.

Lock up your daughters?

Effect on brain of disturbing information repeatedly viewed in visual form – see Restak, 2004.

Tim Gill's Esther Rantzen story – see Gill, 2007 and his website: http://re-thinkingchildhood.com/

Re-establishing free-range play

Guidance for teaching children road-safety rules – see http://think.direct. gov.uk/education/early-years-and-primary/parents/ and www.nidirect.gov. uk/road-safety-advice.

Pass it on...

Active parents tend to have active children – see summary of research in www.sciencedaily.com/releases/2007/11/071126105434.htm.

Chapter 8: Fashion, friendship and fun

A question of identity

Need for parents to help girls navigate marketing messages – see Lamb and Brown, 2006.

Brand Child quote – see Lindstrom, 2003.

The princess culture

Disney princesses – see 'What's wrong with Cinderella' by Peggy Orenstein, *New York Times*, 24 December 2006 www.nytimes.com/2006/12/24/magazine/24princess.t.html?pagewanted=all and Thomas, 2007.

Quote from Abi Moore in 'Role models: someone to look up to' by Kira Cochrane, *Guardian*, 31 October 2010.

Stand well back!

Outdoor play to support children's social and emotional development – see the 2009/2010 London Play report 'Natural play for better mental health' (www. londonplay.org.uk/file/1429.pdf) and Forest Schools www.foresteducation. org plus information on forest kindergartens in Scandinavia www.forestry. gov.uk/pdf/FKreportAppendix.pdf/$file/FKreportAppendix.pdf.

Cool tweens!

The changing definition of tweens – see 'Marketing and Tweens: BFF' Alycia de Mesa, *brandchannel*, 10 October 2005, www.brandchannel.com/features_effect.asp?pf_id=284.

Games website for 'tweenage' girls: www.girlsgogames.com.

For more on the history of 'cool' see Joeri Van den Bergh's article, 18 February 2011   www.howcoolbrandsstayhot.com/2011/02/18/the-history-of-cool/ and on selling 'cool' to teenagers and children – see Del Vecchio, 1997.

Reports on parental concerns about sexualisation of young children – see, for example, 'Parents decry marketers who push sexuality on little girls', Liz Szabo, *USA Today*, 4 December 2011 http://usatoday30.usatoday.com/news/health/wellness/story/2011/04/Parents-decry-marketers-who-push-sexuality-on-little-girls/46021496/1?sms_ss=email&at_xt=4da6398afff4bd17%2Co.

Consuming Kids quote – see the documentary film *Consuming Kids: The Commercialization of Childhood*, directed by Adriana Barbaro and Jeremy Earp, 2008, www.mediaed.org/cgi-bin/commerce.cgi?preadd=action&key=134.

Junk play and junk friendship

Quote about girls' career aspirations – see Lamb and Brown, 2006.

Parent power and tween culture

Noël Janis-Norton's book, *Calmer, Easier, Happier Parenting: The Revolutionary Programme That Transforms Family Life* (Hodder & Stoughton, 2012).

What's hot and what's not?

Statistics on children's use of Facebook before the age of 13 – see the *ChildWise Monitor*, 10 January 2012 www.childwise.co.uk/media/CHILDWISE%20MONITOR%202011-12%20press%20release.pdf and arguments against the lower age-limit for social networking sites 'Mark Zuckerberg: children should be allowed to use Facebook', Matt Warman, *Telegraph*, 24 May 2011.

Virtual social life

Tips and links to resources on supervising children's online social networking, computer and mobile phone use – see www.childnet.com and www.getsafeonline.org/safeguarding-children/safeguarding-children.

The CEOP website www.ceop.police.uk and YouTube clip:www.youtube.com/watch?v=vp5nScG6C5g.

CBBC website: www.bbc.co.uk/cbbc/

Face to virtual face

YouGov survey about smartphone ownership (2012) – see report at http://
   pressoffice.carphonewarehouse.com/news/item/12_million_school_
   children_in_uk_have_accessed_inappropriate_content_on_the/

Information about the four major broadband providers offering to block
   adult content – see 'Parental Internal Controls: BT, TalkTalk, Virgin Media, Sky, Orange and O2's porn block software', Thomas Newton, 10
   September 2012,http://recombu.com/digital/news/parental-internal-controls
   -bt-talktalk-virgin-media-sky-orange-o2_M10934.html.

Kytephone is an example of an app that makes Android phones safer for
   children to use – seehttps://www.kytephone.com/

Mean girls

Relational aggression in girls – see 'Mean Girls and Relational Aggression
   Solutions', Michele Borba, 11 January 2011, www.micheleborba.com/
   blog/2011/01/11/parenting-survival-guide-to-the-mean-girl-scene/

Advice about bullying: www.kidscape.org.ukandwww.beatbullying.org

2011 survey – 46 per cent of children claiming they've been bullied – see
   www.nspcc.org.uk/inform/resourcesforprofessionals/bullying/bullying_
   statistics_wda85732.html.

On helping today's teenage girls navigate through the 'mean girl' scene, see
   the book on which the film was based: Rosalind Wiseman's *Queen Bees and
   Wannabes: Helping Your Daughter Survive Cliques, Gossip, Boyfriends, and the New
   Realities of Girl World* (Three Rivers Press, 2009).

Quote about virtual mean girls – see 'Virtual Violence II: The Real Impact of
   Cyber-Bullying', 6 February 2012www.beatbullying.org.

Coda

UNICEF report (2007): UNICEF Innocenti Research Centre: *An overview of
   child well-being in rich countries: a comprehensive assessment of the lives and well-
   being of children and adolescents in the economically advanced nations.*

Good Childhood report– see Layard and Dunn, 2009.

Statistics showing focus on materialism vs. children's desire to spend time
   with family – see the UNICEF2011 follow-up report 'Children's Well-
   being in UK, Sweden and Spain: The Role of Inequality and Materialism,
   A Qualitative Study' www.unicef.org.uk/Documents/Publications/IP-
   SOS_UNICEF_ChildWellBeingreport.pdf.

Chapter 9: A mind of her own

The perils of people-pleasing

Lyn Mikel Brown and Carol Gilligan, *Meeting at the Crossroads* (Ballantine Books, 1993).

Courtney Martin quote *Perfect Girls, Starving Daughters: How the Quest for Perfection is Harming Young Women* (Berkeley Books, 2008)

The risks of early schoolification

Background on the Early Years Foundation Stage – see House, 2011.

Sebastian Suggate research – see 'Viewing the long-term results of early reading with an Open Eye', in House, 2011.

Studies on long-term effects of an early start on formal learning: Schweinhart, L.J. and Weikhart, D.P., 'Lasting Differences: the High/Scope Preschool Curriculum Study Through Age 23', *Monographs of the High/Scope Educational Research Foundation*, 1997; Howard Friedman and Leslie Martin *The Longevity Project: Surprising Discoveries for Health and Long Life From the Landmark Eight-Decade Study*.

See also 'Why preschool shouldn't be like school' by Alison Gopnik 16 March 2011 www.slate.com/articles/double_x/doublex/2011/03/why_preschool_shouldnt_be_like_school.html.

Sound foundations

Finland's record as top Western country in reading – see the OECD's PISA study www.oecd.org/pisa/pisa2009keyfindings.htm.

The 3Rs – slowing down to learn

The effects of learning to read on the brain – see Wolf, 2008.

Neil Postman quotes – Postman, 1994.

Robert Rekstak quote – Rekstak, 2004.

See also Carr, 2010, Small and Vorgon, 2008.

21st century learners

Louise Robinson quote in 'Textbooks "being replaced by smartphones and e-readers" ' by Graeme Paton, *Daily Telegraph* 28 December 2011 www.telegraph.co.uk/education/educationnews/8979087/Textbooks-being-replaced-by-smartphones-and-e-readers.html.

Barnaby Lenon quote in 'Children becoming "addicted" to computers' by Graeme Paton, *Daily Telegraph* 2 January 2012 www.telegraph.co.uk/education/educationnews/8988082/Children-becoming-addicted-to-computers.html.

Computers in schools

Dr Aric Sigman's quote from an address at *The Child: The True Foundation* conference, London 12 June 2010.

Waldorf School in Silicon Valley: 'A Silicon Valley School That Does Not Compute' Matt Richtel *New York Times*, 22 October 2011.

Quote from Prof Paul Furman – see *New York Times* article above.

Tests, targets, structures and standards

See Mansell 2007 and his website www.educationbynumbers.org.uk/

Under pressure

Quotes from Gillian Low at the Girls School Association conference – 'Leading headmistress: "education has lost its way"' *Independent* 15 November 2010.

Lucie Russell quote from 'Middle-class student exam stress creating mental health time bomb', by Andrew Hough ,*Daily Telegraph*, 21 May 2011.

Well-educated girls...

Half a Wife – Hinsliff, 2011.

...and under-educated boys

Sammi Timimi quote in personal conversation, 2008.

Sexual harassment of girls and teachers 'Sex pest boys targeting not only girls, but teachers too' Adi Bloom, *Times Educational Supplement*, 27 March 2009.

All girls together

'The pseudoscience of single-sex schooling' by Halpern, D.F., Eliot, L., *et al* in *Science*, Vol. 333, September 2011.

Chapter 10: Sex, power...and love

Girls growing older younger

27 per cent of girls losing virginity before the age of 16 – NHS's Health Survey for England, 2011 (www.ic.nhs.uk/article/1732/New-report-reveals-sexual-behaviour-across-the-different-age-groups).

Anglo-Saxon attitudes

Comparisons of teenage pregnancy rates in the UK and in Europe – see www.unicef-irc.org/publications/pdf/repcard3e.pdf (2001), http://news. bbc.co.uk/nol/shared/bsp/hi/pdfs/13_02_07_nn_unicef.pdf (2007), and www.nice.org.uk/niceMedia/documents/teenpreg_evidence_briefing_ summary.pdf (2003) www.fpa.org.uk/professionals/factsheets/teenagers (2011).

Possible causes of Dutch children's higher scores for well-being and lower teenage pregnancy rates – see 'Why are Dutch children so happy?', Kathryn Wescott (http://news.bbc.co.uk/1/hi/6360517.stm).

How to talk to young children about sex – see the Mayo Clinic's 2011 article 'Sex education: Talking to toddlers and preschoolers about sex' (www.mayoclinic.com/health/sex-education/HQ00547/NSECTIONGROUP=2It).

Quotes from *Living Dolls* – see Walters, 2010.

Synonyms of 'cute' – see *Roget's Thesaurus*, 6th edition (Longman, 1982).

The sexualisation of childhood

Quotes from Dr Linda Papadopoulous' 'Sexualisation of Young People Review', 2010, an independent review for the UK Home Secretary www.wrc. org.uk/includes/documents/cm_docs/2010/s/sexualisationyoungpeople. pdf.

On Dr Papadopoulous' involvement with the TV show *Big Brother* and Channel 5 – see www.channel5.com/shows/live-with/meet-the-team/dr-linda-papadopoulos.

The 'porn opt-out clause' is described in Chapter 8 (**Face to virtual face**) and the Parent Port website for registering complaints about media and marketing is at www.parentport.org.uk.

Quote about the power of consumerism in today's culture – see Reg Bailey's report, *Letting Children be Children: Independent Review of the Commercialisation and Sexualisation of Childhood* (Crown, 2011) and the 2012 update: www.education.gov.uk/childrenandyoungpeople/healthandwellbeing/b0074315/ bailey-review.

Sexualisation and feminism

Katie Price's transformation from 'glamour model' to successful businesswoman – see Jenni Murray's article 'Why I admire Katie Price: Former glamour model Jordan is everything Woman's Hour presenter Jenni Murray normally detests... So what has changed her mind?' *Daily Mail*, 1 July 2012.

Book about living as a call girl– see Belle de Jour's (aka Brooke Magnanti)*The Intimate Adventures of a London Call Girl* (Phoenix, 2007).

Books about feminism and how far 'sexual liberation' has gone – see Banyard, 2010, quotes from Walter, 2010 and also Walter, Natasha, *The New Feminism* (Virago Press Ltd, 1998).

Social class and the normalisation of porn

Quote from *Big Brother* creative director Phil Edgar-Jones about his hopes for his daughter – see Walter, 2010.

Sex, freedom and exploitation

Quote that 'women are there to be used and that men are there to use them' – Papadopoulous, 2010 (see above).

For more about porn, misogyny, and the effects on relationships of early introduction to pornography – see Dines, 2010 and Walter, 2010.

Sex, love and power

Quote from feminist writer Michele Roberts – see Walter, 2010.

Current research on romantic love and its relationship to attachment – see 'Common neural activity for long-term and early stage romantic love' Acevedo, B.P., Aron, A. *et al*, *Journal of Social, Cognitive and Affective Neuroscience*, January 2011, also Dr Acevedo's website http://biancaacevedo.net/

Manners maketh man

Wikipedia quote on New College, Oxford – see http://en.wikipedia.org/wiki/New_College,_Oxford (accessed 8 January 2013).

Geoffrey Chaucer's *The Canterbury Tales* is available through Project Gutenberg: www.gutenberg.org/ebooks/2383.

Websites to tell you how to do it: popularized by Neil Strauss in his memoir 'The Game', e.g. Strauss's site www.stylelife.com/ and that of his mentor Ross Jefferies www.seduction.com/

Coda

Quote from girls about 'soppy...emotional and wimpy' boys – see Walter 2010.

Conclusion

Interview with Simon Baron-Cohen, September 2007.

Spread a little empathy

Attachment: 'attachment theory' originated in the work of psychologist John
   Bowlby after the Second World War and the quality of infant attachment
   is now widely accepted as critical to children's overall development: see
   this useful summary www.uea.ac.uk/providingasecurebase/at-
   tachment-theory and this chapter by Bowlby's son about the importance
   of the primary attachment figure www.ecswe.com/downloads/publica-
   tions/QOC-VI/Chapters-10-12.pdf . See also Gerhardt, 2004 and 2010,
   Martin, 2005, James, 2007 and 2010, Sunderland, 2006.
Imitating 'good mothers'. As far as I know, there are no studies showing that
   less 'naturally' empathetic mothers learn by watching others . But successful evidence-based parenting programmes such as the Family Nurse
   Project (in the US the Nurse Family Project) for the parents of young babies, the Triple P and the Incredible Years programmes for families of
   school age children all depend to a large extent on the modelling of parental 'attunement' (see below).

Why motherhood matters

Quote from Gerhardt, 2010.
Naomi Wolf's 'acute social demotion' comes from *Misconceptions* (Anchor
   2003) quoted in Asher, 2011.

What do 'good mothers' do?

I fear I didn't know or can't remember the names of most of the people I've
   spoken to on the subject of 'good mothering' (or the many others simply
   I've watched interacting with babies and toddlers) but I have to acknowledge the many hours of conversation on the subject with Ros Bayley, an
   early years specialist and one of the world's most natural empathisers.
The paper on maternal mind-mindedness that I came across while researching *Toxic Childhood* was Meins, E., Fernyhough, C., Wainwright, R., Clark-
   Carter, D., Gupta, M.D., Fradley, E. and Tuckey, M., 'Pathways to Understanding Mind: Construct Validity and Predictive Validity of Maternal
   Mind-Mindedness' in *Child Development* 74:4 (2003).
'attunement' – see Dr Stacey Annand's website: http://theattunedparent.
   com/ and Zeedyk, 2012

Tuning in to children

Dr Elizabeth Meins spoke about mind-mindedness on *All In the Mind*, BBC
   Radio 4, 18 December 2012.

Trailer for Suzanne Zeedyk's *The Connected Baby* DVD on www.theconnected-baby.org/

Dr Edward Tronick's Still Face experiment www.youtube.com/watch?v =ap-zXGEbZhto .

Roots of Empathy – see www.rootsofempathy.org/ and Gordon, 2005.

O tempora! O mores! (reprise)

The banning of marketing to children under 12: this has been done in Sweden and calls for this or similar action have been made in recent years by the left-wing think tank Compass (2007), the National Union of Teachers (2007), the Mother's Union (2009), Early Childhood Action (2011) and the umbrella organisation Save Childhood (2012).

A campaign calling for an 'opt-in' requirement to view internet pornography was run during 2011–12 by SaferMedia (and gained support from many quarters, including the *Daily Mail*).

The suggestion that marketers conduct research before putting products on the market that could prove harmful to children (e.g. junk food, iPads for tots) was made by Professor Agnes Nairn in a submission to the government's 2012 revisitation of the Bailey Review www.education.gov.uk/ childrenandyoungpeople/healthandwellbeing/b0074315/bailey-review. At present, commercial companies merely say. 'There's no research to prove they're harmful.'

It takes a village (reprise)

Ways of meeting other mothers-to-be or new mums in your local area: in many areas the National Childbirth Trust (www.nct.org.uk) organises both antenatal and postnatal classes; Meet A Mum Association (www.mama.co.uk), or check local library or health centre for details of classes and groups.

Bibliography

Asher, Rebecca, Shattered: Modern Motherhood and the Illusion Of Equality (Harvill Secker, 2011)

Bainbridge, David Teenagers, A Natural History (Portobello Books, 2009)

Banyard, Kate, The Equality Illusion: The Truth About Women and Men Today (Faber and Faber, 2010)

Baron-Cohen, Simon, The Essential Difference: Men, Women and the Extreme Male Brain (Allen Lane, 2003)

Biddulph, Steve, Raising Babies: Why Your Love is Best (HarperThorsons, 2006)

Blakemore, Sarah Jayne and Frith, Uta The Learning Brain (Blackwell, 2005)

Bolen, Jean Shinoda, Goddesses in Everywoman: A New Psychology of Women (Harper Colophon, 1984)

Brizendine, Louann, The Female Brain (Bantam Books, 2006)

Bronson, Po and Merryman, Ashley,Nurtureshock: Why Everything We Think About Raising Our Children is Wrong (Ebury Press, 2009)

Brooks, Libby, The Story of Childhood: Growing Up in Modern Britain (Bloomsbury, 2006)

Bryant, Peter and Bradley, Lynette, Children's Reading Problems: Psychology and Education(Blackwell, 1985)

Carr, Nicholas, The Shallows:How The Internet is Changing the Way we Think, Read and Remember (Atlantic Books, 2010)

Cary, Tanith, Where Has My Little Girl Gone? (Lion Hudson, 2011)

Claxton, Guy, What's the Point of School? (One World, 2008)

Clark, Eric, The Real Toy Story (Black Swan, 2007)

Coloroso, Barbara, The Bully, the Bullied and the Bystander (Piccadilly Press, 2005)

Colvin, Geoff, *Talent is Overrated: What Really Separates World Class Performers From Everybody Else* (Nicholas Brearly Publishing, 2008)

Craig, Carol, *Creating Confidence: a handbook for professionals working with young people* (Centre for Confidence and Wellbeing, 2007)

Cunningham, Hugh, *The Invention of Childhood* (BBC Books, 2006)

Curtis, Adam, *The Century of the Self* (BBC 2002)

Curtis, Adam, *The Trap: What's Happened To Our Dream Of Freedom?* (BBC, 2007)

Deacon, Terrence W., *The Symbolic Species: The Co-Evolution of Language and the Brain* (WW Norton, 1997)

De Waal, Frans, *The Age of Empathy: Nature's Lessons for a Kinder Society* (Broadway, 2007)

Del Vecchio, Gene, *Creating Evercool: A Marketer's Guide to a Kid's Heart* (Pelican, 1997)

Dines, Gail, *Pornland: How Porn Has Hijacked our Sexuality* (Beacon Press, 2010)

Donald, Merlin, *A Mind So Rare: the Evolution of Human Consciousness* (W.W. Norton, 2001)

Dowd, Maureen, *Are Men Necessary?* (Headline Review, 2005)

Durham, M. Gigi, *The Lolita Effect: the Media Sexualisation of Young Girls and What We Can Do About It* (Overlook Press, 2008)

Eliot, Lise, *Pink Brain, Blue Brain: How Small Differences Grow into Troublesome Gaps – and What We Can Do About It* (One World, 2010)

Elkind, PhD, David, *The Hurried Child: Growing Up Too Fast Too Soon* (Da Capo Press; Perseus Books Group, 2001)

Fine, Cordelia, *A Mind of Its Own* (Icon Books, 2006)

Fine, Cordelia, *Delusions of Gender: the Real Science Behind Sex Differences* (Icon, 2010)

Gallagher, Winifred , *Rapt: Attention and the Focused Life* (Penguin Press, 2009)

Geary, David, *Male, Female: The Evolution of Human Sex Differences* (American Psychological Association, 1998)

Gerhardt, Sue, *Why Love Matters: How Affection Shapes a Baby's Brain* (Routledge, 2004)

Gerhardt, Sue, *The Selfish Society: How We All Forgot to Love One Another and Made Money Instead* (Simon & Schuster, 2010)

Gilbert, Daniel, *Stumbling on Happiness* (Harper Perennial, 2007)

Gilbert, Susan, *A Field Guide to Boys and Girls* (Quill, 2000)

Gill, Tim, *No Fear: Growing Up in a Risk-Averse Society* (Gulbenkian Foundation, 2007)

Gilligan, Carol and Richards, David A.J. *The Deepening Darkness: Patriarchy, Resistance and Democracy's Future* (Cambridge University Press, 2009)

Girls' School Association, *Your Daughter: A Guide for Raising Girls* (The Friday Project, 2011)

Gladwell, Malcolm, *Outliers: The Story of Success* (Penguin, 2009)

Goddard Blythe, Sally, *The Well Balanced Child: Movement and Early Learning* (Hawthorn Press, 2004)

Goddard Blythe, Sally, *What Babies and Children Really Need* (Hawthorn Press, 2008)

Goleman Daniel, *Emotional Intelligence: Why It Can Matter More Than IQ* (Bantam Books, 1997)

Goleman Daniel, *Social Intelligence: The New Science of Human Relationships* (Arrow Books, 2007)

Gordon Mary, *Roots of Empathy: Changing the World Child by Child* (Thomas Allen, 2005)

Gopnik A., Meltzoff, A.N., Kuhl, P., *The Scientist in the Crib: What Early Learning Tells Us About the Mind* (Perennial, 2001)

Greenfield, Susan *The Human Brain: A Guided Tour* (London: Phoenix, 1997)

Greenfield, Susan *Tomorrow's People: How 21st Century Technology is Changing the Way we Think and Feel* (Allen Lane, 2003)

Greenfield, Susan, *ID: The Quest For Identity in the 21st Century* (Sceptre, 2008)

Harris, Judith Rich *The Nurture Assumption: Why Children Turn Out the Way they Do* (Pocket Books, 1999)

Harris, Judith Rich, *No Two Alike* (WW Norton and Co, 2007)

Hart Betty and Risley Todd, R., *Meaningful Differences in the Everyday Experience of Young American Children* (Baltimore: Brookes Publishing Co, 1995)

Herschkowitz, Norbert and Herschkowitz, Elinore Chapman, *A Good Start in Life: Understanding Your Child's Brain and Behaviour from Birth to Age 6*, (Dana Press, 2004)

Hinsliff, Gaby, *Half a Wife: the Working Family's Guide to Getting a Life Back* (Chatto and Windus, 2012)

Hobson, Peter, *The Cradle of Thought* (Macmillan, 2002)

Honore, Carl *Under Pressure: Rescuing Our Children From the Culture of Hyper-Parenting* (Orion, 2008)

House, Richard (ed), *TooMuch Too Soon: Early Learning and the Erosion Of Childhood* (Hawthorn Press, 2011)

Jackson, Maggie, *Distracted: The Erosion of Attention and the Coming Dark Age* (Prometheus, 2008)

James, Oliver, *How Not To F*** Them Up: the First Three Years* (Vermilion, 2010)

James, Oliver, *They F*** You Up: How to Survive Family Life* (Bloomsbury, 2007)

James, Oliver, *Affluenza* (Vermilion, 2007)

Jangra, Kate, *Babyhood* DVD (2012). http://babyhood-film.com/

Johnson, Steven, *Everything Bad is Good for You* (Allen Lane 2005)

Juul, Jasper, *Your Competent Child: Toward New Basic Values for the Family* (Ferrar, Straus and Giroux, 2000)

Kagan Jerome, *Galen's Prophecy: Temperament in Human Nature* (Free Association Books, 1994)

Kraemer, Sebastian, 'The Fragile Male' *British Medical Journal*, 321 (December 2000)

Lamb, Sharon and Brown, Lyn Mikel, *Packaging Girlhood: Rescuing Our Daughters From Marketers' Schemes* (St Martin's Press, 2006)

Lannier, Jaron, *You Are Not A Gadget: A Manifesto* (Penguin, 2011)

Lawson, Neal, *All Consuming: How Shopping Got Us into This Mess and How We Can Find our Way Out* (Penguin, 2009)

Layard, Richard, *Happiness: Lessons From a New Science* (Penguin, 2005)

Layard, Richard and Dunn, Judy, *A Good Childhood: Searching For Values in a Competitive Age* (Penguin, 2009)

Lee, Nicky and Sila Lee, *The Parenting Book* (Alpha International, 2009)

Levy, Ariel, *Female Chauvinist Pigs: Women and the Rise of Raunch Culture* (Pocket Books, 2006)

Lindstrom, Martin (with Seybold, Patricia B.), *Brand Child* (Revised Edition) (Kogan Page Limited, 2003)

Linn, Susan, *Consuming Kids: the Hostile Takeover of Childhood* (NY New Press, 2005)

Linn, Susan, *The Case for Make Believe: Saving Play in a Commercialised World* (New Press, 2008)

Livingstone, Tessa, *Child of Our Time: How to Achieve the Best for your Child from Conception to 5 Years* (Bantam Press, 2005)

Louv, Richard, *Last Child in the Woods: Saving our Kids from Nature-Deficit Disorder* (Algonquin Books, 2005)

Mansell, Warwick, *Education By Numbers* (Politicos, 2007)

Marshall, David, *Understanding Children as Consumers* (Sage Publications, 2010)

Martin, Courtney, *Perfect Girls, Starving Daughters: How the Quest for Perfection is Harming Young Women* (2007)

Martin, Paul, *Making Happy People: the Nature of Happiness and its Origins in Childhood* (Fourth Estate, 2005)

Mausen, Susan, *The Winter of Our Disconnect* (Profile Books, 2011)

Mayo, Ed, *Shopping Generation* (National Consumer Council, 2005)

McGilchrist, Iain, *The Master and His Emissary: the Divided Brain and ahe Making of The Western World* (Yale University Press, 2012)

McLean, Carrie and Torchinsky, Jason, *Ad Nauseam: a Survivor's Guide to American Consumer Culture* (Faber and Faber, 2009)

McNeal, James, U., *Kids As Customers: a Handbook of Marketing to Children* (NY: Lexington Books, 1992)

Moir, Anne and Moir, Bill, *Why Men Don't Iron: the New Reality of Gender Differences* (Harper Collins, 1999)

Moran, Caitlin, *How To Be A Woman* (Random House, 2012)

Oldfield, Lynne, *Free To Learn: Introducing Steiner Waldorf Early Childhood Education* (Hawthorn Press, 2001)

Olfman, Sharna (ed), *No Child Left Different* (Praeger, 2006)

Orbach, Susie, *Bodies* (Profile Books, 2010)

Paley, Vivian Gussin, *Boys and Girls: Superheroes in the Dolls' Corner* (University of Chicago Press, 1986)

Palmer, Sue, *Toxic Childhood: how the Modern World is Damaging our Children and What We Can Do About It* (Orion, 2006)

Palmer, Sue, *Detoxing Childhood: What Parents Need to Know to Raise Bright, Balanced Children*(Orion, 2007)

Palmer, Sue *21st Century Boys: How Modern Life is Driving Them Off the Rails and How We Can Get Them Back On Track*(Orion, 2009)

Palmer, Sue and Bayley, Ros, *Foundations of Literacy: a Balanced Approach to Language, Listening and Literacy Skills in the Early Years* (Network Continuum, third edition, 2008)

Pink, Daniel H., *A Whole New Mind: Moving from the Information Age to the Conceptual Age* (Riverhead Books, 2005)

Pinker, Steven, *The Blank State* (Penguin Books, 2003)

Pinker, Susan, *The Sexual Paradox* (Atlantic Books, 2008)

Postman, Neil, *The Disappearance of Childhood* (Vintage Books; Random House – 1994)

Preuschoff, Gisela, *Raising Girls: Why Girls Are Different – and How to Help Them Grow Up Happy and Confident* (Harper Thorsens, 2005)

Restak, Richard, *The New Brain: How the Modern Age is Rewiring Your Mind* (Rodale, 2004

Richardson, Alex, *They Are What You Feed Them* (Harper Collins, 2006)

Ridley, Matt, *Nature via Nurture* (Harper Collins, 2004)

Rifkin, Jeremy, *The Empathic Civilisation: the Race to Global Consciousness in a World Of Crisis* (Tarcher, 2009)

Rosen, Larry D., *Me, MySpace and I: Parenting the Net Generation* (Palgrave MacMillan, 2007)

Royal College of Paediatrics and Child Health, *Helpful Parenting* (Royal College of Paediatrics and Child Health, 2002)

Savage, John, *Teenage: the Creation of Youth Culture* (Viking 2007)

Sax, Leonard, *Why Gender Matters – What Parents and Teachers Need to Know About the Emerging Science of Sex Differences* (Doubleday 2005)

Scholz, Sally J., *Feminism: a Beginner's Guide* (Oneworld Publications, 2010)

Schor, Juliet, *Born to Buy: the Commercialized Child and the New Consumer Culture* (Scribner, 2005)

Shaw MD, Robert, *The Epidemic: The Rot of American Culture, Absentee and Permissive Parenting, and the Resultant Plague of Joyless, Selfish Children* (ReganBooks, an imprint of HarperCollins Publishers – 2003)

Shonkoff, Jack P and Phillips D., (editors) *From Neurons to Neighbourhoods: the Science of Early Childhood Development* (National Academy Press, 2000)

Sigman, Aric, *Remotely Controlled: How Television is Damaging our Lives and What We Can Do About It* (Vermilion, 2005)

Small, Gary and Vorgon, Gigi, *iBrain: surviving the Technological Alteration of the Modern Mind* (Harper, 2008)

Smith, Tracy and Dewar Tammy, *Raising the Village: How Individuals and Communities Can Work Together to Give Our Children a Stronger Start in Life* (BPS Books, 2009)

Sunderland, Margot, *The Science of Parenting: Practical Guidance on Sleep, Crying, Play and Building Emotional Wellbeing for Life* (Dorling Kindersley, 2006)

Tannen, Deborah, *Talking from 9 to 5: Women and Men at Work, Language, Sex and Power* (Virago, 1998)

Thomas, Susan Gregory, *Buy Buy Baby: How Big Business Captures the Ultimate Consumer – Your Baby or Toddler* (Harper Collins, 2007)

Twenge, Jean, *Generation, Me: why Today's Young Americans are More Confident, Assertive, Entitled—and More Miserable Than Ever Before* (Free Press, 2006)

Twenge, Jean and Campbell, Keith, *The Narcissism Epidemic: living in the Age of Entitlement* (Free Press, 2009)

Ward, Sally, *Babytalk* (Century, 2000)

Water, Natasha, *Living Dolls: the Return of Sexism* (Virago, 2010)

Weissbluth, Marc, *Healthy Sleep Habits, Happy Child* (The Random House Publishing Group, 1998)

Wilkinson, Richard and Pickett, Kate, *The Spirit Level: why More Equal Societies Almost Always Do Better* (Allen Lane, 2009)

Winn, Marie, *The Plug-in Drug: Television, Computers, and Family Life* (Penguin Books 2002)

Wolf, Maryanne, *Proust and the Squid: the Story and Science of the Reading Brain* (Icon Books, 2008)

Zeedyk, Suzanne, *The Connected Baby DVD* 2012

For competitions, author interviews,
pre-publication extracts, news and events,
sign up to the monthly

Orion Books Newsletter

at

www.orionbooks.co.uk

Prefer your updates daily?
Follow us @orionbooks